GEOGRAPHY AND REFUGEES

GEOGRAPHY AND REFUGEES
Patterns and processes of change

Edited by Richard Black and Vaughan Robinson

Belhaven Press
London and New York

Co-published in the Americas by Halsted Press
an imprint of John Wiley & Sons

Belhaven Press
(a division of Pinter Publishers Ltd.)
25 Floral Street, Covent Garden, London WC2E 9DS, United Kingdom

First published in 1993

Co-published in the Americas by Halsted Press, an imprint of John Wiley & Sons, Inc., 605 Third Avenue, New York, NY 10158-0012

British Library Cataloguing in Publication Data
A CIP catalogue record for this book is available from the British Library

ISBN 1 85293 227 9

Library of Congress Cataloging-in-Publication Data
Geography and refugees: patterns and processes of change/edited by
    Richard Black and Vaughan Robinson
        p. cm.
    Includes bibliographical references and index.
    ISBN 1-85293-227-9. -- ISBN 0-470-21993-9 (U.S.)
    1. Refugees.   I. Black, Richard, 1964-   . II. Robinson,
Vaughan.
HV640.G46   1993
304.8--dc20   93-15085
                                                                          CIP

ISBN 0 47021 993 9 (in the Americas only)

Typeset by Ewan Smith at 48 Shacklewell Lane, London E8
Printed and bound in Great Britain by Biddles Ltd., Guildford and King's Lynn

Contents

List of figures   vii

List of tables   viii

List of contributors   x

Glossary   xi

Acknowledgements   xiii

Part I   Introduction   1

1   Geography and refugees: current issues
     Richard Black   3

**Part II   Reception, settlement, and repatriation of refugees
            in the Third World**   15

2   From the Kipande to the Kibali: the incorporation of refugees
     and labour migrants in Western Tanzania, 1900–87
     Patricia Daley   17

3   'Internal refugees': the case of the displaced in Khartoum
     Johnathan Bascom   33

4   Return to the promised land: repatriation and resettlement
     of Namibian refugees, 1989–90
     David Simon and Rosemary Preston   47

5   Mass flight in the Middle East: involuntary migration and
     the Gulf conflict, 1990–91
     Nicholas Van Hear   64

Part III Refugees and asylum-seekers in the Developed World   85

6   Refugees and asylum-seekers in Western Europe: new challenges
     Richard Black   87

7   The 'Sweden-wide strategy' of refugee dispersal
     Tomas Hammar   104

8   'Only the women know': powerlessness and marginality in
     three Hmong women's lives
     Kristen Monzel   118

9   North and South: resettling Vietnamese refugees in
    Australia and the UK
    Vaughan Robinson   134

Part IV   New directions, new developments   155

10 Refugees and the environment
    JoAnn McGregor   157

11 Repatriation and information: a theoretical model
    Khalid Koser   171

12 End of the Cold War: end of Afghan relief aid?
    Allan Findlay   185

13 Forced migration and ethnic processes in the former
    Soviet Union
    *Zhanne Zayonchkovskaya, Alexander Kocharyan
    and Galina Vitkovskaya*   198

Part V   Conclusion   209

14 Retrospect and prospect: where next for geography
    and refugee studies?
    Vaughan Robinson   211

Index   217

List of figures

2.1 Refugee influxes into Tanzania 18

3.1 Displaced communities around Khartoum, Sudan 38

4.1 Location of Namibian reception centres for returning refugees 53

5.1 Expatriate workers in the Middle East, late 1980s 65
5.2 Areas in the Middle East covered by UNHCR operations, 1991 71

8.1 *Paj ntaub* embroidery depicting a raid on a Hmong village, and escape through the rainforest and across the Mekong River (artist, Shoua Xiong) 120
8.2 Source areas of Hmong refugees 125
8.3 *Paj ntaub* (detail) of Hmong men reaping the bounty of the rainforest (artist, Lee Lo) 131

11.1 Model of a refugee information system 176

12.1 Afghan villages in North West Frontier Province, Pakistan 189

List of tables

1.1   Countries hosting over 250,000 refugees, 1 January 1991   6
1.2   Emigration, immigration, and asylum-seekers in the UK, 1980–90   8

3.1   Significant populations of internally displaced civilians worldwide,
      early 1992   34

4.1   Age–sex breakdown of returnees to Namibia, 15 September 1989   55
4.2   Namibian RRR Committee expenditure, 1989   59

5.1   Estimates of foreign nationals and their dependents in Kuwait
      and Iraq in mid-1990, and of returnees from the Gulf region
      in 1990–91   66
5.2   Estimates of workers' remittances forgone as a result of the Gulf
      crisis, compared with worldwide remittances in 1989   75

6.1   Asylum-seekers in Western Europe, 1990   91

7.1   Refugee immigration to Sweden 1950–90   105
7.2   Asylum-seekers and persons granted refugee status in Sweden,
      1983–90   108
7.3   Asylum-seekers in Sweden by geographic origin, 1983–90   111
7.4   Classification of Swedish municipalities according to time of
      agreement to participate in dispersal programme, by region   112
7.5   Mean population and number of foreigners in Swedish
      municipalities within each category   113
7.6   Swedish municipalities by average capacity to pay taxes, average
      income, unemployment rate, female labour activity rate and
      percent of apartments available   114
7.7   Refugees admitted to metropolitan and other municipalities in
      Sweden 1985–89   114
7.8   Refugees admitted to Stockholm county and city, 1985–89   115

9.1   Demographic characteristics of Vietnamese refugees in Australia
      and the UK   140
9.2   Regional distribution of Vietnamese in Australia, 1981 and 1986 145
9.3   Regional distribution of the Vietnamese in the UK at resettlement
      and in 1985–88   147
9.4   Urban concentration of the Vietnamese in the UK at resettlement
      and in 1985   148

13.1 Increase in population of indigenous nationalities of the former
      Soviet Union republics, 1959–70   199

13.2 Increase in population of indigenous nationalities of the former
     Soviet Union republics, 1970–79   200
13.3 Increase in population of indigenous nationalities of the former
     Soviet Union republics, 1979–89   201
13.4 Index of population change of different nationalities of the former
     Soviet Union republics, 1979–89   202

List of contributors

Johnathan Bascom, Department of Geography and Planning, East Carolina University, 221 Brewster, Greenville, North Carolina 27858, USA

Richard Black, Department of Geography, King's College London, Strand, London, WC2R 2LS, UK

Patricia Daley, School of Geography, University of Oxford, Mansfield Rd, Oxford, OX1 3BT, UK

Allan Findlay, Applied Population Research Unit, Department of Geography and Topographic Science, University of Glasgow, Glasgow, G12 8QQ, UK

Tomas Hammar, Centre for Research in International Migration and Ethnic Relations, Stockholm University, 10691 Stockholm, Sweden

Khalid Koser, Department of Geography, University College London, 26 Bedford Way, London, WC1H 0AP, UK

JoAnn McGregor, Refugee Studies Programme, Queen Elizabeth House, University of Oxford, 21 St Giles, Oxford, OX1 3LA, UK

Kristen Monzel, Department of Geography, Syracuse University, 343 H.B. Crouse Hall, Syracuse, New York 13244, USA

Vaughan Robinson, Migration Unit, Department of Geography, University College Swansea, Singleton Park, Swansea, SA2 8PP, UK

David Simon, Centre for Developing Areas Research, Department of Geography, Royal Holloway and Bedford New College, University of London, Egham Hill, Egham, Surrey, TW20 0EX, UK

Rosemary Preston, International Centre for Education in Development, Department of Continuing Education, University of Warwick, Coventry, CV4 7AL, UK

Nicholas Van Hear, Refugee Studies Programme, Queen Elizabeth House, University of Oxford, 21 St Giles, Oxford, OX1 3LA, UK

Zhanne Zayonchkovskaya, **Alexander Kocharyan**, and **Galina Vitkovskaya**, Centre of Demography and Human Ecology, Institute of Employment Problems, Academy of Sciences, 16 Malaja Lybjanka St, 10100 Moscow, Russia

Glossary

ACBAR	Agency Coordinating Body for Afghan Refugees (Pakistan)
AMS	National Labour Board (Sweden)
ANC	African National Congress (South Africa)
BRALUP	Bureau of Resource Assessment and Land Use Planning, University of Dar es Salaam (Tanzania)
CAFOD	Catholic Fund for Overseas Development
CCN	Council of Churches of Namibia
COR	Commissioner for Refugees (Sudan)
CRSS	Community Refugee Settlement Scheme (Australia)
DILGEA	Department of Immigration, Local Government and Ethnic Affairs (Australia)
DTA	Democratic Turnhalle Alliance (Namibia)
EC	European Community
ED	Enumeration District (UK)
ECOSOC	United Nations Economic and Social Council
FAO	Food and Agriculture Organization (UN)
GA	United Nations General Assembly
GNP	Gross National Product
GTZ	Deutsche Gesellschaft für Technische Zusammenarbeit (Germany)
IBRD	International Bank for Reconstruction and Development/World Bank
ICARA	International Conference on Aid to Refugees in Africa
IDS	Institute for Development Studies, University of Sussex (UK)
IGADD	Intergovernmental Authority for Drought and Desertification
ILO	International Labour Organization
IMF	International Monetary Fund
IOE	Spanish Institute of Employment
IOM	International Organization for Migration
JCWI	Joint Council for the Welfare of Immigrants (UK)
LGA	Local Government Area (Australia)
MNR	Mozambican National Resistance (Renamo)
NGO	Non-Governmental Organization
NWFP	North West Frontier Province (Pakistan)
OAU	Organization of African Unity
ODI	Overseas Development Institute (UK)
PLAN	Peoples' Liberation Army of Namibia
REST	Relief Society of Tigray
RIDEP	Rural Integrated Development Programme (Tanzania)
RPG	Refugee Policy Group (US)

RPN	Refugee Participation Network (UK)
RRR	Repatriation, Resettlement and Reconstruction Committee (Namibia)
SILABU	Labour Bureau of the Tanganyika Sisal Growers Association
SLORC	State Law and Order Council (Burma)
SOPEMI	Continuous Reporting System on European Migration
SPLA	Sudan Peoples' Liberation Army
SSAC	Squatter Settlement Abolishment Committee (Sudan)
SSCFAD	Senate Standing Committee on Foreign Affairs and Defence (Australia)
SWAPO	South West African Peoples Organization
TCRS	Tanganyika Christian Refugee Service (Tanzania)
TPLF	Tigray People's Liberation Front
UNESCWA	United Nations Economic and Social Commission for Western Asia
UNDP	United Nations Development Programme
UNDRO	United Nations Disaster Relief Organization
UNEP	United Nations Environment Programme
UNFPA	United Nations Fund for Population Activities
UNHCR	United Nations High Commissioner for Refugees
UNICEF	United Nations Childrens Fund
UNLA	Ugandan National Liberation Army
UNOCA	Office for the Coordination of United Nations Humanitarian and Economic Assistance Programs Relating to Afghanistan
UNRISD	United Nations Research Institute for Social Development
UNRWA	United Nations Relief and Works Agency (Palestine)
UNTAG	United Nations Transitional Assistance Group (Namibia)
URT	United Republic of Tanzania
USAID	United States Agency for International Development
USCR	United States Committee for Refugees
USDA	United States Department of Agriculture
WCC	World Council of Churches
WFP	World Food Programme
WHO	World Health Organization
ZIMPEF	Zimbabwe Foundation for Education and Production

Acknowledgements

This book includes material first presented at a joint conference of the Developing Areas Research Group (DARG) and the Population Geography Study Group (PGSG) of the Institute of British Geographers, held at King's College London in September 1991, on 'The Refugee Crisis: geographical perspectives on forced migration', as well as chapters specially commissioned for this volume. The editors would like to thank the contributors to the conference, as well as the Economic and Social Research Council (ESRC), the Nuffield Foundation, DARG and PGSG for their financial support.

The editors would like to thank the various contributors to the volume for agreeing to forgo royalties, which will be donated to the Medical Foundation for the Care of Victims of Torture. In addition, thanks go to Matthew Jowett for organizational support, Liz Traynor of the Department of Geography at King's College London for retyping part of the manuscript, and Guy Lewis and Nicola Jones of University College Swansea for redrawing all of the maps.

Richard Black
Vaughan Robinson

PART I

Introduction

1 Geography and refugees: current issues

Richard Black

Introduction: refugees in the contemporary world

In recent years, academics have been paying increasing attention to a migratory movement that appears to have reached unprecedented levels: that of refugees. Recent volumes broadly from within the discipline of geography include both research monographs (Kuhlman, 1990; Rogge, 1985) and edited volumes (Rogge, 1987), whilst others have addressed explicitly the relationships between refugee studies and disciplines such as political science (Loescher and Monahan, 1989), international relations (Gordenker, 1987) and economic and social history (Bramwell, 1988). This book is intended to build on this growing literature. Its task is to consider the contribution of the discipline of geography to the field of refugee studies, both by presenting several case studies of geographical work on refugees, and through a discussion of substantive issues concerning the relationship between the two fields.

Concern with the scale of the refugee crisis that faces the modern world is not new, of course. Previous studies have almost without exception focused from their outset on the continually worsening nature of the world's refugee problem, citing increasing numbers of refugees in official statistics, and the deadly combination of conflict, economic collapse, and the loss of basic human rights as underpinning an 'unprecedented' situation of 'crisis' proportions (Gordenker, 1987, pp. 2–3). Marrus (1985, p. 1), for example, comments that 'practically everyone contends that the problem is growing, beyond anyone's prediction a generation ago and far beyond the capacity of present national or international institutions to reduce within a short time'. In this sense, academic writing has reflected an overwhelming public pessimism concerning the plight of refugees.

Although it is not suggested that the plight of the world's refugees can be dismissed as either temporary or insignificant – indeed the recent displacement of over one million people from their homes in the former Yugoslavia bears testimony to the enormity of the problem – there are signs, in the early 1990s, that the refugee 'crisis' has begun to take on a rather more contradictory nature. For example, in terms of the forced movement of peoples, the decade certainly began inauspiciously as the Gulf War, and especially its aftermath, added large numbers to the world's displaced population, whilst new or renewed conflict not just in Croatia and Bosnia, but also in Somalia, Liberia, Burma, Bhutan, and the former Soviet Union led to further mass forced displacement. However, at the same time, some regional conflicts appeared to be drawing to a close, with the prospect, according to the United Nations High Commissioner for Refugees (UNHCR), that the 1990s might be a 'decade of repatriation'. The first major repatriation of the decade, the return of some 40,000 people to Namibia, is dealt with in this volume (Chapter 4).

Mirroring and, to a certain extent, explaining this growing contradiction between further mass exodus and repatriation, is a fundamental change in world politics provoked by the dramatic changes in 1990–91 in Eastern Europe and the former Soviet Union. With the decline of one of the world's 'superpowers', and a consolidation of the hegemony of the United States, at least in the political arena, old platitudes about both the causes of, and responses to, the world's refugee 'crisis' have also been undermined. Whilst in some regions, the ending of superpower rivalry has led to a real possibility of a solution to regional conflict, as, for example, in parts of southern Africa, or in Kampuchea, in other areas the vacuum left behind appears to have intensified local rivalries, fragmenting political control and leading to a more bloody phase of conflict. Thus, against western expectations, the withdrawal of Soviet forces from Afghanistan has so far failed to bring a clear end to fighting, rather reorientating it according to underlying local factions and interests (Chapter 12). Meanwhile, in the former Soviet Union itself, the ending of human rights violations by the central state, of which the West has complained for decades, has been accompanied by the emergence of a new set of human rights problems, involving different regions, ethnic and religious groups, and political factions, which threaten more rather than less mass displacement (Chapter 13).

This changing geopolitical context to refugee movements has also had significant implications for the way in which refugee issues are addressed on the international stage. Developments such as the establishment of 'safe havens' for Kurdish refugees inside Iraq, under United Nations supervision (Chapter 5), would have been unthinkable during the era of the Cold War, and may be seen as a new international response, even if this particular 'solution' proves unsustainable or unsuitable in the long term. Elsewhere in the world, US or UN intervention, although clearly not unprecedented (ranging from the UN's role in the Congo crisis, to the US invasion of Grenada), may now be more readily acceptable as a mechanism for upholding human rights and preventing the underlying causes of refugee movements, unhindered by the clash of ideology between East and West. As is discussed in Chapter 12 of this volume, UNHCR began the decade with a fundamental reevaluation of its role in the post–Cold War era, a role that is likely to be different in the future, although no less problematic than before.

It can also be argued that host nation responses to refugee migration have become more contradictory in the last few years. In western nations, for example, and notably in western Europe, the politics of exclusionism, associated with restrictive immigration policies directed at migrant workers in the 1960s and 1970s, has extended to the field of refugees and asylum-seekers. A succession of European countries have passed or are introducing laws designed to stem the flow of asylum-seekers, imposing stiff fines on airlines that bring undocumented travellers, introducing swift and more summary procedures for dealing with asylum claims, and reducing refugees' rights to welfare benefits, legal representation, and rights of appeal against rejected claims. Whilst such measures appear to be supported by significant segments of local populations, however, there are counter-trends: the Sanctuary movement of the US and Canada (Stastny and Tyrnauer, 1992), for example, has some western European counterparts (see Weller, 1992), and religious leaders have been at the forefront of opposition to the Asylum Bill presented to the UK parliament in 1991–92. More significantly, public support for restrictive asylum policies has been coupled with widespread public sympathy for the plight of some refugee groups. Thus there was unease and some public condemnation of attempts, for example, by Turkey, to restrict the movement of Kurdish refugees over its border in 1991, and of the turning back of boats carrying Albanians to Italy, or Haitians to the United States, during the same year.

Geography and refugees

It is in this context of contradictions that this book addresses the role of the discipline of geography in contributing to a greater understanding of refugee problems and policies. The intention is not to present one view of how geographers should or do address the multitude of issues that surround refugee movements. Indeed, the contributions to this volume represent a range of methodological and epistemological standpoints, in which 'geography' might be defined in a variety of ways. At the same time, the focus of the book is not strictly limited to 'refugees' as defined, for example, under the 1951 UN Convention on Refugees (see below). If there is an approach that pervades the book as a whole, it is that refugee migration must be viewed 'in context', meaning that the myriad of connections between different types of 'forced' migration, and the potential cycle of refugee migration and return, should be considered, at least in research terms, as a whole.

Such an integrating approach does not argue that refugee migration is the same as migration in general, and a role for 'refugee studies', such as that outlined by Zetter (1988), is in any case implied in the very focus of the book. However, this approach does provide an opportunity to explore insights gained in the wider field of migration studies, applying these to the particular circumstances of refugees. At the same time, the drawing of a strict and inflexible distinction between 'political' refugees and other kinds of 'economic' migrants is rejected in analytical terms as an oversimplification. Indeed, whilst there is an argument for separating refugees from other migrants in order to ensure humanitarian help at a time of increasing xenophobia against migrants in general, there is a very real sense in which an emphasis on this distinction is being used to justify political attempts to reduce assistance to all migrants, including refugees.

Refugees: definitions and significance

In considering the significance of refugee migration as a subject for geographical enquiry, an attempt must be made to distinguish such migration from migration in general, if only to provide a basis for international comparison. In practice, there is no completely satisfactory definition of a refugee, nor indeed is such a definition likely given the term's significance in international law, for national

Table 1.1 Countries hosting over 250,000 refugees, 1 January 1991

Continent Country	UNHCR total	USCR total
Africa	4,791,600	5,340,800
Malawi	926,700	950,000
Sudan	780,000	717,200
Ethiopia	772,800	534,000
Somalia	460,000	35,000
Zaire	416,000	482,300
Burundi	268,400	107,000
Tanzania	256,200	251,100
Guinea	—	566,000
Europe*	893,100	578,400
Germany	156,100	256,100
Middle East/ South Asia**	6,000,000	9,820,950
Pakistan	3,500,000	3,594,000
Iran	2,500,000	3,150,000
Jordan	—	960,200
Gaza Strip	—	528,700
West Bank	—	430,100
India	—	402,600
Lebanon	—	314,200
Syria	—	293,900
South East Asia	523,600	688,500
China	287,200	14,200
Thailand	—	512,700
North America*	1,508,400	99,300
United States	1,000,000	68,800
Canada	508,400	30,500
Latin America/ Caribbean	1,263,000	119,600
Mexico	356,400	48,500
Costa Rica	278,000	24,300
TOTAL	14,979,700	16,647,550

Sources: UNHCR (1991); USCR (1992)

Notes: * USCR total for Europe and North America refers only to asylum-seekers in 1991, whereas the UNHCR total includes refugees permanently resettled in these countries. USCR records the total number of refugees permanently resettled as 616,400 in Europe, and 1,803,200 in North America.

** UNHCR total for Middle East/South Asia excludes Palestinians. These come under the mandate of UNWRA, who independently estimate their numbers at 2.4 million.

state policy, and for the self-perception of individual displaced people (see, for example, differences in interpretation in this volume, between Chapters 8 and 13). The most widely-used definition is that of the 1951 UN Convention on Refugees, amended by the New York Protocol of 1967, which identifies refugees as people who are 'outside their own country, owing to a well-founded fear of persecution, for reasons of race, religion, nationality, membership of a particular social group, or political opinion'. Working within this 'official' definition, UNHCR estimated that there were around fourteen million refugees in the world at the end of 1991, whilst a more comprehensive analysis by the United States Committee for Refugees, based on the same definition, put the number closer to seventeen million (Table 1.1).

This 'official' definition of a refugee can, however, be seen as inadequate for academic enquiry for a number of reasons. first, in practice, the recognition of refugees is a matter for receiving states, who interpret the Convention and Protocol in a variety of ways (Frelick, 1992). In Africa and Central America, for example, signatories to the OAU Convention on Refugees of 1967, and the OAS Cartagena Declaration of 1985 respectively use a different definition of refugees, which includes those forced to leave their country due to external aggression, occupation or domination (OAU), and by internal conflict or massive violations of human rights (OAS), and such refugees are included in the global figures provided by UNHCR. Meanwhile, there is also a crucial difference in procedure used to determine refugee status broadly between most developed nations, and especially western Europe, and most nations of the Third World. In the former, it is common for countries to accept refugee movements *en masse*, granting refugee status to groups of refugees as they move over an international border. In contrast, in most western countries, claims for asylum by refugees are dealt with on an individual basis, with each individual asylum seeker being forced to demonstrate that he or she has suffered *individual* persecution under the terms of the 1951 Convention before being granted the status of a refugee.

In this book, a rather different approach from that of the politician or lawyer is adopted, in that the focus is on the broader *process* of refugee migration. The thread that draws each of the contributions together is that of people who have been forced to leave their habitual place of residence due primarily to war or persecution. Thus whilst officially-recognized refugees – individuals and groups – are the main concern, one chapter focuses on 'refugees' who do not fall under the 1951 Convention because they are displaced within the borders of their own countries (Chapter 3); whilst others discuss the relationship between 'political' and 'economic' migration (Chapter 2), the phenomenon of 'environmental refugees' (Chapter 10), and refugees from 'man-made' disasters such as the Chernobyl accident (Chapter 13). By including these chapters, it is not intended to reject 'official' definitions of a refugee, or to argue that these groups of people should necessarily be treated in exactly the same way as refugees. Nonetheless, the whole issue of definitions is brought into question, whilst it is suggested that there *are* linkages and parallels between the various types of forced migration discussed, which merit them being treated within one volume. In addition, three further chapters consider what might be described as the final phase of the 'refugee cycle', those who are returning, or are intending to return, to their country of origin (Chapters 4, 11 and 12). This helps to reinforce the point that the migration of refugees cannot be seen as an isolated event, either for the individual migrant, or in a more general sense, but as part of a wider process.

The significance of refugee migration

Given this focus on the broader process of refugee migration, a question must then be asked as to the extent to which the causes and consequences of refugee migration do represent topics of significance to geographers, or more broadly to the field of migration studies. For example, in developed nations of the north, available statistics suggest that refugees, particularly under official definitions, have represented only a tiny proportion of total migrants in recent years, movements in 1992 notwithstanding. In the UK, for example, during the 1980s, the number of asylum-seekers represented less than 3 per cent of total immigration, whilst total emigration was even higher in four out of ten years, leading to a net outflow (Table 1.2). This situation is replicated in western Europe, where 'internal' migration between countries and regions of the European Community vastly outweighs total immigration, not to mention arrivals of asylum-seekers (Chapter 6). Meanwhile, the US admitted just over 120,000 refugees in 1990, compared to a quota of around 270,000 'economic' migrants; this too can be seen as historically insignificant, compared for example to the immigration on average of more than 800,000 each year during the first decade of this century (Simon, 1989).

Table 1.2 Emigration, immigration, and asylum-seekers in the UK, 1980–90

Year	Asylum seekers	Immigrants	Emigrants
1980	2,350	173,000	228,000
1981	2,400	153,000	232,000
1982	4,200	201,000	257,000
1983	4,300	202,000	184,000
1984	3,850	201,000	164,000
1985	5,450	232,000	174,000
1986	4,800	250,000	213,000
1987	5,150	211,000	209,000
1988	5,250	216,000	237,000
1989	15,550	250,000	205,000
1990	25,000	267,000	231,000

Source: UK Annual Abstract of Statistics; Home Office

If the total number of refugees seeking asylum in the developed world to date is small, however, it can nonetheless be argued that refugees have obtained a political significance that outweighs mere numbers. Hammar (1985), for example, has described the 1960s as a decade of labour migration, the 1970s as a decade of family reunification, and the 1980s as a decade of asylum. Whilst this may not be true in terms of the figures for total migration, it does nonetheless reflect the perception of western governments, who have moved to tighten asylum policy throughout the decade. At the same time, in a period of economic recession, the desire to restrict the number of migrants, whilst maintaining a humanitarian stance towards 'genuine' refugees, has brought the asylum question to the centre of government thinking on immigration in general.

Meanwhile, in the Third World, the significance of voluntary 'economic' migration compared to forced 'refugee' migration is much less clear cut, with little in the way of statistics to resolve the issue. Whilst patterns of large-scale labour migration have on the whole remained limited to particular parts of the world, such as migration to the Gulf states and South Africa, from central to north America, and from north Africa to Europe, the list of Third World nations that have experienced large-scale forced migration is both large and growing. The pattern of migration also often contradicts the maxim of economic migration: that movement reflects patterns of structural inequality between nations. In 1991, for example, twenty-seven low-income countries, each with a level of GNP per capita of less than $500, were host to almost half of the total number of refugees in the world.

The fact that a disproportionate share of the burden of hosting refugees falls on the world's poorest nations helps to draw attention to another aspect of the salience of refugee issues to current geographical concerns. For example, the implementation of development projects has increasingly become connected to the question of 'rehabilitating' areas affected by refugee flows, whether as a result of initial flight, or of repatriation. Since the 1960s, there has been discussion in the refugee literature about the necessity to provide 'development' rather than just 'emergency' aid to refugees, and to integrate this with wider development programmes for host areas (Betts, 1969). This formed a major conclusion of the second International Conference on Aid to Refugees in Africa (ICARA II), which set the tone for refugee aid in the 1980s. There are now also an increasing number of cases in which the linkage should work the other way around: development projects for specific areas must take into account the needs and opportunities afforded by refugee or returnee populations located within them.

There is also a theoretical sense in which the study of refugees is of particular interest to geographers and other social scientists, in that an understanding of socio-economic or political processes under the specific conditions of refugee migration may provide crucial insights into the operation of these processes at a more general level. For example, in many refugee situations, individuals and communities must act to rebuild social networks, economic structures, and patterns of political expression and representation, often in adverse circumstances. The evolution of these structures may be rapid compared to that in more 'stable' populations, providing the researcher with a unique opportunity to document and explain social and economic change. Similarly, the planning of assistance programmes for refugees may start with a relatively 'clean sheet', affording more direct evaluation of its results and pitfalls. This should not be taken to imply that refugees, or the areas into which they move, are somehow without any history: indeed an ahistorical approach might be seen as one of the primary inadequacies of some existing studies of refugees, which have treated them as 'exceptional' populations (Black, 1991). Nonetheless, elements may be drawn from the study of refugee migration that are of relevance not just to refugees, but to broader questions of economic and social development.

There is also clearly a humanitarian element to the study of refugee migration, which is present throughout the contributions to this volume. One might debate for a long time the extent to which geographers should be involved in humanitarian questions, but this would seem a logical response to the calls both of those who argue for a geography or social science that acts to empower the disenfranchised (Wisner, 1988), of which refugees are a classic group, and of those who argue for geographical research to address the major issues of public concern (Douglas, 1986).

The significance of geography

A question also arises regarding to what extent the discipline of geography can provide specific skills or perspectives which help to explain the conditions of the world's refugee population. Here again, there is a definitional problem, since there are many perspectives in a subject which often regards itself as somewhat 'interdisciplinary'. A preliminary discussion in Black (1991) outlines three areas in which geographical work to date has been concentrated, namely in explanation of the causes of refugee migration; discussion of the consequences of refugee movements for planning, and uneven development in the Third World; and analysis of the (spatial) patterns generated by resettlement of refugees in the developed world. However, none of these areas of research could be considered as exclusive to geographers, and only perhaps the last might be regarded as 'geographical', at least in a traditional sense.

In terms of this book, it is perhaps easiest to deal first with what is not being attempted. It is not intended, for example, to provide a 'geography *of* refugees', if indeed such a thing could exist at all. Rather, a number of themes are explored, each of which reflects a geographical perspective of relevance to the wider field of refugee studies. Thus a major concern of geography has involved discussion of the relationship between people and the environment, and this is considered here both in terms of the environmental consequences of refugee movements, and whether it is possible to identify a category of 'environmental refugees' (Chapter 10). Another significant strand of modern geography concerns the development of spatial patterns in the human landscape, and this is examined in relation to both planned and spontaneous patterns of dispersal and resegregation of refugees in a variety of local and national contexts (Chapters 7 and 9). A third important focus of current geographical writing in general centres on the significance of 'place' in generating distinctive social, economic and political processes. The relevance of this to the study of refugees might be seen, for example, in the role of conflicting claims to places as 'homelands' with specific ideological significance, which have helped to perpetuate conflict and worsen the situation of many refugee populations. Here, there is a focus on the ambiguous nature of the term 'home', and on the mistaken notion that refugees will necessarily wish, or be able, to return to a specific place called 'home' during or after particular conflicts (Chapters 5 and 12).

Meanwhile, the interest of geographers in patterns of social segregation is not limited, for example, to purely spatial patterns, and the wider issues of social and economic differentiation of refugees and their hosts are also dealt with here. Such questions are addressed in subsequent chapters both on the basis of detailed historical analysis (Chapter 2), and with regard to contemporary processes (Chapters 3 and 6). Refugees themselves must also evolve strategies to deal with displacement and the process of marginalization that this often entails, strategies that may involve varying approaches to integration in host societies (Chapter 8), and attempts to return to their country of origin (Chapter 11). Finally, planning questions concerning the movement, settlement, and resettlement of refugees also relate directly to a long-standing geographical concern with planning issues and planning policy, from the conditions which force people to flee (Chapter 13), to best practice in resettlement (Chapters 7 and 9), and policies which may facilitate their return (Chapter 4).

Structure of the book

The remaining chapters of this book are divided into three main sections. These deal in turn with the experiences of refugees and refugee policy in the two distinct 'worlds' already alluded to, the 'Third World', and the 'developed world' of advanced industrialized countries respectively, followed by a section which focuses on new developments in refugee research and refugee policy. This reflects significant differences in the situation of refugees in rich and poor nations of the world, and provides an opportunity to focus directly on issues of practical and theoretical importance for future research.

In Part II, four chapters address different aspects of refugee reception, settlement and repatriation in countries of the Third World, with a particular emphasis on Africa, which is currently host to over a third of the world's refugees. In Chapter 2, the migration of the Burundi people to Tanzania, and their settlement in the latter country, is placed in the context of both colonial and post-colonial political economic structures. It is argued that both the movement of, and Tanzanian policy towards, first 'economic' migrants, and more recently 'political' refugees can be considered as part of a continuum rather than as discrete events, with the dictates of the Tanzanian plantation economy representing a major controlling variable. Chapter 3 examines the current situation of over one million displaced people in Khartoum, focusing on attempts by the Sudanese authorities to forcibly resettle such 'internal refugees' away from the capital. The chapter argues strongly that those populations displaced within the borders of their own countries risk being ignored by the international community, despite their considerable need for humanitarian aid.

In contrast, Chapter 4 provides a detailed analysis of the high-profile, and largely successful, operation to repatriate and resettle Namibian refugees returning to their home country after independence. Far from being forgotten, the Namibian experience is held up as a model for future repatriation programmes, although its high cost might raise some reservations. Chapter 5 then considers one of the largest and most rapid forced displacements since World War II, in which it is estimated that up to five million people have been forced to leave either their own country, or the country in which they were living as migrant workers, as a result of the Gulf War. This chapter highlights the fact that displacement arising directly from the Allied attack on Kuwait and Iraq was much lower than originally expected, whereas it was those – such as migrant workers and ethnic minorities – who were already marginalized and disenfranchised, who have been most affected by displacement, both before and after the war itself. Once again, high-profile and well-organized assistance to certain sections of the displaced population has not been extended to all, with those internally-displaced within Iraq suffering in particular from a lack of world attention.

In Part III, discussion turns to the 'developed world', where there are both refugees resettled from parts of the Third World (mainly Southeast Asia), and others who have applied directly for asylum in these countries. In Chapter 6, the potential for integration of refugees in western Europe is considered. Here, it is suggested that solutions can be found to the integration of refugees at a national level, although for these to be successful, a challenge must be made both to the rising trend of xenophobia, and to state policies which have increased marginalisation and vulnerability of refugees and asylum-seekers. One particular policy trend has been to try to disperse refugees to various cities, in order to alleviate the 'burden' of refugee assistance on particular localities. This is discussed in Chapter 7, using as an example the specific case of Sweden. The author argues that a well-intentioned policy was rapidly overtaken by events, forcing it to a point where it appeared increasingly restrictive.

Chapter 8 then switches attention from state policy to the strategies of refugees themselves in dealing with their 'new life', in this case in the United States. Through a case study of the experiences of one Hmong family from the highlands of Laos, the themes of powerlessness and marginality are stressed, and generational differences in addressing these problems are explored. Chapter 9 maintains the focus on resettlement from Southeast Asia, comparing policy responses to the arrival of Vietnamese refugees in the UK and Australia. Short-term and restrictive measures in the former country are contrasted with the latter's attempt to build a broader-based policy which includes a commitment to multi-culturalism.

Finally, in Parts IV and V, five chapters address current themes in both refugee policy and refugee research. Chapter 10 approaches the topical question of the relationship of refugees and the environment from two distinct angles: the 'environmental consequences' of refugee movements, and the existence of so-called 'environmental refugees'. In both cases, it is argued that generalized environmental arguments are used to legitimize political actions, with little real understanding of environmental processes. The importance of detailed local case studies, and an awareness of environmental variability, are stressed. In Chapter 11, meanwhile, a theoretical approach to another major current concern of policy makers – repatriation – is put forward. Again, it is argued that it is necessary to understand the actions and strategies of potential returnees, rather than make unwarranted generalizations. A model for such research, which draws on advances in the field of return migration in general, is presented. Chapter 12 continues the focus on repatriation, here in the case of Afghanistan, where predictions of a large-scale return after the withdrawal of Soviet forces have, at the time of writing, proved unfounded. This chapter also examines the role of UNHCR in relief aid to Afghan refugees, and the reformulation of UNHCR policy in response to political developments in the region. Chapter 13 focuses on the potential for mass movement of refugees in the countries of the former Soviet Union, drawing on results from the 1990 Soviet census on the distribution of ethnic minorities.

In the final chapter, the involvement of geographers in the field of refugee studies is returned to again, both in the light of contributions to this book, and the conference from which it was drawn, and also in the context of previous reviews of research in refugee studies by each of the editors, both within and outside the discipline of geography. It is hoped that the work presented in the following chapters will be of interest, both for its focus on detailed case studies, and for attempts to highlight the wider relevance of geographical work on refugees. Nonetheless, it is clear that a considerable amount remains to be done in addressing one of the most pressing problems of our age.

References

Betts, T., 1969, 'Zonal rural development in Africa', *Journal of Modern African Studies*, 7 (1): 149–53.

Black, R., 1991, 'Refugees and displaced persons: geographical perspectives and research directions', *Progress in Human Geography*, 15 (3): 281–98.

Bramwell, A.L., ed., 1988, *Refugees in the age of total war*, Unwin Hyman, London.

Douglas, I., 'The unity of geography is obvious', *Transactions, Institute of British Geographers*, 11 (4): 459–63.

Frelick, B., 1992, 'Call them what they are: refugees', in *World refugee survey, 1992*, United States Committee for Refugees, Washington, DC, 12–17.

Gordenker, L., 1987, *Refugees in international politics*, Croom Helm, London.

Hammar, T., ed., 1985, *European immigration policy: a comparative study*, Cambridge University Press, Cambridge, UK.

Kuhlman, T., 1990, *Burden or boon? Eritrean refugees in the Sudan*, Zed Books, London.

Loescher, G. and Monahan, L., eds, 1989, *Refugees and international relations*, Oxford University Press, Oxford.

Marrus, M.R., 1985, *The unwanted: European refugees in the twentieth century*, Oxford University Press, Oxford.

Rogge, J.R., 1985, *Too many, too long: Sudan's twenty year refugee dilemma*, Rowman & Allenheld, Totowa, New Jersey.

Rogge, J.R., ed., 1987, *Refugees: a Third World dilemma*, Rowman & Littlefield, Totowa, New Jersey.

Simon, J., 1989, *The economic consequences of immigration*, Basil Blackwell, Oxford.

Stastny, C. and Tyrnauer, G., 1992, 'Sanctuary in Canada', in V. Robinson, ed., *The international refugee crisis: British and Canadian responses*, Macmillan, London.

UNHCR (United Nations High Commissioner for Refugees), 1991, *An instrument of peace: for forty years, UNHCR alongside refugees*, Presidenza del Consiglio dei Ministri, Dipartimento per l'Informazione e l'Editoria, Rome.

USCR (United States Committee for Refugees), 1992, *World refugee survey*, 1991, USCR, Washington, DC.

Weller, P., 1992, 'Sanctuary in Britain', in V. Robinson, ed., *The international refugee crisis: British and Canadian responses*, Macmillan, London.

Wisner, B., 1988, *Power and need in Africa*, Earthscan, London.

Zetter, R., 1988, 'Refugees and refugee studies: a label and an agenda', *Journal of Refugee Studies*, 1 (1): 1–6.

PART II

Reception, settlement, and repatriation
of refugees in the Third World

2 From the Kipande to the Kibali: the incorporation of refugees and labour migrants in Western Tanzania, 1900–87

Patricia Daley

Introduction

Refugee migration is viewed as distinctly different from economically motivated migration, and yet similarities exist in the way both groups are incorporated into host societies by receiving states. It is the contention of this chapter that host government policy on the incorporation of refugees may be closely associated with the demands of the labour market. To illustrate this, the chapter links the 1972 displacement of Barundi refugees to earlier migrations to East Africa's sisal, coffee and cotton plantations during colonial rule. Using labour market criteria and development priorities as determining factors in the incorporation of Barundi refugees in Western Tanzania, it questions the extent to which the settlement of refugees, with its substantial inputs of international aid, represents a purely humanitarian and altruistic solution to the refugee crisis. A discussion of the contemporary spatial pattern of Barundi refugee migration and settlement within Tanzania takes place after a historical materialist analysis of the development of the region as peripheral to the core areas of capitalist development. Links are drawn between the in-migration and settlement of Barundi refugees, and the Barundi people's role in the social and economic history of the region and the country at large, through an analysis of their involvement in earlier migrant labour flows and settler populations. This historical – and more recent potential – contribution of Barundi migrants to the Tanzanian economy provides the basis for the analysis of state attempts to incorporate Barundi refugees into contemporary Tanzanian society as semi-proletarianized direct producers and labour migrants.

From the 1950s, internal conflicts within neighbouring states have periodically forced a considerable number of refugees to seek sanctuary in Tanzania. By 1987, about 90 per cent of Tanzania's refugees were concentrated in the western regions of Kigoma, Tabora and Rukwa (Figure 2.1). Western Tanzania (known as Western Province during the British colonial period) has received refugees from Zaire (1964 onwards), Rwanda (1959–64), Burundi (1972 onwards) and Uganda (1971–85), amounting to an estimated 200,500 people. With the exception of a small number of repatriated Zaireans and Ugandans, most have remained in this zone since arrival. Following the organized rural settlement policy of the 1970s, Barundi refugees became concentrated in Rukwa region, comprising in 1987 an estimated 15 per cent of the region's population. They live mainly in Mpanda district, where together with other refugee groups they constitute some 43 per cent of its population.

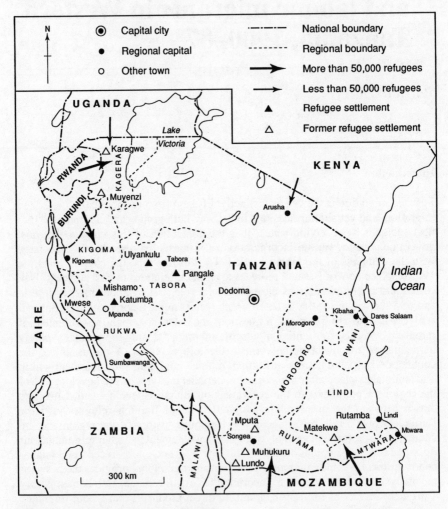

Figure 2.1 Refugee influxes into Tanzania

Population and ecology

Western Tanzania, due to certain ecological and demographic features, was in the pre-colonial era a haven for refuge-seekers and pioneer settlers. However, it emerged from the colonial period as a backward, underdeveloped area relative to other parts of the country. The cumulative effect of its integration into the world capitalist system was a massive reduction in its population and a stagnation of its economy, as Africans were coerced into labour migration, became subjected to forced labour, and succumbed to new diseases such as cerebro-spinal meningitis and influenza (Tambila, 1981). The development and promotion of settler plantation agriculture and the tolerance of African commodity production in the more accessible areas of Tanganyika[1] territory created a demand for labour which exceeded local supply. Western Province's isolation from the main ports made it unprofitable to encourage export activities. It was therefore integrated into the capitalist system as a supplier of wage labour to the plantations and mining concerns of the territory (Orde-Browne, 1946; Rodney *et al.*,1983). Its peripheral position persisted into the independence period, owing to entrenched regional differentiation and the operation of economic policies which perpetuated under-development (Wayne, 1975; Rodney *et al.*, 1983).

As part of its rural development strategy, the independent state discouraged labour migration, and adopted policies aimed at intensifying commodity production within the dominant peasant domestic unit. Although the zone has a plentiful supply of under-utilized land, immediate economic benefits were hindered by the extensive areas of low population density and enormous ecological constraints. In 1955 about 20,000 km^2 of Western Province was estimated to be covered by miombo woodland[2] and 60 per cent of the land area infested by the tsetse fly which was notorious for its associated diseases of trypanosomiasis in cattle and sleeping sickness in humans. The colonial remedy for the diseases was to forcibly move the people into settlement schemes or concentrations in an effort to control human contact with the fly. An estimated 15 per cent of the population of Tabora district, 13 per cent of Uha's and 10 per cent of Ufipa's were resettled (Tambila, 1981). Entomological evidence now shows how the concentration of people, rather than reducing the spread of the fly and halting the disease, acted only to aggravate them (Kjekshus, 1977). In fact sleeping sickness concentrations accrued more benefits to the colonial state than to the Africans they were intended to protect.

Towards the end of the British period, population concentration had clearly taken on a developmental rationale (HMSO, 1948). Health reasons continued to be quoted when people were forcibly being moved, but other assorted motives such as administrative expediency, labour recruitment, soil preservation and game concentration explain why the concentration measures retained their popularity among administrators. Throughout the 1940s, and in independent Tanzania, the concentration measure has been positively advocated as an administrative device to be pursued for reasons of 'development' (Kjekshus, 1977, p. 178).

Migrant labour from Ruanda-Urundi

Due to its proximity to the high density states of Rwanda and Burundi to the north and its separation by the lake from the Zairean kingdoms of Northern Zambia, Western Tanzania has traditionally been an area of in-migration or refuge. Migrants of Tutsi or Tusi background who were said to have originated from Rwanda and Burundi (formerly Ruanda-Urundi) settled in Western Tanganyika over two hundred years ago, and some eventually dominated the peoples of Buha, Uvinza and Ufipa between 1700 and 1921 (Wayne, 1975). In the Kasulu and Kigoma districts of Kigoma region, the Tutsi hegemony survived the colonial period, being bolstered by the colonial state until 1962 when chieftainship was abolished by the newly-independent Tanganyika. The demise of the Tutsi aristocracy was to have favourable ramifications for the in-coming Bahutu refugees in 1972.

During the colonial period Barundi peasants migrated to Tanganyika and settled among the dispersed Waha. Between the 1948 and 1957 census years the Barundi recorded the highest percentage increase (35 per cent) of any group in Tanganyika. Since the Barundi had no colonially defined tribal area, their rapid increase could be attributed to migration from Ruanda-Urundi. Colonial officers had difficulty detecting the newcomers since they shared a common language and culture. Furthermore, families became divided by territorial boundaries after the border between the mandated territories of Ruanda-Urundi and Tanganyika was designated in 1922. However, interaction in the form of cross-border trade and marital unions persists up to today. To date, most of the Barundi refugee families living in Tanzania have non-refugee relations in Kigoma region (Lugusha, 1980). This is exemplified by an incident in 1972, when the Tanzanian Member of Parliament for Manyovu-Kasulu got caught up in the conflict and was killed whilst visiting relatives on the other side of the border (*Daily News*, May 1972).

Labour migration from Ruanda-Urundi during the twentieth century was a direct response to the presence of the colonial state in Eastern and Central Africa. There was no scope for settler agricultural development in Ruanda-Urundi, where all cultivable land was heavily populated. Isolation in terms of distance from the world market, poor internal communication, plus the tight control exerted over their subjects and the economies by the local rulers, hampered for a considerable period of time any attempt by the Belgians to develop a colonial cash economy. In contrast, neighbouring British territories had seen, during the period of German colonization (1895–1918), development of settler plantation agriculture with sisal and coffee in Tanganyika and peasant cash crop production, cotton and coffee in Uganda. British territories were generally sparsely populated, with labour tied to peasant agriculture. A survey by the UN Trusteeship Council (1957) showed that the population density of Ruanda-Urundi was 81.2 per km^2, exceeding that of 'all African territories under United Nations Trusteeship as well as neighbouring countries.' In contrast, Tanganyika had a population density of five per km^2 and the potential local labour force was either small or unwilling to leave their traditional occupation, since the work on European plantations was arduous and poorly paid with unsatisfactory conditions of employment. The system whereby workers were allocated a series of tasks to complete within a specified period of time, before receiving payment, discouraged local workers. Recruits were penalized and subjected to fines, corporal punishment or imprisonment if they failed to complete their eighteen-month to three-year contracts. Under such terms of employment, desertion was the most popular form of resistance employed by the workers.

The colonial administration, faced with the major problem of securing labour from the peasantry, set up in 1926 a labour department specifically to recruit labour for government work and for the estates. The introduction of poll and hut taxes, which could only be paid in cash, linked with developments in transport, forced many workers to 'sell themselves for wages'. Taxation was used as the best method of securing labour. After the British took over Western Tanganyika from the Belgians in 1921, a poll tax was systematically collected. Orde-Browne (1946) stated that 'pressure by taxation provided forced labour in a much less obvious way than outright slavery' (p. 30). By 1936 the number of recruiters in the province numbered twenty-one, even though attempts were made in the 1930s to limit their number to two main firms in order to halt the spread of sleeping sickness. Such was the need to earn wages that people travelled to other areas to be recruited (Tambila, 1981; Sago, 1983). The term 'distance labour' refers to labour migrants travelling long distances to the plantations – for example, from Western and Southern Tanzania, as well as Rwanda and Burundi. The formation of SILABU (Labour Bureau of the Tanganyika Sisal Growers Association) in 1944, and later of the Labour Supply Corporation, signified a deliberate attempt to capture labour, especially 'distance labour'.

By this time migrants from Ruanda-Urundi formed a significant component of local recruitment. The introduction of forced labour for road and building construction, forced cash cropping, and taxation, linked with the prolonged famines of 1928–29 and 1941–44, were added incentives for Barundi migrants to travel distances of up to 900 miles to find work.

During the 1940s tea plantations in Kenya were requesting permission to recruit labour from Ruanda-Urundi (Orde-Browne, 1946). By 1950 the Belgians estimated that over 675,000 migrants from Belgian territory were in Uganda and Tanganyika, of which 157,000 were in Tanganyika (UN Trusteeship Council, 1957). However, the exact magnitude of the labour force migrating to Tanganyika was difficult to determine due to the uncontrolled nature of the flow and confusion with resident Barundi and Banyaruanda. As labour contractors were operating from the 1920s in the border regions, it is likely that the Barundi were among the first migrants. Most of the labour from the province migrated independently to the estates. This pattern may have been followed by the majority of Rundi and Ruanda. A provincial commissioner indicated that about 50 per cent of the recruits during the 1930s were immigrants from Belgian territory.

The British authorities in Tanganyika, being well aware of the labour demands of their territory, positively encouraged the flow of migrants, although the physical condition of workers coming from Ruanda-Urundi was of some concern. They were described as a 'miserably poor lot', dressed in rags and prone to suffer from malaria, relapsing fever and enteritis. Ruanda migrants especially were said to have a poor physique, whilst the Rundi had the highest reputation as labourers (Richards, 1954). During the 1930s, the colonial authorities placed restrictions on recruitment in areas near the borders in order to prevent the spread of sleeping sickness. However, by 1946 the demand for labour led the government to enact Orde-Browne's recommendations of the channelling of migrants from Ruanda-Urundi into well-defined routes, and their maintenance for two weeks in reception camps with medical facilities. By 1955 labour recruiters from British territories were actively engaged in Ruanda-Urundi.

Sisal estates of the Tanga, Coast and Dar es Salaam districts were the main destinations. From the 1920s to the 1960s, the sisal industry was the largest employer of labour in Tanganyika, with over 386,000 workers in 1956, of which 52,000 were from other territories. Migrants from Ruanda-Urundi and the furthest provinces of Tanganyika were 'distance labour' and were therefore provided with free housing. Working conditions on the estates were generally poor, and resulted in high labour turnover and absenteeism. In 1956, 48 per cent of recruited and volunteered labour deserted. Estate owners were aware of the importance of immigrant labour from Belgian and Portuguese territories, since 21 per cent of them worked as cutters, the most arduous task on the estates (Guillebaud, 1958). The colonial administration had attempted to obtain improved conditions on the estates in order to stabilize the workforce in close proximity to the estates, but to no avail.

The sisal plantations continued to be the major employer of migrant labour in the post-independence period. However, the collapse in the price of sisal, mechanization, stabilization of the workforce, and immigration restrictions had effectively reduced the flow of migrant labour. The socialist ideology of the independent Tanzanian state in the 1960s had an adverse impact on the wage labour market. As Raikes (1983) points out, the state 'officially disapproved' of labour hiring, as being 'inconsistent with its policies' (p. 288).

In recent years, the working conditions of the labourers from Ruanda-Urundi appeared to have improved very little since the 1920s. Raikes (1983) also notes that Banyarwanda and Barundi who are normally denied access to land in Tanzania, are among the worst paid and most badly treated labour force in the country. It seems that the stigma attached to sisal workers, particularly the Waha, also extended to the Barundi. However, the next wave of Barundi entered independent Tanzania not as labour migrants but as refugees.

The in-migration of refugees: the Banyarwanda

The Banyarwanda were the first group of refugees from a post-colonial state to seek refuge in independent Tanzania. Over 10,000 refugees crossed the border into the north-western districts of Ngara and Karagwe. Tanzania not being signatory to any international conventions, the warm reception extended to the refugees by the Tanzania government party was partly the result of political sympathies with the Batutsi movement as an anti-colonial liberation struggle, as well as being the expression of a traditional attitude towards refuge-seekers. This was particularly strong in this instance, where kin relations and friends lived on the other side of the border, and where the Banyarwanda and Barundi were already renowned in the territory for their involvement in labour migration. Several districts offered to take refugees; Bukoba took 3,500, Karagwe 1,600 and Biharamulo 1,300, all of these being labour-intensive coffee-growing areas (*Tanganyika Standard*, March 1962). The historical alignment of the refugee group with one particular ethnic group in Ngara district resulted in their acceptance by that group and rejection by others. In Ngara district, the Bugufi chiefdom was hostile to the Batutsi refugees who had past links with the Tusi rulers of their enemies, the Washubi. The Washubi, along with the Wanyambo, because of the historical connection welcomed the refugees and gave them land (Yeld, 1967).

According to Yeld (1967) the Washubi thought the refugees would boost their numbers and subsequently their representation on local councils, and help to eradicate the tsetse fly. Moreover, the government was aware of the potential agricultural contribution the refugees could make to the region. Initially the

Tanzanian government policy was to disperse the refugees among the local population of the border districts.

Certainly the tradition of labour migration from Ruanda-Urundi into Tanganyika affected the way in which the refugees were perceived by the authorities and the people. The authorities distributed some refugees as casual labourers among Wahaya families in Bukoba district. Gasarasi (1976) noted this was a humiliating experience for the refugees; former pastoralists and lords under *Ubuhake* (a clientele system; see Maquet, 1961) were forced to work on banana and coffee plantations, and most Wahaya saw the refugees as free labour. Bukoba district was already a destination for seasonal labour from Burundi to work as coffee pickers. Migrant labour was held in low esteem by the locals and the refugees were treated with contempt. Destitute refugees could expect no hospitality when moving into areas of labour shortage. Nevertheless, the prospect of wage labour was attractive. A study which focused on the defection of Banyarwanda refugees from settlement schemes in Burundi to neighbouring East African countries included, among the reasons for flight, the greater possibility of obtaining wage labour in Tanganyika territory (Yeld, 1967).

Because of pressure from the Rwanda government and the Organization of African Unity (OAU), which was at that time establishing its commission on refugees and trying to implement its principle of non-interference in the affairs of member states, the Tanganyika government was encouraged to enact policies which curtailed the movement of refugees. Many of the refugees were supporters of the Inyenzi guerrilla group, which had made repeated incursions into Rwanda from bases in Uganda and Tanganyika. A settlement scheme programme was finally launched in 1962, against the wishes of the Banyarwanda, at Muyenzi in Ngara district, 50 miles from the border and 180 miles from the regional headquarters. Aid came mainly from the League of Red Cross, UNHCR and voluntary agencies: the British Red Cross, Oxfam, the Swedish Churches, Lutheran World Federation's Tanganyika Christian Refugee Service (TCRS) and the World Council of Churches (WCC). An estimated $100,000 was needed; Oxfam gave $32,900, UNHCR $33,600 and the US government gave food aid.

The isolation of Muyenzi, along with the inadequacy of water supplies and the presence of predatory wild animals, all contributed to the problem of converting pastoralists into cultivators. Inequalities within the refugee group meant that rich refugees could establish a sound economic base by reverting to cattle-rearing. Cattle were obtained from Sukumaland and Burundi. In 1976, at the time of Gasarasi's survey, only 3,000 of the original 10,000 refugees remained at Muyenzi. Many fled the settlements for Burundi during the villagization programmes of 1974, when they were requested to move into *ujamaa* villages (communal villages established by the Tanzanian state) (Gasarasi, 1976; McHenry, 1979).

In 1964 and 1965, a further 3,000 Banyarwanda were resettled from Goma in Kivu Province, Zaire, to Mwesi in Mpanda district. Mwesi is a remote highland area, some 130 km from the district headquarters of Mpanda town (Figure 2.1). It is a relatively under-populated area, which unlike most parts of the district is free from the tsetse fly at the higher altitudes. With a temperate climate and moderately fertile soils, Mwesi was earmarked as a potential development area, but its location in a peripheral traditional labour migration district made it a low-priority area in terms of development funds, until the resettlement of the refugees.

Initially, Mwesi was designed to resettle 10,000 Banyarwanda refugees from Burundi. When it became apparent that the refugees from Burundi were not going to arrive, the agency was instructed by the government to continue with the expansion of the settlement. The refugee agency was informed by the Ministry of Agriculture that, 'if the original refugees do not arrive, there is a strong possibility that others from different parts of Africa may arrive'.

The possibilities of attracting humanitarian development funds to such remote areas meant that any refugee community was welcomed. Thus the 10,000 Barundi refugees were replaced by 3,000 refugees from Kivu province in Zaire. Just over half moved between early November and late December 1964, and the second group of 1,300 moved between 19 May and 18 June 1965. The Mwesi highlands being environmentally similar to their homeland enabled the Banyarwanda to establish their traditional occupation of pastoralism along with the cultivation of grains. In 1986, a livestock survey found 5,864 cows and goats within the settlement, and some twenty-eight herds in the surrounding area. Extensive grain cultivation is developing with the presence of a Munyarwanda-owned tractor hire service. From the 1986 harvest, Mwesi contributed 10 and 11 per cent of the district cooperative's maize and beans respectively.

Mwesi's refugee population decreased to 2,290 in 1975 following considerable out-migration to Burundi or to other parts of Tanzania, namely Kigoma region and the local towns of Sumbawanga and Mpanda. Out-migration accelerated after the citizenship decree of 1980. The extension of citizenship to the Banyarwanda is unique in Africa and Tanzania. Gasarasi (1990) attributed this singular benevolent act to utilitarian considerations and the need to stabilize a politically vulnerable group. However, other influential factors were the relatively small size of the group and their already disintegrating settlements, and an increased awareness by the government that a politically demobilized refugee group would ensure continued good relations with the Rwanda government at a time when cooperation was needed over the proposed Kagera river basin development. More significant, Gasarasi (1990) has shown that a number of Banyarwanda were, under the existing naturalization laws, eligible for citizenship and that many had submitted applications prior to the decree. The state was therefore capitalizing on what had become a *de facto* situation, therefore, increasing the international standing of the Tanzanian state and leadership in the field of refugee assistance (former President Nyerere was awarded the Hansen medal for services to refugees in 1983), and reassuring neighbouring countries of its commitment to preventing the use of its territory for subversion.

As a consequence, the Banyarwanda are no longer considered refugees, and Mwesi has ceased to be an official refugee settlement, even though the processing of citizenship applications has been unnecessarily slow and complicated, and ten years later remains incomplete (Gasarasi, 1990). The proportion of Banyarwanda at Mwesi has fallen from about 50 to 28 per cent of Mwesi's population, due to their out-migration and the in-migration of Wachagga, Wafipa and Wapimbwe. Settlement of these groups was stimulated by the provision of basic services, and in the case of the Wachagga, actively encouraged by the government (URT, 1969) with the intention of ameliorating the land pressure problem of the Kilimanjaro region and opening up Mwesi for greater state accumulation.

Barundi refugees: patterns of migration

Refugees first started fleeing Burundi as early as October 1965, after the failed Bahutu coup, and later in 1969 after the threat of a coup resulted in reprisals by the Batutsi-controlled state on the Bahutu population. However, the majority of the refugees fled after May 1972, when, following another unsuccessful coup, further reprisals by the Batutsi-controlled government culminated in 200,000 people being murdered and over 150,000 fleeing to the neighbouring countries of Rwanda to the north, Tanzania to the east, and Zaire to the west. At the end of 1973, some 90,000 Barundi nationals were in exile, 50,000 in Tanzania, 30,000 in Zaire and 10,000 in Rwanda.

The refugees came mainly from the southern districts of Burundi, where in 1972 the fighting was particularly intense. The existence of past interaction with the Waha resulted initially in what has been termed 'traditional African hospitality' in refugee literature. The scarcity of resources in Africa's rural areas and the integration of African peasant communities into the capitalist system have meant that today the myth of traditional hospitality can be used as a euphemism for exploitation of refugee labour. Alternatively, in conditions of extreme poverty and scarce resources it may even result in the deterioration of the living conditions of the hosts (Chambers, 1979; Kibreab, 1983; Yeld, 1967).

When the Barundi first crossed the border, the earliest arrivals did have relatives in the adjacent areas who took initial responsibility for them. This is indicated by the fact that over 5,000 of the 8,696 refugees registered by 13 May 1972 were collected by relatives living in the Kigoma area (*Daily News*, 13 May 1972). One month later, an estimated 8,000 refugees were staying with relatives, more than twice the number in the government camp at Pangale, which was 420 km from the border. Many refugees may have escaped registration by moving direct to the homes of their relatives, especially those with some familiarity with the territory.

Every effort was made to enforce the government policy, in accordance with the OAU recommendations, that refugees be moved over 50 km from the border. Local people and party officials were encouraged to report refugees and ensure their removal to Pangale. The government policy of settling refugees in organized schemes frequently caused them to be rooted out by the authorities and forcibly moved. Even if 'traditional hospitality' existed among the Waha, in this case national considerations overruled local sentiment and kinship.

Forced settlement: the move to Ulyankulu, Katumba and Mishamo

The origin of the settlement solution to the refugee problem has been discussed elsewhere (Holborn, 1972; Gasarasi, 1984). In the context of the spatial reorganization of rural dwellers in Western Tanzania, it was in essence the old colonial strategy of settlement schemes located in areas where the tsetse dominates. The refugees, once provided with basic services, were to become pioneers and developers of the periphery. When in August 1972 the refugee population at Pangale had reached 18,000, the state and the donors (UNHCR and TCRS) selected a site for their settlement at Ulyankulu, some 85 km from Tabora town in the direction of Urambo. A feasibility study was carried out by FAO, UNHCR, WHO and the Tanzanian government, as the result of which an area of 750 km² was considered suitable for an estimated refugee population of 18,000 (*Daily News*, 28 August 1972). Ulyankulu, situated within the miombo woodland area, contained swamps, was infested with tsetse flies and was therefore sparsely populated. Most of its original population was forcibly moved to sleeping sickness settlements during the colonial period. The area was designated in 1965 by the World Bank for the development of a tobacco complex aimed at establishing 15,000 Tanzanians as cooperative tobacco growers. The local member of parliament was keen to have the refugee population, not only to boost the members of his constituency, but also to provide cheap labour for local farmers, as well as to increase the cash crop output of the area.

In September 1972 refugees began moving to the settlement in groups of 500 per day, where they were registered and allocated plots of 3.5 hectares per household, on which they were expected to construct their homes and cultivate. Simple farming implements were provided. By the end of 1972, some 3,215 plots had been surveyed and 250 km² of additional land was made available. A rapid increase in Ulyankulu's population ensued. Large-scale movements from the border during the months of February to June raised the population to 46,500 (TCRS, Annual Report, 1974).

In August 1972 a second site was chosen at Katumba in Mpanda district for some 10,000 refugees. Katumba was selected from five sites chosen by the government. Its situation in miombo woodland some 400 km from the border and 25 km north-east of Mpanda town and on the branch railway line between Kaliua and Mpanda made it suitable for containment and yet accessible to other regions. The settlement site was also an area earmarked by the government for tobacco production. The first refugees, some 3,000, moved to Katumba in May 1973. At the end of the year Katumba had a population of 7,513, and by July 1974 its population had increased to 45,130. The sudden rise in the settlement's refugee population was the result of the villagization policy of the Tanzanian government. During the 1974 forced villagization programme of 'Operation Kigoma' many self-settled refugees fled from the border regions into the settlements. TCRS estimated that at times some 3,000 refugees were arriving per week. At the end of 1975, over 51,000 refugees were in Katumba and by 1976 the settlement had attained a population of 54,440. Considerable pressure was placed on the physical resources of Ulyankulu and Katumba, and this increase occurred in the light of a 1974 survey by the donors which suggested that the settlements could be expanded to support a viable population of 45,000 refugees each. Both settlements were thus overpopulated. At the end of 1976, Ulyankulu's population was 59,000, well beyond its estimated carrying capacity. Ulyankulu was then the fourth largest population concentration in the country. To reduce the effects of overpopulation, a viability study recommended the relocation of 30,000 people (UNHCR, 1977). With the cooperation of UNHCR, the state selected a further site at Mishamo in Mpanda district.

Mishamo is located on the Mpanda–Uvinza road at a distance of 130 km from the border, 125 km from Mpanda town, and 80 km from the nearest village. Prior to the settlement of refugees the area was relatively unpopulated, since most of the peasants scattered across the area were resettled in the nearby village of Mpanda

Ndogo during the villagization programme of 1974. Mishamo covers an area of 2,050 km² and was planned to take an estimated population of 25,000 from Ulyankulu and 10–20,000 from Kigoma region. Refugees were first moved to the settlement in 1978, and by December 1979 the settlement contained some 25,000 from Ulyankulu and 2,169 from Kigoma. The smaller than expected population from Kigoma region reflected the resistance of the estimated 22,000 refugees in the border area to resettlement. This forced the government to reach an agreement with UNHCR for the provision of development aid to those villages with a significant refugee population.

Refugees and development policy in the periphery

Because of state-controlled organized settlement, the spatial distribution of refugee groups in Western Tanzania is such that most are settled over 100 km from their respective borders. Even with the relative porosity of the border and the difficult terrain of the border regions, the government has managed to place 82 per cent of the Barundi refugee population in organized settlements, whose total population is estimated to be around 154,400. Mpanda district, in particular, has a disproportionate amount of refugees. In 1967 the district's population was just over 60,000; thus the 1970s in-migration of refugees doubled its population in the space of eight years.

By the 1978 census refugees comprised 43 per cent of Mpanda population and 6.6 per cent of the population of the newly-formed Rukwa region (URT, 1981). Today Katumba, with a population of 66,885, is by far the largest concentration of rural dwellers in Western Tanzania. Restrictions on mobility, and the necessity for a *Kibali* (pass) in order to leave the settlements, place the refugees literally in the category of 'captured' peasantry. Only a few enterprising businessmen have managed to carry out their occupations outside the settlement boundaries without the permission of the Ministry of Home Affairs. They, however, are subjected to frequent police raids and repatriation to the settlements. Apart from the need to gain control over the productive capacity of the Barundi, the reluctance of the Tanzanian state to encourage mass naturalization can be attributed also to the size of the group, the effect it would have on local political representation, and the possibility that freedom of movement would stimulate unwanted migration to urban centres.

With the fall in the world price of raw materials (especially sisal) in the 1960s, the promotion of Western Tanzania as a labour reserve subsided. However, these peripheral areas retained their remote and impoverished character and low levels of development of infrastructures, and contributed little to the export-oriented market of the national economy. In the 1970s the massive reorganization of the rural population into 'development' villages was indicative of the state's determination to control the peasantry and monetarize the rural sector. The failure of the Tanzanian state to further the expansion of peasant cash crop production was linked to its inability to cater for the welfare needs of the rural populace.

Consequently, donor-financed rural integrated development projects (RIDEPs) were conceived in the early 1970s, whereby the country was divided amongst western countries. Each of the thirty-two regions in the country was assigned either to a developed country in the western or eastern bloc, or to the World Bank and United Nations organizations like FAO and UNDP. Each region was to receive a team of experts from the foster country, whose task was to concentrate aid in multi-sectoral projects. The rationale put forward by organizations such as the World Bank was that increased services would encourage farmers to partici-pate further in cash cropping. Foreign experts were needed because of the ineffi-ciency of local organizations. The activities encompassed in an integrated project, meanwhile, were expected to give donors direct control over the rural develop-ment process.

The creation of Rukwa region in 1974 was part of this nationwide attempt by the independent state to attract development aid to peripheral areas. Rukwa was adopted by the Norwegians, who described the region as 'potentially the greatest remaining agricultural zone in Africa' (NORAD/NORCONSULT, 1982). Rukwa is certainly representative of the low-density, high-potential regions of Tanzania. A 1976 Bureau of Resource Assessment and Land Use Planning of the University of Dar es Salaam (BRALUP) report identified the peasants as 'the strongest productive force in the region with 97 per cent of the cropped area and most of the livestock' (Sandberg, 1976, p. 77). Yet only 3 per cent of the land area is cultivated, while 40 per cent is considered suitable for agriculture (University of Dar es Salaam, 1984). Intensification of peasant production has been seen as the most viable means of extracting a surplus: 'a mere four per cent increase of the productivity of existing peasant fields would more than off-set the entire produc-tion from the state farm and ranches' (Sandberg, 1976, p. 77). BRALUP identified two major roles for the region, first as a region of food surplus in deficit areas, secondly as a region of in-migration for the settlement of populations from regions of land shortage. Not surprisingly, from as early as the 1960s the state has tried to attract population from high-density areas like Kilimanjaro and Mwanza to these peripheral regions. The unenthusiastic response from Tanzanians made the arrival of some 100,000 refugees a blessing in disguise. Furthermore, in 1981, the Tanzanian state was considering the settlement of some 300,000 Banyarwanda refugees/immigrants in Rukwa region, the bulk of whom were to be located in Mpanda district (NORAD/NORCONSULT 1982).

The settlement of the refugee communities conformed to the requirements of the RIDEP. Along with the provision of minimal services, cash cropping of tobacco and basic staples was vigorously promoted within the settlement. Within five years the refugees in the Mpanda area became the district's major producers of crops sold to marketing boards. By 1986, they had brought 36,890 hectares under cultivation, producing all of the district's marketed tobacco and 80 and 99 per cent of its maize and beans respectively. Rukwa, through the productivity of the refugee population, has become one of the 'big four' food-producing regions of Tanzania. This observation is supported by the Regional Agricultural Officer, who commented that 'with the arrival of the refugees at Mwesi, Katumba and Mishamo, the production of crops, especially maize has greatly increased in the region' (*Daily News*, 1 July 1985).

The presence of the refugees thus serves two functions: firstly to expand peasant agricultural production and secondly to fulfil the casual labour require-ments of the local and even national economies. The state has tried to get the refugees to participate in more coordinated labour migration to plantations, as state-owned plantations have been permitted directly to recruit labour in the settlements. Recently in an attempt to revive the sisal industry, shortage of labour has resulted in a renewed state-sponsored recruitment drive in the traditional labour reserve which included the refugee settlements. Direct recruitment was carried out under the auspices of the Ministry of Labour and Manpower Development in the former labour reserves of western Tanzania. It was to this end that during 1982 the ministry undertook a survey of labour demands in the settlement. In 1986 the Tea Authority recruited some 600 Katumba men to work on plantations in Mbeya region. Many deserted and returned to the settlement before their contracts expired. Labour shortages on plantations and the recent state concessions to large-scale agriculture imply that recruitment will increase in former labour reserves such as Mpanda district. Refugees, with restrictions on their independent search for employment outside the settlement, find themselves drawn to employment which is sanctioned by the state. It is unlikely that the Tanzanian state will encourage greater labour market flexibility for fear of competition with nationals and exodus from the remote settlement areas.

It is anticipated that in the 1990s marketed output by the refugees will stagnate or decline as numerous economic, ecological and spatial constraints on household production begin to manifest themselves. Within the restricted geographical area of the settlements, production has intensified to the extent that land degradation is becoming apparent in the close-settled zones. This situation is aggravated by the ineffective marketing policies of the monopolistic regional cooperative union, which frequently cause delayed payments to farmers and inadequate supplies of highly capitalized inputs. The resultant squeeze on production has created a crisis in household production as peasants adopt multiple survival strategies to meet the costs of subsistence. Ensuring food supplies to the domestic unit has been paramount, as the majority of households continue to emphasize food crops, spurning the vigorously promoted cash crop, tobacco, with its slightly improved extension services. Increased producer prices and the removal of input subsidies as proposed in the economic liberalization policies of structural adjustment programmes will do little to alter the historically precarious nature of production in western Tanzania. In sum, the objective conditions of production and distribution in the Mpanda area have not only affected the surplus appropriation by the state but have also limited the development of a thriving parallel market in food commodities, so much in evidence elsewhere in Tanzania. Therefore peasants cannot easily withdraw from commodity relations with the state marketing agencies. They can only affect the intensity of the relationship by exercising some control over the types of crops grown.

Conclusion

Western Tanzania, refuge for the majority of Barundi refugees, has been characterized by low population density, infrastructural impoverishment and economic backwardness. These characteristics owe their origin partially to the colonial period, when economic and settlement policies forced people into labour migration and sleeping sickness concentrations, thus contributing to depopulation, increasing loss of ecological control, and low levels of agricultural development.

Migrants, whether moving as settlers or for labour, have been an essential feature of the history of Western Tanzania. The establishment of independent political units altered the dominant character of cross-border migration, and those fleeing political persecution could be drawn under the new humanitarian umbrella. Moreover, with accorded refugee status came an increased awareness of the rights of refugees to externally-derived material assistance, which has meant that the patterns of their distribution within the host countries is well coordinated and may even be linked to the labour requirements of the hosts. In this respect Barundi refugees can be placed at the end of a continuum of labour migrants to Tanzania.

As settlement schemes have been seen by the colonial and post-colonial states as a strategy for gaining control over the productive capacity of the peasantry, from sleeping sickness concentrations to *ujamaa* villages, it is not surprising that refugee schemes might function as part of the development policy of the Tanzanian state. However, the difficulties now faced by the refugee settlements were evident in those previous schemes for nationals, where failure to stimulate production has been attributed to several factors, from the coercive nature of state apparatus and subsequent peasant resistance, to the declining terms of trade for cash crops (Bernstein, 1981). One significant difference between schemes for nationals and those for refugees is that the latter enabled dispossessed people to re-establish their households and community structures relatively quickly, and according to Kibreab (1987) helped them to regain the confidence and self-respect which were destroyed by uprooting and flight. As with Kibreab's (1990) study of Ethiopian settlements in Sudan, a combination of land, labour, technological and ecological constraints hinder the prospect of self-reliance which appears to be unattainable under the deteriorating economic conditions of the host country. This situation is not peculiar to refugees: it epitomizes the plight of the majority of direct producers in Tanzania, where integration for refugees refers to their incorporation in the wider economic system as peasants or labour migrants. No other aspect of this multi-faceted term has been given serious consideration as restrictions on movement and political participation continue to prevent refugees who pay taxes from having any role in activities central to their existence.

Notes

1. Mainland Tanzania was known as Tanganyika during the British colonial period. The name Tanzania arose after its unification with Zanzibar in 1964.
2. Miombo is a single-storey woodland with a light closed canopy, dominated by trees of the Genera Brachystegia and Julbernardia type, which may vary in height from 4 m to about 15 m. There are a few scattered shrubs under the canopy (Mansfield *et al.*, quoted in King, 1977, pp. 3–4).

References

Bernstein, H., 1981, 'Notes on state and the peasantry: the Tanzanian case', *Review of African Political Economy*, **21**: 44–62.
Chambers, R., 1979, 'Rural refugees in Africa: what the eye does not see', *Disasters*, **3** (4):

381–92.

Daily News, Newspaper, Dar es Salaam, 1972–87.

Gasarasi, C.P., 1976, *The life of a refugee settlement: the case of Muyenzi in Ngara District,* United Nations High Commissioner for Refugees, Geneva.

Gasarasi, C.P., 1984, *The tripartite approach to the resettlement and the integration of rural refugees in Tanzania,* Research Report no. 71, Scandinavian Institute for African Studies, Uppsala, Sweden.

Gasarasi, C.P., 1990, 'The mass naturalization and further integration of Rwandese refugees in Tanzania: process, problems and prospects', *Journal of Refugee Studies,* 3 (2): 88–109.

Guillebaud, C.W., 1958, *An economic survey of the sisal industry of Tanganyika: Tanganyika Sisal Growers Association,* James Nesbi, Welwyn, UK.

HMSO (His Majesty's Stationery Office), 1948, *African population of Tanganyika territory, geographical and tribal studies,* Government Printer, Dar es Salaam.

Holborn, L., 1972, *Refugees: a challenge of our time: the role of UNHCR,* Scarecrow Press, Metuchen, New Jersey.

Kibreab, G., 1983, *Reflections on the African refugee problem: a critical analysis of some basic assumptions,* Research Report no. 67. Scandinavian Institute for African Studies, Uppsala, Sweden.

Kibreab, G., 1987, *Refugees and development in Africa: the case of Eritrea,* Red Sea Press, Trenton, New Jersey.

Kibreab, G., 1990, *The Sudan: from subsistence to wage labor: refugee settlements in the central and eastern Sudan,* Red Sea Press, Trenton, New Jersey.

King, R.B., 1977, *Land resources of the Rukwa region: a provisional assessment,* BRALUP Research Report no. 24, new series, University of Dar es Salaam Press.

Kjekshus, H., 1977, *Ecology control and economic development in East African history,* Heinemann, London.

Lugusha, E.A., 1980, *A preliminary report of a socio-economic survey of spontaneously settled refugees in Kigoma region,* Department of Sociology, University of Dar es Salaam.

Maquet, J., 1961, *The premise of inequality in Rwanda,* Oxford University Press, Oxford.

McHenry, D., 1979, *Tanzania's ujamaa villages,* University of California Press, Berkeley, California.

NORAD/NORCONSULT, 1982, *Rukwa Water Master Plan, 10 (3), Final Report,* NORAD/NORCONSULT, Oslo.

Orde-Browne, G. StJ., 1946, *Labour conditions in East Africa,* HMSO, London.

Raikes, P., 1983, 'Rural differentiation and class formation in Tanzania', *Journal of Peasant Studies,* 5 (3): 385–325.

Richards, A., ed., 1954, *Economic development and tribal change: a study of immigrant labour in Buganda,* Heffer & Sons, Cambridge.

Rodney, W., Tambila, K. and Sago, L., 1983, *Migrant labour in Tanzania during the colonial period. Case studies of recruitment and conditions of labour in the sisal industry,* Institut für Africa-Kunde, Hamburg.

Sago, L., 1983, 'Labour reservoir: the Kigoma case', in W. Rodney *et al., Migrant labour in Tanzania during the colonial period. Case studies of recruitment and conditions of labour in the sisal industry,* Institut für Africa-Kunde, Hamburg.

Sandberg, A., 1976, *Rukwa Rural Integrated Development Programme, Draft Report, Part 1,* BRALUP, University of Dar es Salaam.

Tambila, K., 1981, 'A History of the Rukwa region (Tanzania) ca. 1870–1940: aspects of economic and social chance from pre-colonial to colonial times', Ph.D. thesis, Hamburg University.

Tanganyika Standard, Newspaper, Dar es Salaam.

University of Dar es Salaam, 1984, *Atlas of the natural, physical features and agricultural*

32   *Patricia Daley*

potential of the Rukwa region, Institute of Resource Assessment and Clark University, Massachusetts.

UN Trusteeship Council, 1957, *Committee on rural economic development: study of population, land utilization and land system in Ruanda-Urundi*, UN Trusteeship Council.

URT (United Republic of Tanzania), 1969, *Second five year plan. July 1969–June 1974, Vol. 11*, URT, Dar es Salaam.

URT, 1981, *Population census. Volumes II & VII, 1978,* Bureau of Statistics, Ministry of Planning and Economic Affairs, URT, Dar es Salaam.

UNHCR (United Nations High Commissioner for Refugees), 1977, *Report on a UNHCR-sponsored viability report on Ulyankulu and Katumba, May 1977*, UNHCR, Geneva.

Wayne, J., 1975, 'Colonialism and underdevelopment in Kigoma region, Tanzania: social structural view', *Canadian Review of Sociology and Anthropology*, **12** (3): 316–32.

Yeld, R., 1967, 'The resettlement of refugees', in R. Apthorpe, ed., *Land Settlement and Rural development in Eastern Africa*, Nkanga Transition Books Ltd, Kampala.

Further reading

Armstrong, A., 1987, 'Refugee settlement schemes in Tanzania', *Land Reform, Land Settlement and Cooperatives*, **1–2**: 83–108.

Daley, P., 1991, 'Gender displacement and social reproduction: settling Burundian refugees in western Tanzania', *Journal of Refugee Studies*, **4** (3): 248–66.

Kibreab, G., 1985, *African refugees: reflections on the African refugee problem*, Africa World Press, Trenton, New Jersey.

Raikes, P., 1983, 'Rural differentiation and class formation in Tanzania', *Journal of Peasant Studies*, **5** (3): 385–325.

Rodney, W., Tambila, K. and Sago, L., 1983, *Migrant labour in Tanzania during the colonial period. Case studies of recruitment and conditions of labour in the sisal industry*, Institut für Africa-Kunde, Hamburg.

3 'Internal refugees': the case of the displaced in Khartoum

Johnathan Bascom

Introduction

Internally displaced persons are the forgotten half of the millions of people who have been forced to migrate from their area of customary habitation. The global total of involuntary migrants is divided between international refugees and internal displacees. At any given time, the global total of internally displaced persons is usually comparable to, or greater, than that of international refugees. In early 1992, for example, there were more than twenty-three million people who had fled to havens within their country of citizenship in addition to almost seventeen million persons outside their home country (USCR, 1992).

Despite their significant number and the fact that most flee from the same well-founded fears of persecution as cross-border refugees, internally displaced persons receive far less protection, assistance, and research attention. Because they do not, or cannot, leave the country of their citizenship, 'internal refugees' do not receive the protection provided by the Geneva Convention or the assistance offered by the United Nations High Commissioner for Refugees.[1] In spite of the fact that these movements are of considerable social, economic and demographic significance, little or no attempt has been made to examine impelled population movements within developing countries (Hugo, 1987). The current state of the literature on internal refugees is likened to the limited amount which existed for international refugees at the beginning of the 1980s. In sum, internally displaced people in dozens of countries are subject to inconsistent *ad hoc* responses from the donor community, reinforced further by the marked disparity in attention they receive from the academic community.

This chapter relies on the case of one country to demonstrate the vulnerability of internal refugees in general. Among twenty-nine countries with 'significant' populations of internally displaced citizens, Sudan ranks number one (see Table 3.1). Conservative estimates suggest that at least four million people are displaced within Sudan. Nearly one million of them inhabit the metropolitan area of Khartoum.[2] The vast majority of these people fled to the capital to escape the brutalities of a protracted civil war in the southern region of the country, exacerbated further by drought, a series of famines, the erosion of their agricultural production systems, and finally, the collapse of their former way of life. During the last two years, however, the problem of their displacement has taken on another new dimension. In April 1991 the Sudanese government began a massive demolition and relocation campaign designed to rid the capital of the displaced population.

Table 3.1 Significant populations of internally displaced civilians worldwide, early 1992*

Region Country	Displaced people
Africa	
Sudan	4,750,000
South Africa	4,100,000
Mozambique	2,000,000
Angola	1,000,000
Ethiopia/Eritrea	1,000,000
Liberia	500,000
Somalia	500,000 – 1,000,000
Uganda	300,000
Sierra Leone	145,000
Rwanda	100,000
Senegal	12,000
East Africa and Pacific	
Burma	1,000,000
Philippines	900,000 – 1,500,000
Sri Lanka	600,000
Cambodia	180,000
Europe and North America	
Commonwealth of Independent States	750,000
Former Yugoslavia	557,000
Cyprus	210,000 – 268,000
Turkey	30,000
Middle East and South Asia	
Afghanistan	2,000,000
Lebanon	750,000
Iraq	700,000
India	85,000
Latin America	
Nicaragua	350,000
El Salvador	200,000 – 400,000
Peru	200,000
Columbia	150,000
Guatemala	150,000
Honduras	7,000
TOTAL	19,001,000 – 22,169,000

Source: USCR, 1992

Note: * Because some form of registration almost always occurs upon the arrival of international refugees, the quality of data for displaced populations beyond national boundaries is better than for those within them. Therefore, this table presents only 'significant' populations and the figures constitute reported estimates at best.

The conditions under which more than 400,000 people have been dispossessed and relocated to desert sites outside Khartoum illustrates the dire need for new measures on behalf of internally displaced people worldwide.

Definitions: critical issues beneath the semantics

Harrell-Bond (1986) has highlighted the 'politics of nomenclature' associated with labelling refugees. In similar fashion, a number of important issues underlie the semantics associated with internally displaced persons. Internal dislocation is the product of several factors, many of which are often interrelated, such as political conflict (i.e. ethno-religious unrest, outright civil war, revolution, terrorism or expulsion); ecological degradation, including famines and other so-called 'natural disasters' which are increasingly a product of human responsibility; and technological developments like agricultural mechanization, hydro-electric schemes, or resettlement programs (Hansen and Oliver-Smith, 1982). Internally dislocated persons are, by definition, forced by one condition or another to migrate from their homes and settle elsewhere within the country.

The vast majority of internally dislocated persons are forced to flee civil strife for safer havens. Most, therefore, fall within the classic dictionary definition of a refugee as 'one who flees to a place of safety' (Demko and Wood, 1987). In keeping with this kind of broadly-formulated criterion, Clark (1989) employs the term 'internal refugees' as a means to recognize a class of people who are compelled by armed conflict to migrate from their home to a location elsewhere within the country. 'Refugee' is also a more evocative term that connotes the need for entitlement. As such it is a useful designator to advocate protection, assistance, and attention for internally displaced persons.

The issue of status, however, can also be argued in the opposite direction. Rogge (1987) for example, suggests that the political push factor that causes many rural–urban refugees – and, by extension, displaced persons as well – to take flight is merely a catalyst to already existing desires and aspirations to become part of the urbanization process occurring in Africa. Arguments like this minimize the differences between voluntary and involuntary migration. Governments often take this line of argument further. When tension peaked in early 1985, for example, the internally displaced population in Khartoum were referred to collectively as 'vagabonds'. The Governor of Khartoum told journalists that the 690,000 'alien elements' from remote areas had sneaked into the capital. He also announced plans by the government to remove 'squatters' as 'a prelude to deporting them to production sites in various provinces' (Timberlake, 1985, p. 189). Rhetorical designations like 'squatters', 'vagabonds' or 'alien elements' render internally displaced citizens as collective entities without rights. At minimum, governments use such terms to help evade their responsibility for creating, or responding to, the depravation of their own displaced citizens. Frequently, however, a shift in semantics helps justify harsh action on the part of the government against displacees (e.g. 'squatters' become a physical problem to be rectified by the Ministry of Housing which is, in fact, overseeing the current destruction of displaced communities in Khartoum).

Internal refugees often remain 'hidden' for other reasons as well. Foreign refugee movements often occur *en masse*, and thereby become high-profile media events which host governments can actively encourage in order to elicit international assistance. In contrast, displaced persons tend to migrate gradually and blend more readily into the indigenous population. Moreover, they are generally 'quarantined' from media attention. Because the presence of large displaced communities and the treatment they receive are politically charged issues, governments tend to resist media coverage as well as relief efforts as a 'violation of national sovereignty'. Herein lies the crux issue at stake: national sovereignty versus international responsibility. Legally speaking, internal refugees remain under the sovereignty of the state and, thereby, beyond the purview of direct international intervention. Attempts to deal with mass exodus must rely on the consent of governments to operate – often the very perpetrators of the human rights abuses that give rise to displacement. The tragic history of displaced persons who have fled to Khartoum illustrates the serious consequences of this system, thereby underscoring the need for more 'points of entry and leverage' for internal displacees worldwide.

The Khartoum case study

The capital area of Khartoum is comprised of the three cities – Khartoum, Khartoum North and Omdurman – which straddle the juncture of the Nile rivers. Like many African cities, it offers the largest concentration of economic activities in the country. Hence, well-established chains of migration between peripheral regions and the capital acted as conduits for two major conflict-induced flows during the 1980s.

The exodus to Khartoum

The first great influx of displaced persons came to the capital as a result of the collapse of traditional rainfed farming in the western portion of the country. During the last twenty-five years the Sudanese state has actively encouraged the expansion of mechanized agriculture in rainfed areas to the virtual neglect of peasant agriculture (Bascom, 1990). Vast tracts of land, usually in one thousand feddans units (1 feddan = 2.57 ha), have been leased to private operators for nominal fees or expropriated outright. Scheme operators move in and pay off or evict traditional farmers, exclude nomads' herds from grazing except on harvest stubble (for which they are charged), clear off trees and the remaining vegetative cover, often by fire, and then deep plough through the soil for planting sorghum and sesame. After a few quick yields deplete the soil, the scheme is abandoned and operators move on to another site. Between 1964 and 1984 sorghum yields in Sudan steadily declined from 400 kg per feddan to 200 kg per feddan (Carter, 1986, p. 8).

Land degradation and declining food security, combined with minimal agricultural and industrial investment, set the stage for a devastating famine and a massive migration out of the western region, in particular. The 1984–5 famine, known as *sona jafaf* or 'the year of hunger', was the worst this century (De Waal, 1989). Despite the failure of rains in 1984, President Nimeri refused to admit the impending crisis, which crucially delayed the request for international aid and the flow of assistance to drought victims. The subsequent famine affected more than ten million Sudanese people, killed more than 250,000, and forced tens of thousands to move in desperation, many of whom came to Khartoum from the Darfur and North Kordofan areas from late 1984 to early 1986.

A second great wave of displaced persons entered Khartoum as a result of a protracted civil war in the southern region of the country. Southerners began fleeing to Khartoum when a fragile federation between the north and the south began to collapse in the early 1980s. In 1986, government-armed militias pillaged village after village in northern Bahr el Ghazal and Upper Nile provinces. Tens of thousands fled northward to Khartoum or eastward and out of the country. In 1987, the Southern People's Liberation Army (SPLA) besieged the principal southern cities – Wau, Malakal, Juba and Aweil – and rendered food supplies tenuous at best. Although thousands evacuated into the so-called 'transition zone' between the north and the south, tens of thousands, and then, hundreds of thousands more moved onward to Khartoum. A survey undertaken in early 1987 estimated that southerners constituted 62 per cent of the displaced population (Bassan, cited in Burr, 1990, p. 10). In sum, the recent failure to address the deterioration of food security or resolve the ongoing civil war has meant that those problems have come 'home to roost' in the national capital by way of no less than 845,000 displaced persons.

Life for the displaced in Khartoum

The Khartoum displaced have had to establish homes and negotiate livelihoods in spite of their own severe impoverishment, as well as encountering indifference or open hostility from the resident population. In the words of one displaced person:

> They do not accept any outsider to come and settle among them ... They consider whoever is black and comes from the West and South as an outsider. Once you find them in such a hostile attitude, you find yourself obliged to leave ... Then we said, since there is an empty area, it is better to leave and we left. (Manga and Miller, 1988, p. 20)

Not surprisingly, most southerners were forced either to settle on wasteland lots within the city (e.g. garbage dumps) or move to the margins of the three cities. In addition to small enclaves within the city, sizeable communities formed along the northwest and southwest rim of Omdurman, the northern and eastern edge of Khartoum North, and just beyond the greenbelt flanking the southern portion of Khartoum (see Figure 3.1).

The first initiative by a non-governmental organization to help southern displaced began on the eastern edge of Khartoum North (Burr, 1990). Like many other sites for displaced persons, Hag Yusif benefited from no essential services. Also known as Hag Yusif 'Carton', from the thousands of shacks built from whatever refuse could be salvaged, this site offered no health clinic, no school and no clean water. Some males found work as labourers in the booming construction industry, boosted by speculators who invested their 'earnings' from a lucrative black-market exchange rate into house construction. Women found it difficult to

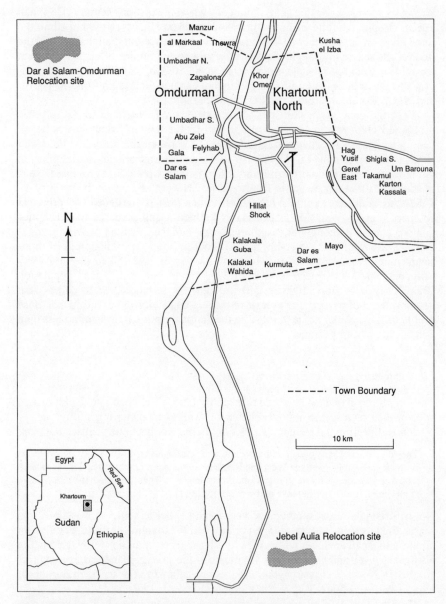

Figure 3.1 Displaced communities around Khartoum, Sudan

compete with Ethiopian refugee women for low-paying, domestic service jobs (Kebbede, 1991). To generate income, some turned to brewing sorghum beer (*marissa*) despite the constant threat of reprisals from the local police for breaking the ban on the production and consumption of alcohol under Islamic law. Children obtained income for the household by selling petty commodities like matches, cigarettes, peanuts, fruits, soaps or gum. Whatever their total earnings, households purchased five basic necessities: foodstuffs (principally grain), water (brought by donkey-pulled tanks), charcoal, kerosene for lamps (there was no electricity) and transportation for any member who travelled into Khartoum to work.

Contrary to the stereotypes of chaotic squalor that often dominate perceptions of such settlements, a distinct social structure can be found within most displaced communities. The inhabitants of Hag Yusif, for example, formed villages as the site expanded eastward to encompass as many as 200,000 displaced persons (Burr, 1990, p. 7). The first inhabitants of one village – Takamul – created a committee to supervise and organize installation of new-comers, resist efforts to expropriate their land, and mediate conflicts within the community that might provoke the intervention of the government. The committee made construction according to official norms its ultimate goal, hoping to draw sufficient attention and apprecia- tion from officials to obtain the recognition of the Ministry of Housing:

> We only directed them [the inhabitants] that everybody should reserve a piece of land which is just enough for him. No one should catch a big piece, otherwise the matter would turn into business ... If someone starts constructing on the road, we tell him 'this is not proper, this road is needed and necessary for me and for you too; it will help in land planning' ... We used to instruct people in this way ... And right from the beginning we warn them against constructing in carton. This is because constructions in carton are vulnerable to fire. Therefore we asked them to build their houses of mud. We said it's better to surround the houses with walls so that the roads may become clear. In fact there are sites which we left for general services: hospital, market, schools, mosques, churches ... That means all the people of the area agree on a certain space and the members of the committee tell the people 'no one should construct here; we reserve it for a general purpose'. We are waiting for the government to arrange the place ... We are waiting to see what the government is going to do with us. (Manga and Miller, 1988, p. 19)

Further clan or village clustering exists within the villages that subdivide the larger settlements. Ethnic clustering is not unique to displaced in Khartoum; it is a typical feature of the migratory process which helps maintain links with home and expedite the process of assimilation for new-comers to cities (Hill, 1977; Lightfoot, 1979; Peil, 1981). When demolition campaigns occur, however, the destruction of social fabric within displaced communities is often as serious as the destruction of physical structures *per se*.

The demolition campaigns

Like other African capitals atop their urban hierarchy, Khartoum has long at- tracted incoming migrants from rural areas. Even before the influx of internally displaced persons in the mid-1980s, the Sudanese government resorted to force as a means to remove rural migrants who occupied open spaces. In July 1978, for example, the most viable portions of the squatter community were evicted from unsightly cardboard and sacking huts during the OAU meetings in Khartoum, then forcibly relocated to sites outside of the city. As early as 1981, members of the Khartoum Bar Association protested against such policies, basing their claim on the provision of freedom of movement and residence for all citizens except – and it was an important exception – 'for reasons of security and public health' (Burr, 1990, p. 3).

Since then, the same kind of rationale (i.e. concerns over increasing urban crime, unrest, unsanitary conditions and food prices) have been used to justify different policies and practices regarding the internally displaced community in Khartoum. In April 1987, the government of Sadiq el Mahdi initiated a campaign of forced expulsions (*kashas*) to deter southerners from living in the tri-city area. Although the campaign involved serious human rights concerns (rapes, looting, deaths and confiscated documents) the *kasha* operation – like its predecessors – was sporadic in nature, limited in scale, and responsive to an international media campaign. Although Mahdi's government made evident its desire to restore the Arab character of the capital, the prospect of incurring severe criticism seemed to deter it from reinstating another *kasha* campaign.

When Sadiq el Mahdi was deposed from power on 30 June 1989, the fortunes of the Khartoum displaced were shifted to a fifteen-member Revolutionary Command Council headed by Omar al-Bashir. The change in power constituted a distinct shift toward Islamic fundamentalism, and thereby posed a new threat to the southern displaced community, in particular. At first international donors were promised there would be no forcible evictions of displaced persons, but soon thereafter were informed that the Revolutionary Command Council regarded the issue of the Khartoum displaced a domestic matter under its purview. During the next year and a half, the military junta's stance toward the displaced communities in the capital steadily hardened. Resettlement sites were chosen outside the city limits of Omdurman and Khartoum. In April 1991, the Council of Ministers announced the government's intention to move all of the Khartoum displaced out of the city by the end of the year. Since then, more than 400,000 people have been forcibly relocated to desert sites outside the city under a 'squatter settlement abolishment' program. The ongoing campaign is unparalleled, not only in its scope and intensity, but in its insensitivity to pressure mounted by the media or the international community.

In March and April 1991 mass demolition of displaced and 'squatter' areas started in Omdurman. Members of several communities – Gamayer, 6 April, and Khor Omer – were relocated to a settlement site named Dar el Salam Omdurman outside the western edge of the city (see Figure 3.1). International non-governmental organizations were excluded from providing assistance to their earlier target beneficiaries, now resettled in the new 'squatter absorption' camps. In June, the Squatter Settlement Abolishment Committee (SSAC) launched demolition programs in three more settlements – Takamul, Shingla South, and Shingla North – located in Khartoum North. During the fall of 1991 an estimated 150,000 people were dispossessed by demolition teams working in various parts of the capital.

Three days before Christmas the campaign took on a new level of intensity when the SSAC turned to the southern portion of the city. A demolition team, consisting of a judge, the army, police, security forces and social workers came with orders to raze to the ground hundreds of homes in the Kurmuta portion of the larger Dar el Salam settlement. The threatened citizens presented a memorandum demanding that the demolition cease, and formed a human belt around their area. The judge tried to address the inhabitants of the area using a loudspeaker, but was dismissed by a volley of stones. The army responded, first with tear gas, and then with submachine guns. Thirteen squatters were killed, eighty-one were wounded, and the bulldozers began work (Hassan, 1991). On Christmas Eve the homeless were ordered to mount trucks with what scant belongings they had salvaged and were driven to a barren resettlement site near Jebel Aulia, 40 km south of the city.

The British Ambassador and the Dutch Chargé d'Affairs representing the European Community both lodged official protests over the aggressive manner of the Kurmuta relocation. Amid the outcry, however, government authorities announced that the relocation of 60,000 more displaced people in Kusha (Khartoum North) would commence (Ellis, 1992, p. 7). During the rest of January 1992 the government attempted to relocate approximately 40,000 people from the Kusha community. Little or no notification of the intention to be moved or the time at which it would take place was given. Areas were cordoned off by armed troops, leaving inhabitants with little option than to comply with the instructions to dismantle their shelters or watch them be destroyed. Although people were permitted to take possessions, small ruminants and shelter materials with them, community members were not told by the authorities where they were going. In late January, the government implemented the relocation of another 60,000 displaced people from Zagalona community to the same barren site west of Omdurman.

The new site for the relocated from Gamayer, 6 April, Khor Omer, el Markesi, Takamul, Shingla South, Shingla North, Kusha, el Izba and Zagalona extends over an area 6 km^2 in size. The camp is expanding westward into the desert (there are no trees within sight of the settlement). The relocated inhabitants have constructed tents made of sacks, cardboard and scraps of wood. The water supply for the camp is entirely dependent on daily delivery by tanker trucks. When members of the US Agency for International Development (USAID) were escorted to the new site by the Khartoum State Minister of Housing, they asked how people could remain employed without transportation to their jobs at 15 km away. The minister's reply, 'They can walk', illustrates the issue of socio-economic sustainability as well as that of humanitarian treatment at stake.

The government's rationale for the demolition and relocation campaign is a product of many factors. At a more immediate level, they include the perceived threat to 'society and the environment' posed by the displaced community, eviction of squatters from valuable agricultural land on the White Nile, the assertion of urban land owners of their rights to land inhabited by squatters, and conformity with a recent World Bank study outlining a new urban plan for Khartoum. Many plots inhabited by displaced persons have been sold to civil servants and Sudanese working abroad. Having already received payment for the land (much of which came in hard currency), now the government must clear the sites, delineate lots, and convey legal titles to the new owners. At another level, however, there is little doubt that this campaign symbolizes three themes at the political nexus of the country. The 'squatter abolishment campaign' counters the alleged influence of the Umma political party, who have been charged with importing Westerners into the capital; it also mitigates the presence of the southerners in the capital, a group that are at distinct ethnic, religious and political odds with the Arab government; whilst vivifying the marked shift towards Islamic fundamentalism on the part of the current regime in power.

Before the current campaign began in April 1991, it seemed possible that as long as the international community showed concern for the displaced in Khartoum, egregious examples of abuses against them, particularly any forced relocation, could be halted (Burr, 1990). Since then, however, protests by the international community have been ineffective in slowing demolitions or relocations, or in moderating the conditions under which they have been conducted. Four indigenous agencies are allowed to provide assistance to newly relocated communities (three Muslim agencies and the Sudan Council of Churches), but international non-governmental organizations (NGOs) have been prohibited from providing any direct assistance. Access to sites by observers is either denied altogether, or carefully monitored in the company of governmental officials. In effect, the Sudanese government has conveyed a 'we will do as we choose' sentiment to its observers. This heavy-handed response to 'internal refugees' is particularly striking in view of the fact that the Sudanese government had earned international recognition and acclaim for its overall tolerance and hospitality in accommodating close to one million international refugees from neighbouring countries (Rogge, 1985).

Alternative solutions to forcible relocation

Four alternatives to demolition and relocation exist for Khartoum's displaced population. In essence, they constitute the three basic durable solutions for international refugees – integration, repatriation, and third country resettlement. First, despite the obvious risk of encouraging more displacees to come to the capital, the displaced already in Khartoum could be better integrated by way of common types of urban development programs (e.g. installation of essential services, upgrading shelter facilities, income-generation and small credit schemes). Secondly, displaced persons could be repatriated to their areas of origin. Doing so would depend on securing routes of safe passage, preparing appropriate areas for displaced repatriation, and then supporting participants in the process. Two forms of 'third country resettlement' have been proposed as a third alternative. The first is the establishment of conflict-free zones in productive rural areas into which displaced persons could be transported and then supported with integrated rural development projects. Undoubtedly these 'peace zones' would be sited in the transition zone between the north and the south (e.g. the Renk area of northern Upper Nile province). The second form of 'third country resettlement' involves relocating displaced persons from Khartoum and other Sudanese cities to refugee camps in eastern Sudan. Tripartite negotiations between the Sudan, Eritrea and UNHCR have moved slowly, hampering the implementation of a resettlement program. Twenty-two camps are currently occupied by as many as 200,000 Eritrean refugees. Once vacated these camps might be an alternative, but there is little doubt that any attempt to transport mainly non-Muslim southerners to relatively isolated sites in the east would provoke severe criticism and stiff resistance. For its part, the government has conveyed mixed messages of support for each of these alternatives. As might be expected, enthusiasm for repatriation is growing among southerners in the face of the ongoing demolitions and relocations. If any alternative is deployed in the future, most likely it would be implemented on a pilot basis, especially in view of the prevailing uncertainty of events in Sudan, the heavy criticism that an unsuccessful attempt might engender, and the possibility of evaluating a project before the commitment of substantial resources.

Conclusion: rights and responsibilities

The current campaign in Khartoum is not unique to Sudan or, for that matter, to Africa. In recent years the media has witnessed the plight of displaced people within Afghanistan, El Salvador, Ethiopia, Mozambique, Iraq and the former Yugoslavia. The demolition and relocation campaign in Khartoum poses once again the question of what can be done on behalf of highly vulnerable populations comprising displaced persons. Who will be the voice for these voiceless people?

Heroic efforts by dedicated individuals and organizations to assist internal refugees are not sufficient. For many observers, as Rogge (1990) suggests, 'the needs of and the responses to the displaced problem should be seen and dealt with as human rights issues' (p. 19). Contexts like Sudan – where the government has imprisoned dissidents, banned organizations that traditionally defend human rights (the Bar Association and Doctors' Union), distanced NGOs from the displaced community, and has remained unresponsive to repeated protests from the diplomatic community – suggest the need for universal protection rights that transcend the particulars of a specific place, time, and political confluence.[3]

The chief concern among much of the international community centres on the *voluntariness of participation* in any programmes involving relocation (Rogge, 1990, p. 19). Key issues include, for example, ample notification of the intention to move members of a community, allowance of UN observation teams to monitor the process in an unhampered manner, and the provision of services at least comparable to those available at the previous settlement site. Whether or not these issues are broached in 'displaced conventions' likened to those that exist for refugees, some legal terms of reference are necessary to modulate the conditions which displaced people must endure.

There are two prominent obstacles to the process of framing terms of protection for displaced persons – how a displaced person is defined, and what time period or conditions determine how long a person is considered to remain displaced. Both are complex issues that require in-depth research and debate. Implicit to the term 'displaced' is the notion that migration was undertaken involuntarily. However, there are degrees of involuntariness which, in turn, are a manifestation of the levels and intensities of political, economic, or environmental pressures that exist at the point of origin (Rogge, 1990). Moreover, after the departure 'moment' at which they leave home, displaced persons move back and forth across a continuum of adjustment and integration. Obviously, the cessation of conflict and their voluntary choice to return or not can terminate displacement. When displaced persons remain in domestic asylum indefinitely, however, the task of determining when they cease being displaced is a more challenging one. Setting 'boundary lines' in these contexts will require serious investigation.

The particulars of differentiating one displaced person from another are difficult indeed. Nonetheless, it is critical to recognize that most international refugees are granted status on the basis of a *mass determination* (Clark, 1989; see also Chapter 1). Likewise, what is more important for internal refugees is a systematic way to recognize the existence of this class of displaced people, identify their special needs, and mandate responsibility for meeting those needs. 'Solidarity rights' or 'majority human rights' are necessary when the nation-state is either too weak or too much the instrument of the ruling class to protect or provide the conditions for achievement of people's rights (Falk, cited in Shepherd, 1987, p. 13). This emphasis is even more relevant given that people in developing regions still think about human rights largely in collective and communal terms (Ake, 1987).

Secondly, the provision of assistance to host governments must be unified, consistent, and discerning. Forging unified positions among the international community – donor agencies, diplomatic envoys, and NGOs – is particularly important in lieu of formalized protection for internal refugees. Cooperative and, thereby, more forcible expressions of concern are necessary, but so are well-conceived positions regarding assistance. Donor assistance can be used as the 'carrot' or the 'stick', making the provision of more assistance contingent on responding to humanitarian and socio-economic concerns or withholding assistance in order to press for an ongoing activity to stop. The timing and manner in which donors assist can be important bargaining tools as well. In sum, a thin, but critical dividing line exists between providing humanitarian assistance to those in need and encouraging the government authorities who oversee demolition and relocation campaigns to cause more suffering.

Thirdly, internal displacement deserves considerably more attention by researchers. During the last decade the plight of international refugees has become the subject of considerable academic interest (Black, 1991). The vast majority of internally displaced persons are 'refugees' in every respect apart from the fact that they do not, or can not, cross an international boundary. To date, however, the movement of internal refugees has attracted little research or attention, despite the fact that such movements are growing large in scale, frequent in occurrence, and profound in their impact. On one hand, the dichotomy between internal and international displacement needs to be addressed by way of comparative analysis. The time is indeed '... ripe for the development of the impact and consequences of forced migrations that incorporate both internal and international refugee movements' (Hugo, 1987, p. 298). On the other hand, our analysis needs to move beyond the use of motivation and boundaries as the bases for deriving both categories. In terms of analysis, much can be gained by placing both forms of involuntary migration into the larger context of migration theory (Richmond, 1988), particularly given the structural pressures posed by an ever-tightening global political economy.

Fourthly, the United Nations must continue to build a more strident and active position on the matter of displaced persons. Even as the methods and objectives of war have changed dramatically during the twentieth century, so has the incidence of conflict-induced displacement. Now over 97 per cent of all armed conflict situations are internal ones (Clay, cited in Clark, 1989, p. 20). There is no reason to think there will be fewer internal refugees in the future, but millions of people will be condemned to unnecessary suffering every year as long as each instance is treated as an isolated case (Clark, 1989).

In the aftermath of the Gulf War, the United Nations did authorize an unprecedented humanitarian intervention to protect Kurds in Iraq. This precedent, extended again for Croatians and Muslims in the former Yugoslavia, needs to be strengthened further in order to build a basis for a systematic response to mass migration and internal displacement. During 1992, the General Assembly is debating formal mechanisms as well as institutional vehicles to protect and assist internal refugees (Frankel, 1991, p. 18E). Once again the fundamental issue of sovereignty is at stake. Whatever the mandate, raising the *advantage* or privileged position of the United Nations is necessary in order to mitigate the conditions that internally displaced persons must face and to intervene more assertively on their behalf.

Notes

1. UNHCR has only become involved with internally displaced persons in rare and special cases. They include, for example, some cases of repatriation of international refugees to areas where displaced persons exist as well or instances when the UN Secretary-General requests to use its 'good offices' (Clark, 1989, p. 23). In addition to recent instances in Iraq and the former Yugoslavia, UNHCR has – at the specific initiation of the country concerned – assisted persons displaced by civil war within Lebanon, Angola and Vietnam (Hugo, 1987).
2. Estimates of the number of displacees in the Khartoum metropolitan region range widely from as low as six hundred thousand to as high as three million (Rogge, 1990, p. 20). The Emergency Unit of the United Nations Development Programme, which has monitored carefully the status of Khartoum's displaced since 1988, generally uses an estimate of 845,000.
3. In Sudan, churches have found themselves in the unusual position of carrying the human rights flag virtually alone. On 13 January 1992, central security ordered the Catholic church to hand over all copies of a booklet entitled 'The truth shall make you free', which in moderate but firm language accused the government of treating non-Muslims as 'guests in their own country' (Ellis, 1992, p. 7).

References

Ake, C., 1987, 'The African context of human rights', *Africa Today*, **34** (1–2): 5–11.

Bascom, J., 1990, 'Food, wages and profits: mechanized schemes and the Sudanese state', *Economic Geography*, **66** (2): 140–55.

Black, R., 1991, Refugees and displaced persons: geographical perspectives and research directions', *Progress in Human Geography*, **15** (3): 281–98.

Burr, M., 1990, *Khartoum's displaced persons: a decade of despair*, United States Committee for Refugees, Washington DC.

Carter, N., ed., 1986, *Sudan: the roots of famine*, Report for Oxfam, Oxford.

Clark, L., 1989, Internal refugees: the hidden half, in *World Refugee Survey 1989*, United States Committee for Refugees, Washington, DC.

Demko, G. and Wood. W., 1987, 'International refugees: a geographical perspective', *Journal of Geography*, **86** (5): 225–28.

De Waal, A., 1989, *Famine that kills: Darfur, Sudan, 1984–85*, Clarendon Press, Oxford.

Ellis, S., ed., 1992, 'Sudan: the politics of human rights', *Africa Confidential*, 24 January, p. 7.

Frankel, M., 1991, 'New solutions for new refugees', *New York Times*, 10 November, p. 18E.

Hansen, A., Oliver-Smith, A., eds, 1982, *Involuntary migration and resettlement: the problems and responses of dislocated people*, Westview Press, Boulder, Colorado.

Harrell-Bond, B.E., 1986, 'Refugee issues', *Third World Affairs*, pp. 311–19.

Hassan, A.H., 1991, '13 squatters shot dead in shanty quarter', *New Horizon*, 25 December, p. 2.

Hill, P., 1977, *Population, prosperity and poverty: Rural Kano 1900 and 1970*, Cambridge University Press, London.

Hugo, G., 1987, 'Postwar refugee migration in southeast Asia: patterns, problems and policies', in J.R. Rogge, ed., *Refugees, a third world dilemma*, Rowman & Littlefield, Totowa, New Jersey.

Kebbede, G., 1991, 'The agonies of displacement: Ethiopian women refugees in Khartoum, Sudan', *GeoJournal*, **23** (2): 99–106.

Lightfoot, P., 1979, 'Spatial distribution and cohesion of resettled communities', in L. Gosling, ed., *Population resettlement in the Mekong river basin*, University of North Carolina, Chapel Hill.

Manga, A. and Miller, C., 1988, 'Urbanization and migration: case study of Takamul community in Khartoum North', Report for United Nations Emergency Unit, Khartoum.

Peil, M., 1981, *Cities and suburbs: urban life in West Africa*, Africana Publishing Company, New York.

Richmond, A., 1988, 'Sociological theories of international migration: the case of refugees', *Current Sociology*, **36** (2): 7–25.

Rogge, J.R., 1985, *Too many, too long: Sudan's twenty-year refugee dilemma*, Rowman & Allanheld, Totowa, New Jersey.

Rogge, J.R., 1987, 'Urban refugees in Africa: some changing dimensions to Africa's refugee problem, with special reference to Sudan', *Migration World*, **14** (4): 7–13.

Rogge, J.R., 1990, 'Relocation and repatriation of displaced persons in Sudan', Report to the Minister of Relief and Displaced Persons Affairs, Khartoum, 27 June.

Shepherd, G., 1987, 'Global majority rights: the African context', *Africa Today*, **34** (1–2): 13–26.

Timberlake, L., 1985, *Africa in crisis: the causes, the cures of environmental bankruptcy*, International Institute for Environment and Development, London & Washington, DC.

USCR (United States Committee for Refugees), 1992, *World refugee survey, 1991*, USCR, Washington DC.

Van Hear, N., 1991, 'Mass migration and mass displacement during and after the gulf war', *Refugee Participation Network*, **10**: 29–31.

Further reading

Burr, M., 1990, *Khartoum's displaced persons: a decade of despair*, United States Committee for Refugees, Washington DC.

Clark, L., 1989, 'Internal refugees: the hidden half', in *World refugee survey, 1989*, United States Committee for Refugees, Washington DC.

Hansen, A. and Oliver-Smith, A., eds, 1982, *Involuntary migration and resettlement: the problems and responses of dislocated people*, Westview Press, Boulder, Colorado.

Hugo, G., 1987, 'Postwar refugee migration in southeast Asia: patterns, problems and policies', in J.R. Rogge, ed., *Refugees, a third world dilemma*, Rowman & Littlefield, Totowa, New Jersey.

Richmond, A., 1988, 'Sociological theories of international migration: the case of refugees', *Current Sociology*, **36** (2): 7–25.

4 Return to the promised land: repatriation and resettlement of Namibian refugees, 1989–1990

David Simon and Rosemary Preston

Introduction

Africa is currently struggling to cope with some five million refugees amid continuing political upheaval and unprecedented economic and environmental crises. The recent Liberian conflict alone forced over 650,000 people to seek sanctuary beyond their country's borders, while the number of refugees from the Horn of Africa, Mozambique and other familiar war zones has continued to grow. In an otherwise 'bleak year for Africa's refugees', the 'one cause for celebration' during 1990 was Namibia's independence in March following the voluntary repatriation of over 43,000 refugees (UNHCR, 1990a).

Namibian independence on 21 March 1990 represented the culmination of a long and bitter anti-colonial liberation struggle against German and then South African rule. The guerrilla insurgency, launched by SWAPO from Angola in August 1966, was second in duration in Africa only to that of the ANC against white minority rule in South Africa itself. Namibia's right to independence had been agreed during the mid-1970s by all the parties involved in negotiations which culminated in the adoption of UN Security Council Resolutions 432 and 435 in 1978. These established a complex framework, set of conditions and timetable to reach internationally recognised independence under UN supervision.

Key elements of the package were the monitoring of a ceasefire which was to initiate the process, a phased withdrawal of South African forces, the voluntary repatriation of exiles and refugees, the repeal of all remaining discriminatory legislation, and the creation of conditions conducive to the holding of free and fair elections. These elections, to be held seven months after the implementation of Resolution 435 began (provided that the other transitional arrangements had been satisfactorily completed) would establish a Constituent Assembly charged with drawing up and approving a constitution ahead of independence. The entire process was to be overseen and coordinated by a specially established United Nations Transitional Assistance Group (UNTAG), headed by a Special Representative of the UN Secretary General. Implementation was originally envisaged for 1978, but the timetable unravelled over certain technicalities. Successive delaying tactics by South Africa and the US frustrated attempts to reactivate the process for over a decade. It was only the end of the Cold War and the subsequent

US–Soviet agreement to end regional conflicts in the Third World, coupled with accelerating changes in South Africa, that led ultimately to the signing of the Angola–Namibia Accords in December 1988. This presaged the implementation of Resolution 435 as from 1 April 1989 (Simon, 1991).

The high level of publicity and international support, at a cost of over US$39 million or almost $900 per capita, which this apparent drop in the continental ocean received, can be understood only in terms of Namibia's special international status and bitterly contested history. In addressing the Namibian repatriation process and its aftermath, this chapter seeks both to highlight a remarkable exercise and to contribute to the wider literature on repatriation, which remains underdeveloped relative to other aspects of refugee studies. Against the backdrop of comparable repatriation exercises, including that following Zimbabwean independence a decade earlier, the chapter outlines the course of the Namibian programme and discusses preliminary research findings on the post-resettlement fortunes of returnees. The inevitable problems associated with proposed assistance programmes under current post-war conditions in northern Namibia, from where most of the returnees originated, are also discussed.

Repatriation in context

Of the three durable outcomes of asylum, the voluntary return of refugees to their country of origin is currently preferred by the international community to long-term settlement in the host country or resettlement in a third country (Crisp, 1984; Harrell-Bond, 1989; Rogge and Akol, 1989). Although statistics are notoriously unreliable, there is little doubt that most refugees returning from exile do so on their own initiative, without government or agency assistance and outside the framework of international protection (Cuny and Stein, 1989). This process is sometimes known as self-repatriation (see Chapter 11 of this volume). Stein (1990), quoting UNHCR, compares 4,400 Mozambicans given assistance to return with some 208,000 (98 per cent) who had returned unaided, as of the end of December 1989. Meanwhile, in relation to the continent-wide estimate of 3.5 million Africans who returned over the period 1971–90, Namibia's 43,500 exiles who were assisted to return appear no more than a modestly sized group (Rogge, 1991).

If the contemporary interest in refugee studies is characterised by its youthfulness (Adelman, 1989), research into repatriation is in its infancy. Thus it is pulled in one direction by the need for links with established social theory – with theories of migration in contexts of political and economic change in general, and of return migration in particular – and, in another, by attempts to define its own parameters. At a recent conference on Repatriation in Africa (UNRISD, 1991), Jackson (1991) attempted to locate his comparative study of return to Zimbabwe, prior to independence in 1980 and again in 1988 after the Matabeleland conflicts, within the context of the contemporary political economy and labour process. Also with reference to Zimbabwe, Makanya (1991) insisted on the need to understand the factors underlying departure in the first place, as a prerequisite for any analysis of repatriation. This is particularly important where, as in the Zimbabwean case, the opportunity for political restructuring occurs. Gasarasi (1990) argues that research into return from exile should be embedded within theories of return migration, but then does not extend the conceptual framework of his Namibian research beyond other studies of repatriation.

Writers such as Rogge and Stein are concerned with the diversity of factors that comprise any single repatriation and responses to it, and with the comparison of different such movements. These efforts are essentially leading to the construction of typologies which will serve as frames of reference for future studies of the return from exile. In such endeavours, return flows are differentiated by, for example, size, rate, and whether they are sponsored or self-initiated. Returnees are disaggregated by categories – age, sex, family, ethnic, economic, vulnerable – and the repatriation itself is also broken down into processes and stages – preparation, departure, travel, arrival, dispersal and integration – at which different actors – governments of host and home countries, assisting agencies and local people – perform specific roles (Rogge, 1991; Stein, 1990, 1991).

Implicitly, this approach is similar to that used in past decades by geographers and sociologists to describe differential migratory movements within and between countries. While such writing was criticised for its failure to account for the influence of capital accumulation in underdeveloped areas and its implications for migration of the transition from subsistence production to wage labour, synthetic writing on the macro-level political and economic contexts of involuntary migration and return from exile is only now beginning.

While not claiming any systematic theoretical advances, this chapter blends these two approaches. It accepts that return from exile, in this case organised repatriation, may have well-defined stages. It suggests that there may be similarities in the characteristics of these stages in different contexts, when there are other features common to the return. As such, it therefore compares aspects of other return movements in Africa to the planning, execution and post-return situation of repatriation to Namibia.

Experience elsewhere of relevance to Namibia

On the basis of research undertaken to date, it would seem that events associated with the repatriation to Zimbabwe at the time of independence in 1980 provide the closest model for what was to occur in Namibia a decade later. Like Namibians, many Zimbabweans had sought refuge beyond their country's borders from the repression and violence of a settler regime. Over 200,000 returned joyfully *en masse*, in anticipation of independence, to assert their democratic rights and vote. This similarity was certainly appreciated by Namibians, many of whom, both officially and unofficially, made visits to Zimbabwe to learn from the repatriation experience there and to optimise the planning of their own return (Preston, 1990). Nevertheless, there are also some obvious differences between the two experiences, reflecting different global conditions, the respective scales of repatriation, the identities of the brokers of the peace agreement and sponsors of the repatriation, and specific local factors.

Jackson (1991) describes how, in a remarkably brief exercise costing an estimated $5 million, UNHCR's budget of $1.2 million was put towards assisting the return of some 70,000 Zimbabwean exiles. Estimates of the incidence of unassisted return range from 70,000 to 140,000. The organised return took place in two waves, with able-bodied adults and families preceding the more vulnerable groups comprising unaccompanied school children and the infirm. Of overriding concern was the need for as many eligible voters as possible to be in Zimbabwe for the election. To this end, it is thought that two-thirds of the 35,000 who comprised the first phase were expecting to vote.

Reports from UNHCR representatives and NGO observers at entry points suggest that the Rhodesian forces were keen to turn back those returning and to prevent them participating in the elections. Everywhere, it seems, nationalistic fervour, joy and party commitment meant that the harassment and delaying tactics were of little avail (De Wolf, 1981; Jackson, 1991; Makanya, 1991). For Jackson, Phase Three of the repatriation was marked by the transition of responsibility from international organisations to the national government and local NGOs, in which a network of religious organisations proved critical in tracing families, organising transport to places throughout the country and providing all kinds of other assistance. Both he and De Wolf describe the difficulties of this transition, given the devastation of physical and social infrastructure that had occurred, in particular the damage to the national transport system.

Makanya (1991) stresses the importance of the rigorous ideological training in exile, certainly in Mozambique, in which the ideal of returning to a free state, the will to work in national reconstruction and loyalty to the party were fostered. The effectiveness of this training, she suggests, was in some measure due to the strong international support for such activities among exiles from Rhodesia in neighbouring states (Makanya, 1991). The intention was to continue such political socialisation in Zimbabwe by keeping exiled children in the same school groups after return. This scheme collapsed when the students came to realise that the quality of the education they were being given differed significantly from that in national schools and was in no way advantageous (De Wolf, 1981).

Unlike individual and small group return, the experience of organised, large-scale return from exile is one of convergence. People come together to re-enter their country of origin at specially designated points, usually under the blanket of complex, internationally arranged legal protection (see Goodwin-Gill, 1989, on legal and policy issues). At such points, provision will have been made for their reception, documentation, health review and basic needs. Such population movements are consequently easy to observe and monitor. In contrast, exiles who return independently tend to be spatially and temporally dispersed and therefore difficult to observe systematically. This is almost invariably so in the case of those who return in flight from some new threat to their existence in their country of refuge (Stein, 1991). Recently, however, there have also been studies of refugee-initiated return movements by those who could be said to be more pulled than pushed (e.g. Wilson and Nunes, 1991).

After arrival, with the dispersal of those who have returned to the places where they expect to reside, even those who came as part of a highly organised group lose their conspicuousness. At this stage, some categories of returnee become visible while others drop from view. In the public eye is the fate and conduct of those who succeed in becoming leaders, capitalising on opportunities of education and administration while abroad. Of concern regarding the maintenance of the status quo is the frustration of those who, expecting such preferment (on the basis of qualifications and experience or as compensation for their role in the struggle), fail to obtain it. Some governments seek to avert such difficulties by making special employment provision or providing compensation (in the form of land or credit, for example). However, such action seems likely to be as fraught with difficulties as is taking no action at all, on the grounds that once people have returned there is no reason or justification in distinguishing them from the rest of the population.

In 1972, the Sudanese government instituted a policy of returning former civil servants to their previous posts, often alongside those who had replaced them. However, this had to be abandoned in 1974, since the long-term duplication of salaries could not be justified or afforded (Akol, 1991). In Zimbabwe, the reported arrogance of some returnees assuming senior positions on the basis of qualifications earned abroad, often some years earlier, but without work experience, led to administrative difficulties until systems of training were introduced to assist their resolution (Preston, 1991b; Cohen, 1991).

Less conspicuous but far more numerous are those who return to rural areas. In Zimbabwe's rural sector, many ex-combatants and other returned exiles still lack land and the means of generating a satisfactory livelihood ten years after independence. Fears have been expressed that these groups pose a potential threat to national security. In Matabeleland, where economic prospects on the land are particularly poor, it is suggested that circular movements in and out of the country occur as disaffection leads to further conflict and a return to exile (Jackson, 1991). Prospective returnees to Mozambique have made constant visits to appraise the range of opportunities available (Wilson and Nunes, 1991). Many, failing to see satisfactory change in security or economic prospects, have returned to exile across the border (Preston, 1991a). Elsewhere, in Chad for example, action taken by the government to provide some assistance to returnees to rural areas was disregarded by those with higher expectations (Alhabo and Passang, 1991). Similar observations in Sudan have led Akol to conclude that states preparing for the mass return of exiles should cease to make assumptions about either the intended place of settlement or mode of economic insertion. The severance of refugees from primary production, not only of the minority who acquire education and professional experience but also of those in camps dependent on centralised service distribution, has been found to be linked to an attitudinal change, discouraging former subsistence producers from work on the land (Akol, 1987). The same caution exists in the case of the reintegration of erstwhile combatants. In many instances, in discussion at the UNRISD conference, reference was made to destabilising tactics adopted by former fighters, frustrated at what they perceived to be the inadequate provision for their needs as compensation for their life-risking contributions to change in – or maintenance of – the political order (UNRISD, 1991).

At a micro level, information is now becoming available about the psycho-social tensions that emerge once the euphoria of return has subsided and people with very different life worlds struggle to make a living and construct relationships (Allen, 1991). In Zimbabwe, observers note the distressing separation of conflict/exile-bonded groups, as members are reunited with lost families in different places (De Wolf, 1981). Comments are made on the difficulty experienced in local integration, and the returnees' propensity to drift away again in search of peer solidarity. Cases are also cited of women who fought, became leaders or who acquired education in exile, beyond what they would have obtained if they had remained at home. On return they are found to suppress or be pressurised to suppress their skills and experience in order to resume traditional community roles (Preston, 1991b).

Similarly, the disabled may become invisible if they are not among the few who find rehabilitation and training opportunities. In Zimbabwe, the ZIMFEP (Zimbabwe Foundation for Education and Production) schools, for returning exiles, provided training from the outset for those disabled in the war. Subsequently, other special schools were created for all war wounded. Their continued existence indicates that such assistance should be planned to last over a long period of time.

The Namibian repatriation exercise

Implementation of Resolution 435 was almost sabotaged at the outset by a fierce outbreak of fighting between South African and SWAPO forces on 1 April 1989, before UNTAG was fully deployed. Over 300 people were killed as euphoria turned to gloom and deep suspicion at the impartiality and effectiveness of Maarti Ahtisaari, the UN Special Representative, and UNTAG in standing up to the South Africans. Remarkably, therefore, the process was salvaged and ultimately completed successfully approximately on schedule, despite numerous subsequent hurdles. The South African Administrator General sought to limit UNTAG's role and effectiveness so as to restrict legislative changes, enable elements of the security apparatus to escape confinement and monitoring, and generally to hamper SWAPO's election campaign by every possible means (Asante and Asombang, 1989; Bender, 1989; Manning, 1989; Stiff, 1989; Bush, 1990; Cliffe, 1990; Leys, 1990; Simon, 1991). Recent revelations by former operatives have attested to the vast scale of South Africa's covert propaganda, disinformation and intimidation campaign. These allegations prompted the South African Foreign Minister to disclose funding of over R100 million for anti-SWAPO parties during the election campaign, including at least R65 million for the Democratic Turnhalle Alliance (DTA).[1]

Institutional arrangements and legal background

Against this background, it is hardly surprising that the repatriation exercise faced many legal, political and practical obstacles. Overall responsibility for the operation lay with the UNHCR, who contracted the Council of Churches in Namibia (CCN) as their local partners in April 1989. To this end, a dedicated and largely autonomous implementing agency, the Repatriation, Resettlement and Reconstruction Committee (RRR Committee) was established within the CCN. Its principal task was the reception and short-term care of returnees prior to their departure for homes or other chosen destinations. This involved the identification and subsequent preparation of suitable reception centres, the care and feeding of returnees in these centres, the tracing of relatives and making of travel arrangements.

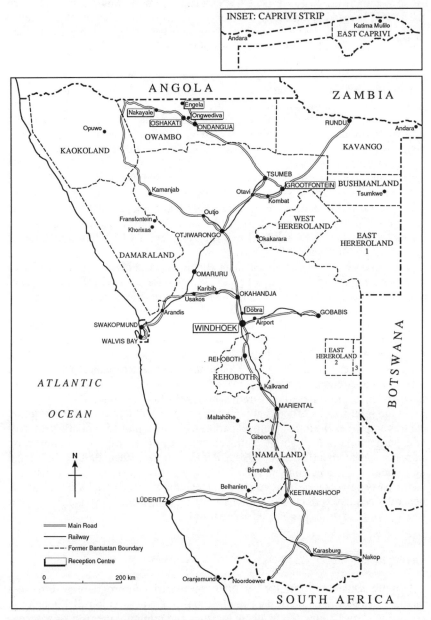

Figure 4.1 Location of Namibian reception centres for returning refugees

Over 300 local RRR committees were established countrywide to assist in this process. UNHCR retained overall responsibility for operations, and for the related negotiations, through UNTAG and the Special Representative, with the South

African authorities. In this respect the Namibian operation was exceptional, since the UNHCR mandate normally ends once refugees and exiles in its care reach their own countries. The extension of its mandate in this case was deemed necessary in view of Namibia's special status and the international community's responsibility for it through the UN.

The UNHCR was responsible for arrangements outside Namibia, including the registration of Namibians abroad, administration of vaccinations and medical treatment, travel arrangements from the countries of asylum or residence to Namibia, shipment of personal belongings and associated logistics. Since Resolution 435 stipulated that repatriation was to be entirely voluntary, all beneficiaries were required to sign voluntary repatriation forms to that effect. Freedom of access to all refugees and exiles by UNHCR staff was therefore also required, especially since many of the Namibians in Angola and Zambia, the two principal host countries, were in SWAPO-controlled refugee camps or guerrilla bases. Equally, the rights of non-SWAPO refugees had to be guaranteed. These and related arrangements were made possible under the terms of tripartite protocols signed by the UNHCR, SWAPO and the Angolan and Zambian governments (Gasarasi, 1990; Mwase, 1990).

A second set of legal prerequisites for commencement of the actual repatriation concerned legislation covering a general amnesty for political offences, citizenship rights, electoral provisions and the repeal of discriminatory statutes which inhibited free association and could be used to victimise or intimidate returnees. Negotiations between the UN Special Representative and South African Administrator General on each of these proved extremely difficult and protracted, for reasons already mentioned. Ultimately, however, the Administrator General was forced to back down; anything less would have been unacceptable to the UN, the international community and most black Namibians, thus jeopardising the entire independence process. Administrative arrangements regarding formalities and access to returnees by officials at points of entry, the administration of reception centres and the exclusion of political parties from them proved similarly problematic, particularly in the light of continued evidence of security force intimidation in northern Namibia (Gasarasi, 1990; RRR Committee, 1989, 1990, 1991). Final agreement was reached only in June 1989. In mid-May, a six-member reconnaissance party of refugees from Angola and Zambia had delivered a qualified but generally positive verdict on conditions and arrangements for the repatriation after a week-long visit.

The repatriation exercise

Originally scheduled for mid-May 1989, the repatriation programme suffered a month's delay on account of the complications in the negotiations. Ultimately, it commenced on 12 June. To facilitate logistics and minimise the risks of confrontation – albeit at greater financial cost – repatriation took place by air, with only three entry points, namely Windhoek Airport and the military airbases at Grootfontein in the northeast of the commercial farming area and at Ondangwa in central Ovamboland (Figure 4.1). On completion of formalities, returnees were transported to one of five tented reception centres on church property: Döbra,

Okahandja or Mariabronn in the case of Windhoek, and Ongwediva or Engela for arrivals at Ondangwa. They were immunised, fed, accommodated, and treated medically if necessary, for up to seven days in these centres, during which time relatives were traced or other onward arrangements made. Three hot meals per day, complying with specified nutritional standards, were provided by a catering firm. If required, the RRR Committee also provided transport to a series of drop-off points in returnees' home areas.

The rate of repatriation accelerated rapidly after the start, although many people from northern Namibia elected to arrive in Windhoek on account of lingering fears about security and intimidation in the north. At one stage the reception centres around Windhoek were filled to overflowing. Many of the SWAPO leadership returned on 18 June, although President Nujoma delayed his homecoming until 14 September for security and protocol reasons. Thereafter, the flow of returnees declined and by the time the main operation ended in October, over 42,000 had been brought home. The largest number, over 12,500 were received at Döbra.

Table 4.1 provides details of the 41,088 returnees enumerated by 15 September 1989. Just over 56 per cent were male, an imbalance which arose almost entirely amongst adults (18+). Meanwhile, the overall demographic breakdown of the returnees – a majority of adults rather than children – contrasts strongly with that of the national population. This is no more than a reflection of the fact that it was primarily teenagers and younger adults who fled into exile at various times over the previous thirty or so years, together with the consequent disruption to conventional family life and structures, especially in neighbouring countries.

Table 4.1 Age–sex breakdown of returnees to Namibia, 15 September 1989

Age	Male	Female	Total	%
0–2	2,038	2,126	4,164	10.1
3–5	1,846	1,956	3,802	9.3
6–11	1,657	1,661	3,318	8.1
12–17	1,067	585	1,652	4.0
18+	16,438	11,714	28,152	68.5
TOTAL	23,046	18,042	41,088	100.0
%	56.1	43.9	100.0	—

Source: WCC (1989)

Out of a total of thirty-two different countries of origin, Namibia's two northern neighbours, Angola and Zambia, accounted for 95 per cent of the total number of returnees. A large proportion of returnees (over 50 per cent) possessed some professional skills, however loosely defined. Data suggest that by mid-1990, returnees at the top of the occupational range included, for example, 370 medical doctors, dentists and nurses; and 196 architects, engineers and technicians.

Although some were immediately engaged to assist in RRR-related work, under-took full-time political activities, or found other jobs, returnee unemployment has, from the beginning, been high. This issue will be discussed in the following section.

It was a requirement of Resolution 435 that the repatriation be completed in time to permit the returnees to register for and participate fully in the elections. Inevitably, not everyone wanted or was able to do so, and a trickle of returnees continued throughout the remainder of 1989 and 1990 as, for example, students abroad completed their courses or personal circumstances permitted. While the repatriation machinery remained in place, these latecomers received the same treatment and rations as their predecessors. By 31 March 1990, ten days after independence, 43,387 official returnees had been processed (WCC, 1990). UNHCR ended its operation in June of that year, and closed its Windhoek office in August.

Returnees without homes or other immediate accommodation were transported to one of some fifty secondary reception centres at church premises around the country, where longer stays were permitted. Additional prefabricated housing units were supplied for the purpose, while food rations and a small monthly allowance were provided by the World Food Programme (WFP) through the RRR Committee. Almost 12,000 returnees utilised these secondary centres but by the beginning of 1990 only 233 'genuinely homeless people' remained. The figure had fallen to 100 in September 1990, and responsibility for the small number remaining when the last secondary centres were closed at the end of 1990 was assumed by the Namibian Ministry of Lands, Resettlement and Rehabilitation (RRR Committee, 1991).

Disabled returnees, especially those requiring longer-term care and rehabilita-tion, represent a particularly vulnerable group, and special arrangements were therefore made for them. Twenty-five retarded and seventeen blind children were accommodated and provided with nursing and training at existing church medical facilities at Engela in Ovamboland. Up to a hundred people with physical disabili-ties, including war wounded, were initially catered for at Nakayale, another church centre in Ovamboland. Those unable to rejoin their families were trained in market gardening (RRR Committee, 1991). Beyond this, a shipment of second-hand prosthetic limbs was arranged from the UK by one of the authors (Simon) as a stopgap until local limb manufacturing and fitting centres, currently under construction, come on stream. Obviously, these will cater for the disabled popu-lation at large, not only returnees.

The RRR Committee programme continued to assist returnees for up to a full calendar year from the date of their repatriation. To ensure adequate nutrition without burdening often hard-pressed relatives, the WFP provided food rations, through RRR, on a monthly basis at ninety-six distribution points around the country. Where necessary, UNTAG transport was utilised for this purpose (RRR Committee, 1991). For those returning with few possessions and facing problems in obtaining employment, these rations provided a lifeline.

Once under way, the smoothness and efficiency of the repatriation exercise was remarkable. It has been labelled an outstanding success by those heading the operation, other UN officials, the Namibian government and international com-munity. Nevertheless, there were occasional problems. These included the deaths in transit of two children; unannounced night arrivals in Windhoek of aircraft bearing returnees; missing luggage; and distributional difficulties with food rations in certain localities. Right-wing politicians and newspapers regularly accused the UNHCR and RRR Committee of partiality and of favouring SWAPO. Gasarasi (1990) also documents allegations of this nature made by a former UNHCR employee in Windhoek but on balance he concurs with the generally held view that UNHCR/RRR undertook their tasks conscientiously, with meticulous attention to the need for even-handedness. As with UNTAG in general, officials adopted a dignified and businesslike stance, denying serious allegations while refusing to engage in mudslinging.

Returnees also spoke highly of the caring treatment they received during a time of extreme emotional difficulty as they left friends and places of exile en route to their own country – for many of them a very different place from the one they fled many years previously – and prepared to be reunited with long lost family and friends. Emotional scenes were repeated up and down the country, in remote southern villages, crowded Windhoek townships and isolated northern homesteads as returnees reached the end of their long journeys (Williams, 1990b; RRR Committee, 1991). Sometimes there was disbelief as siblings or children not heard from since their departure, and occasionally rumoured to have perished in exile or combat, arrived at the family hearth. Inevitably, too, there was grief as loved ones failed to return after the last incoming flight had landed.

As in Zimbabwe ten years before, in addition to difficulties of adaptation, returnees faced intimidation by security force elements. This was most acute in northern Namibia, continuing until after the elections in November 1989. The perpetrators commonly posed as rank and file DTA supporters. Harassment, much of it violent, was directed at the population at large in an effort to undermine support for SWAPO, but party officials and returnees, as known and identifiable cadres, were often singled out for particular attention. Although the AG and police denied these allegations, many were substantiated by UNTAG personnel, other observers or community leaders. It is also apparent that many returnees were followed or even assisted in getting home by undercover agents intent on discovering their identities and addresses (Gasarasi, 1990). Initially, too, some reactionary rural headmen sought to prohibit SWAPO returnees from land under their control. In most cases, however, community pressure or official sanction reversed these decisions. Generally speaking, the warmth of welcome accorded by local communities to their own returnees as well as those originally from elsewhere was quite remarkable (RRR Committee, 1989, 1990, 1991; Gasarasi, 1990).

Two controversies: inflated refugee figures and ex-detainees

Remarkably little has been said in any quarter about the vast gap between the 80–90,000 refugees whom SWAPO had long claimed to be outside Namibia, and for whom it had received aid from the international donor community, and the roughly 45,000 who registered under the Resolution 435 repatriation scheme. A certain element of the discrepancy may be accounted for by deaths in combat during the latter stages of the fighting, and by those Namibians who settled and married in their place of exile, mostly in southern Angola, and decided not to return. Nonetheless, the gap provides an indication of the difficulty of compiling accurate refugee statistics more generally.

A related matter is the return of some 250 detainees formerly held by SWAPO as alleged South African spies. Many of these detainees had been abused, tortured and imprisoned under appalling conditions. On return, some renewed their loyalty to SWAPO and were reintegrated into the party, the most able subsequently even receiving prominent political or civil service positions. However, others denounced SWAPO and joined the opposition, some also establishing a small new political movement (Gasarasi, 1990). This issue has a long and controversial history which is beyond the scope of this chapter. In essence, until the implementation of Resolution 435 was assured, SWAPO had consistently denied allegations since 1985/86, by the so-called Parents' Committee in Windhoek and the International Society for Human Rights, that they were holding or torturing political prisoners. They responded by charging their accusers with seeking to discredit SWAPO, in cahoots with South Africa. Even since the release of these detainees, the SWAPO leadership has unfortunately not acted to resolve the issue and put it behind them. Theo Ben Guriab, the Foreign Minister-designate, was alone in trying to do so ahead of independence and, in the face of pressure from colleagues, he ultimately had to retract his earlier statements. Although clearly an issue comparable to abuses against detainees and the civilian population at large by South African forces, the problem should be formally laid to rest rather than being left to fester. Under the circumstances, controversy flared anew with the appointment of the alleged head torturer, Solomon 'Jesus' Hawala as Head of the Army in October 1990 (Simon, 1991).

Persistent claims by the Parents' Committee and some ex-detainees, in particular, that more prisoners remained in Angola, prompted mediation by the churches and then a formal investigation by UNTAG. Its mission to Angola failed to find any such evidence. Since independence, the government has remained under pressure on the issue, and after much procrastination, negotiation and an inconclusive report by an all-party committee of the National Assembly into the position of all dead and missing people during the war, the International Committee of the Red Cross finally agreed in mid-1991 to pursue the matter in Angola.

Costs and financing

In April 1989, UNHCR budgeted an amount of $38.5 million for its Namibian repatriation operation, comprising $9.5 million (24.6 per cent) for international transport, $7.8 million (20.3 per cent) for pre-departure and post-arrival supplies and services, $6.0 million (15.6 per cent) for local transport in countries of asylum and in Namibia, $6.6 million (17.1 per cent) for programme support and administration, and $5.2 million (13.5 per cent) for the purchase and pre-positioning of foodstuffs. The main donor pledges towards this sum had been made by the Nordic countries ($10 million), USA ($5 million), Japan ($2.6 million), European Community ($2 million) and Canada ($1.6 million) (UNHCR, 1990b). By September 1989, however, only $30 million of the budgeted requirements had been raised (*Namibian*, 14 September 1989). Final expenditure figures were not available at the time of writing, although the total had reached $39.1 million by October

1989. This overspend resulted principally from the exclusive use of air transport for the actual repatriation – encompassing 452 chartered flights altogether – on account of security concerns and accessibility problems by land, and delays in moving some of the early returnees out of reception centres to their homes in the north during periods of increased intimidation (Gasarasi, 1990). The RRR Committee's audited accounts for the 1989 calendar year showed expenditure of R22.24 million (Table 4.2), of which UNHCR provided over three-quarters, CCN 22 per cent and UNICEF 1.4 per cent (RRR Committee, 1990). In January 1990, the RRR Committee's estimated budget of expenditure for 1990 was almost R20.4 million, or $8.64 million (WCC, 1990).

Table 4.2 Namibian RRR Committee expenditure, 1989

Department/activity	CCN	UNHCR	UNICEF	Total	%
	(in thousands of Rands)				
Administration/finance	530	682	–	1,212	5.4
Reception centres	547	3,125	–	3,673	16.5
Food in reception centres	–	1,090	–	1,090	4.9
Food distributed to returnees	–	1,621	–	1,621	7.3
Transport	1,694	5,233	–	6,297	31.1
Logistics	722	3,540	–	4,262	19.2
Rehabilitation/health	164	226	–	390	1.8
Information	59	–	–	59	0.3
Secondary centres	135	1,145	–	1,280	5.8
Pastoral counselling	33	–	–	33	0.2
Tracing service	–	395	–	395	1.8
Education	898	–	302	1200	5.4
Contingencies	99	–	–	99	0.4
TOTAL	4,882	17,058	302	22,242	100.1
%	22.0	75.6	1.4	100.0	

Source: calculated from RRR Committee (1990)

Note: Figures compiled from *The Namibian*, 3 May 1991, 8 May 1991; 17 May 1991, 24 May 1991, 12 July 1991, and 26 July 1991.

Issues and problems beyond repatriation: Namibia now

While there is now considerable written material on the planning and process of repatriating Namibian refugees, information on the extent to which exiles have achieved social and economic integration is scarce. However, although it is policy that returnees should not be given preferential treatment over the population at large, it has for some time been apparent that the experiences of reinsertion for them, and adjustment to their presence on the part of those who remained behind, are qualitatively different and should be addressed. By early 1990, voice was being given to some of these difficulties. In the May 1990 special issue of the UNHCR magazine, *Refugees*, celebrating the return to Namibia, there is a case study from Ovamboland which reveals the embarrassment experienced by some returnees at being kept by their families who remained behind, a sentiment matched by disappointment at the lack of opportunities and infrastructural support.

Not surprisingly, given that as many as 35,000 exiles may have returned initially to rural areas in northern Namibia, 33,000 to Ovamboland alone, information about the situation of the majority is patchy. In the most detailed study to date of returnees in Ovamboland, Tapscott challenges what he sees as the two assumptions upon which the repatriation was based: that those returning would be accommodated by those members of their families who had remained in Namibia, and that they would be absorbed into the private and public sectors of the labour market. This latter assumption was made in the light of the need for people with skills to replace those who had left for South Africa before or at independence, and the knowledge that most of the returnees had received some education or training in exile (Tapscott and Mulongeni, 1990). This report makes no mention of the extent to which, as observed elsewhere, former subsistence producers without new skills are resisting the resumption of primary production on principle or because it no longer coincides with their ambitions.

A UNICEF nutrition survey in April 1990 (quoted by Tapscott and Mulongeni, 1990) discovered that only 7 per cent of returnees had found formal sector employment and that no more than 36 per cent were active in subsistence production. This left 57 per cent who were described as economically inactive. Independently, the Otto Benecke Stiftung, which provided vocational training scholarships to Namibians in exile, found that only 10 per cent – of the 270 for whom they have information – had obtained employment by the end of 1990 (Otto Benecke Stiftung, 1991). Tapscott and Mulongeni list a series of reasons for this situation, including the lack of knowledge of how to go about finding employment; lack of access to job information via radio or newspapers; and delays in reaching prospective employers once word comes through about vacancies or the possibility of work. The lack of funds to cover the cost of transport to job interviews is a further impediment (Williams, 1990a). Other problems encountered include the lack of adequate fluency in English or Afrikaans (the lingua franca); a failure or reluctance by employers to recognise qualifications and experience obtained in many countries abroad, especially in eastern Europe, Cuba and parts of Africa; having to take biased written examinations or to possess unfair linguistic abilities; and employer discrimination against returnees in general on account of their assumed support for SWAPO. At the end of August 1991, it appeared that some 50–60 per cent of the returnees were still unable to find employment, but no detailed breakdown or distribution of this unemployment is available.

The difficulties of economic integration are likely to have exacerbated those of domestic integration and family and economic reconstruction. As is commonly observed with respect to returning migrants, difficulties are experienced in resuming their previous productive and social roles, while they often resist full reidentification with community culture. Although the general picture is not known, the situation of assertive young women accustomed to leadership has already been observed (Tapscott and Mulongeni, 1990), in ways again reminiscent of Zimbabwe a decade ago. As elsewhere, the demands of former fighters for compensation, with demonstrations held in Windhoek in pursuit of this claim, have been documented consistently in the Namibian press. Moreover, wide coverage was given to the embarrassment caused when South Africa agreed to compensate its former soldiers before SWAPO had its own arrangements for PLAN fighters in place. After prolonged public exchanges between the two governments, former combatants on both sides received payouts. General resentment has also been expressed at the conspicuous wealth of those appointed to senior government and other secure positions.

Without carefully constructed research into the extent of the difficulties apparently being experienced by returnees, it is difficult to assess the representativeness and spread of the problems identified. Efforts have been made to take stock of lessons from this experience by agencies which will be involved in similar repatriations elsewhere in the future. Notwithstanding the uniqueness of several facets of the Namibian operation – namely the policy and operational context having been established by the UN Security Council, rather than by tripartite agreement, the scale of the airlift, and pressure of time – UNHCR has undertaken a critical evaluation of its contribution to the exercise and made recommendations to enhance future performance (UNHCR, 1990b). The evaluation covered the period from the pre-planning stage to the end of the agency's involvement in mid-1990. The report identifies 177 lessons to be learned, including the need for overall planning guidelines, staff training and continuity, budgetary security, and a rehearsal of distribution and transport systems. In addition, vulnerable groups should be identified prior to departure and procedures for tracing families on return simplified. Some of the eighty NGOs, largely church agencies, which proved crucial in assisting returnees to reach their communities of origin, are also preparing reports on their activities.

Conclusion

As with other cases of planned mass return of refugees, the abiding memory of that to Namibia will be a story of success (Allen, 1991; Jackson, 1991; Makanya, 1991; RRR Committee, 1991). As elsewhere, however, with the passage of time, the picture of the return and its consequences becomes less uniform. Individual experiences, positive and negative, become known and commonalities with other repatriations become apparent. Already, it seems that there are similarities between the processes and stages of the Namibian experience and those of other countries, so that they can in some measure be linked to the nascent typologies of repatriation to which reference has been made. Only with time will it be possible to review the processes affecting economic and social reintegration in Namibia and the extent to which this conforms to patterns of repatriation and other forms of return migration elsewhere. Meanwhile, by comparing some of the events in Namibia with those associated with other repatriating groups, this chapter has underlined the complexity of the process of return and the diversity of experience, confirming Rogge's contention that repatriation is a far from simple solution to exile (Rogge, 1991).

References

Adelman, H., 1989, *Refugee research: past, present and future*, Centre for Refugee Studies, York University, Ontario.

Akol, J.O., 1987, 'Southern Sudanese refugees: their repatriation and resettlement after the Addis Ababa Agreement', in J.R. Rogge, ed., *Refugees: a third world dilemma*, Rowman & Littlefield, New Jersey.

Akol, J.O., 1991, *Social and economic aspects of reintegration of returnees: Southern Sudan's experience, 1972–1974*, United Nations Research Institute for Social Development (UNRISD), Geneva.

Alhabo, M. and Passang, M., 1991, *Socio–economic aspects of repatriation assistance: the case of Chad*, UNRISD, Geneva (infra).

Allen, T., 1991, *Repatriation to northern Uganda: a view from below*, UNRISD, Geneva (infra).

Asante, S. and Asombang, W., 1989, 'An independent Namibia: the future facing SWAPO', *Third World Quarterly*, **11** (3): 1–9

Bender, G., 1989, 'Peacemaking in southern Africa: the Luanda–Pretoria tug-of-war', *Third World Quarterly*, **11** (2): 15–30.

Bush, R., 1990, 'The Namibian election process: just about free and fair', *Review of African Political Economy*, **45/46**: 151–57.

Cliffe, L., 1990, 'Namibia postscript: the election results', *Review of African Political Economy*, **45/46**: 157–58.

Cohen, C., 1991, 'Educational administration in Namibia: the colonial and immediate post-independence periods', D.Phil. thesis, University of Oxford.

Crisp, J.F., 1984, 'Voluntary repatriation programmes for African refugees: a critical examination', *Refugee Issues*, **1** (2): 1–23.

Cuny, F. and Stein, B., 1989, 'Prospects for and promotion of spontaneous repatriation', in G. Loescher and L. Monahan, eds, *Refugees and International Relations*, Oxford University Press, Oxford.

De Wolf, S., 1981, 'The resettlement and rehabilitation of refugees in the Umtali area', paper presented at the University of Michigan, December 1981.

Gasarasi, C.P., 1990, 'UN Resolution 435 and the repatriation of Namibian exiles', *Journal of Refugee Studies*, **3** (4): 340–64.

Goodwin-Gill, G., 1989, 'Voluntary repatriation: legal and policy issues', in G. Loescher and L. Monahan, eds, *Refugees and international relations*, Oxford University Press, Oxford.

Harrell-Bond, B.E., 1989, 'Repatriation: under what conditions is it the most desirable solution for refugees?', *African Studies Review*, **32** (1): 41–69.

Jackson, J.C., 1991, *Refugees, repatriation and reconstruction: an account of Zimbabwe's post-Lancaster House repatriations*, UNRISD, Geneva (infra).

Leys, C., 1990, 'The security situation and the transfer of power in Namibia', *Review of African Political Economy*, **45/46**: 142–51.

Manning, P., 1989, 'Namibia's independence: what has happened to Resolution 435?', *Review of African Political Economy*, **44**: 63–72.

Makanya, S.T., 1991, *The desire to return: an examination of the effects of the experiences of Zimbabwean refugees in the neighbouring countries on their repatriation at the end of the liberation war*, UNRISD, Geneva (infra).

Mwase, N.R.L., 1990, 'The repatriation, rehabilitation and resettlement of Namibian refugees at independence', *Community Development Journal*, **25** (2): 113–22.

The Namibian, Newspaper, Windhoek, 1989–91.

Otto Benecke Stiftung, 1991, *Annual Report*, Otto Benecke Stiftung, Windhoek.

Preston, R., 1990, Notes of interviews with Stella Makanya, School of Social Work, University of Zimbabwe and Fay Cheung, Minister of Education, Zimbabwe, December 1990.

Preston, R., 1991a, *Report to an inter-agency mission on education for Mozambican refugees in Malawi and Zimbabwe*, United Nations Development Programme, New York.

Preston, R., 1991b, Notes of interview with Dawson Sanangore, Director of the Department of Social Welfare, Zimbabwe, March 1991.

Rogge, J.R., 1991, *Repatriation of refugees: a not-so-simple optimum solution*, UNRISD, Geneva (infra).

Rogge, J.R. and Akol, J.O., 1989, 'Repatriation: its role in resolving Africa's refugee dilemma', *International Migration Review*, **23** (2): 184–200.

RRR Committee (Repatriation, Resettlement and Reconstruction Committee), 1989–90, *CCN/RRR Weekly Newsletter*, Council of Churches of Namibia/Repatriation, Resettlement and Reconstruction Committee (CCN/RRR), Windhoek (supplement to *The Namibian* during the repatriation exercise).

RRR Committee, 1990, *Narrative Reports*, CCN/RRR, Windhoek.

RRR Committee, 1991, *Mission Accomplished*, CCN/RRR, Windhoek.

Simon, D., 1991, 'Independent Namibia one year on', *Conflict Studies*, **239**, Research Institute for the Study of Conflict and Terrorism, London.

Stein, B.N., 1990, 'Patterns of spontaneous voluntary repatriation and its implications for policy and program', Paper presented to meeting on 'Repatriation under conflict: the Central American case', Center for Immigration Policy, Georgetown University.

Stein, B.N., 1991, *The actual and desirable link between programmes of ad hoc assistance to return movements and long-term development programmes for the local areas where refugees return*, UNRISD, Geneva (infra).

Stiff, P., 1989, *Nine days of war: Namibia before, during and after*, Lemur, Alberton, RSA.

Tapscott, C. and Mulongeni, B., 1990, *An evaluation of the welfare and future prospects of repatriated Namibians in northern Namibia*, Namibian Institute of Social and Economic Research, Windhoek.

UNHCR (United Nations High Commissioner for Refugees), 1990a, 'Africa: a continent in crisis', *Refugees*, **81**: 9–11.

UNHCR, 1990b, *Namibia repatriation operation: lessons learned survey*, UNHCR, Geneva.

UNRISD (United Nations Research Institute for Social Development), 1991, Symposium on social and economic aspects of mass voluntary return of refugees from one African country to another, Harare, 12–14 March.

Williams, T., 1990a, 'UNTAG: walking a tightrope', *Refugees*, **75**: 13–14.

Williams, T., 1990b, 'No place like home', *Refugees*, **75**: 39–40.

Wilson, K. and Nunes, J., 1991, *Repatriating Mozambicans: past experiences, ongoing programmes and future dilemmas*, UNRISD, Geneva (supra).

WCC (World Council of Churches), 1989, *Namibia: Situation Report, 1–6*, WCC, Geneva.

WCC, 1990, *Namibia: Situation Report, 7–8*, WCC, Geneva

Further reading

Gasarasi, C.P., 1990, 'UN resolution 435 and the repatriation of Namibian exiles', *Journal of Refugee Studies*, **3** (4): 340–364.

Goodwin-Gill, G., 1989, 'Voluntary repatriation: legal and policy issues, in G. Loescher and L. Monahan, eds, *Refugees and international relations*, Oxford University Press, Oxford.

Harrell-Bond, B.E., 1989, 'Repatriation: under what conditions is it the most desirable solution for refugees?', *African Studies Review*, **32** (1): 41–69.

Rogge, J.R. and Akol, J.O., 1989, 'Repatriation: its role in resolving Africa's refugee dilemma', *International Migration Review*, **23** (2): 184–200.

Simon, D., 1991, 'Independent Namibia One Year On', *Conflict Studies*, **239**, Research Institute for the Study of Conflict and Terrorism, London.

5 Mass flight in the Middle East: involuntary migration and the Gulf conflict, 1990–1991

Nicholas Van Hear

Introduction

The number of people uprooted in the Middle East since the invasion of Kuwait by Iraq on 2 August 1990 may total between four and five million, one of the largest mass displacements in recent times, and possibly the most far-reaching in terms of the number of countries affected since the Second World War. This chapter reviews the forms of mass displacement the Gulf conflict set in motion and begins to assess the impact of this forced migration in the region and beyond.

The mass displacement occurred in five main waves, which featured almost every kind of forced migration. First, in the wake of the invasion, came the mass flight of mainly migrant workers and professionals from Iraq and Kuwait into Jordan and other neighbouring countries. This movement was closely followed by the mass expulsion of Yemenis from Saudi Arabia. These two migrations took place between August and December 1990 and may have involved more than two million people. The second period, from the outbreak of the war in January 1991 until the cease-fire, featured a smaller wave of displacement. About 65,000 people are thought to have left the war zone during this period, although the numbers displaced within Iraq and Kuwait may have been much larger. The mass flight of up to two million Iraqi Kurds and Shias towards Turkey and Iran in the wake of the uprisings and their suppression in northern and southern Iraq formed the third wave of forced migration; large numbers of people also sought refuge from the Iraqi military in Iraq's mountains or marshes. A complex pattern of displacement meanwhile emerged in southern Iraq, Kuwait and Saudi Arabia involving what might be called stranded people or *de facto* refugees thrown up in the course of the allied bombing, the ground war and the aftermath of the civil war. By May 1991 a fourth period – the mass return of refugees from Turkey and Iran – was under way. By July 1991, almost all of those who had fled for Turkey and most of those who had fled to Iran had returned to within Iraq's borders, although not necessarily to their homes. Large numbers of people remained displaced within Iraq against the background of the political and military stalemate that prevailed for the rest of 1991; there was further large-scale flight in the wake of Iraqi military attacks. A fifth period of displacement gathered momentum in mid-1991 with the renewed exodus of Iraqis and of Jordanians and Palestinians from

Kuwait. There remained large numbers of stranded people scattered around southern Iraq, Saudi Arabia and Jordan.

This chapter elaborates this periodisation and considers the impact of the mass displacement on some of the populations and countries affected. It underlines the unprecedented diversity of the mass migration and displacement, both in terms of the nationalities and countries involved and in terms of the forms of involuntary movement. The chapter concludes by indicating some of the implications of this diversity for the forced migration 'regime' – the configuration of international law, institutions and practice that has evolved to deal with refugees and displaced people.

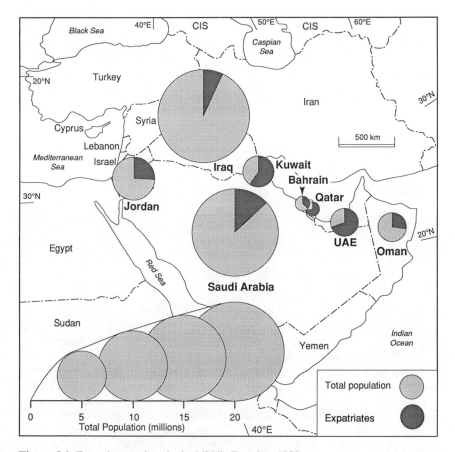

Figure 5.1 Expatriate workers in the Middle East, late 1980s

The flight of migrant workers, August–December 1990

It is thought that the oil boom of the 1970s had attracted more than five million foreign workers to the oil-producing countries of the Middle East by the mid-1980s (Figure 5.1). Estimates vary greatly, but perhaps half of these expatriates were drawn from other Arab countries – principally Egyptians, other North Africans, Yemenis, Jordanians and displaced Palestinians. Most of the remainder were from south and south-east Asia. Expatriate workers in Iraq and Kuwait may have accounted for more than one-third of the total in the region (Owen, 1985; Birks *et al.*, 1988; Amjad, 1989; FAO, 1990; Appleyard, 1991).

Table 5.1 Estimates of foreign nationals and their dependents in Kuwait and Iraq, mid-1990, and of returnees from the Gulf region in 1990–91 (thousands)

Country of origin	Kuwait Workers	Kuwait Dependents	Iraq Workers	Iraq Dependents	Returnees in 1990/91
Egypt	180	35	850	50	500–700
Yemen[1]	7	16	1	1	750–850
Jordan/Palestine	110	400	5	22	300[2]
Lebanon	20	20	15	5	60
Sudan	12	3	190	10	35–200
Syria	–	–	–	–	50–130
India	130	42	7	2	180–200
Pakistan	77	13	7	2	90–142
Sri Lanka	79	21	1	0	73–101
Bangladesh	70	4	15	0	64–90
China	–	–	60[3]	–	60
Philippines	38	7	7	2	30–55
Vietnam	–	–	16	–	8–16
Thailand	–	–	–	–	10

Sources: ILO, 1991b; US General Accounting Office, 1991; IOM, 1991; UN ESCWA, 1991; Abdalla, 1991; UNDP, 1991b.

Notes: 1. The People's Democratic Republic of Yemen and the Yemen Arab Republic were unified in 1990 to form the Republic of Yemen. The figures cited in this table and elsewhere in this chapter combine those for the two former republics. There were said to be about one million Yemenis in Saudi Arabia towards the end of the 1980s, but there was controversy about this figure (Findlay, 1987), and thus of the number of returnees in 1990–91. The most commonly cited figures were 800,000 returnees from Saudi Arabia and 30,000 via Jordan.

2. There were estimated to be 605,000 Jordanians/Palestinians in the six Gulf Cooperation Council countries (Bahrain, Kuwait, Oman, Qatar, Saudi Arabia and the United Arab Emirates) on the eve of the Gulf crisis. 300,000 Jordanians and Palestinians moved to Jordan, mostly from Kuwait, with about 10 per cent from Saudi Arabia. In addition there were said to be 54,000 returnees to the Occupied Territories, of whom 26,000 had been working in Kuwait and the remainder in Saudi Arabia and other Gulf states (UN ESCWA, 1991; UNDP, 1991b).

3. Total number of workers reported to be in Iraq and Kuwait.

This pattern of migration was profoundly disrupted by the mass exodus following the invasion of Kuwait by Iraq on 2 August 1990. By the end of 1990 perhaps two million foreign nationals had left their countries of residence and work as tensions rose in the region (Table 5.1). Further outflows of foreign nationals occurred in 1991 (Van Hear, 1991a, 1991b; Graham-Brown, 1991).

Flight from Kuwait and Iraq

Most of those leaving Kuwait and Iraq passed through Jordan. By the end of 1990 more than a million people are thought to have entered the country, the great majority en route to other destinations. Returnees to Jordan, including Palestinians holding Jordanian documents, numbered up to 250,000. Perhaps half of the 865,000 third country nationals passing through Jordan were Egyptians; others were migrants from Yemen, India, Bangladesh, Pakistan, Sri Lanka, the Philippines and Sudan. Most of the 60,000 evacuees who left through Turkey were from Bangladesh, Pakistan, Sri Lanka, Vietnam and Eastern Europe, together with some 5,000 Turkish nationals. Some 100,000 people entered Iran, of whom 70,000 were Iranians or Kuwaitis and most of the remainder Pakistanis. Of 60,000 people who left Iraq for Syria, about 50,000 were Syrians. Many of these involuntary migrants lost assets and belongings and reported harassment en route (Van Hear, 1991a; US General Accounting Office, 1991).

Many of the evacuees in this first wave of mass exodus, including most of the Egyptians, made their own way home with minimal assistance. About 350,000 migrants were repatriated by their governments (US General Accounting Office, 1991); the Indian authorities were among the most conscientious in flying home their own and other south Asian nationals. By the end of 1990, nearly 156,000 foreign residents in Iraq and Kuwait had been evacuated under the airlift overseen by the International Organization for Migration (IOM), mainly from Jordan, but also from Iraq itself, Turkey and Iran (IOM, 1990–91).

The repatriation of evacuees from Jordan and other countries to which they fled was a considerable achievement by the governments and international agencies involved. That the number in camps in Jordan was reduced from 110,000 at its peak to less than 35,000 by mid-September is evidence of the effectiveness of the evacuation effort by land and air. By early December 1990 very few people were left in the camps in Jordan (UNDRO, 1990a). After initial confusion as thousands of migrants made for the Jordanian border with Iraq, a relatively effective relief operation was set in motion. After early problems, coordination appears to have been effective among the Jordanian authorities, the international agencies and the many NGOs that engaged themselves in the emergency (UNDRO, 1990a, 1990b; UN Office, 1990; US General Accounting Office, 1991).

Smaller-scale reception, evacuation and relief operations were mounted in Iran, Syria and Turkey. To provide coordination at the regional level, the UN Secretary General appointed a personal representative for humanitarian assistance relating to the Gulf crisis. While this appointment had little impact on the effort to assist migrant worker evacuees, the representative (later designated executive delegate) was to come to greater prominence after the mass exodus of Kurdish and

Shia refugees from Iraq (US General Accounting Office, 1991; UN Office, 1990; IOM, 1990–91).

The mass expulsion of Yemenis from Saudi Arabia

While international attention was focused on the plight of migrants moving from Iraq and Kuwait and their evacuation to their countries of origin, the Gulf crisis was generating another, largely unnoticed mass exodus from Saudi Arabia (Van Hear, 1991a). From mid-August 1990, increasing numbers of Yemenis began to leave Saudi Arabia as a result of tensions between the two countries arising partly from what the Saudis saw as the Yemen government's support for Iraq. Then, in September, the Saudi authorities made far-reaching changes to the rules governing work and residence permits for the large Yemeni community in the kingdom (see Findlay, 1987, for a discussion of the controversy over the number of Yemenis abroad). The changes removed many of the exemptions enjoyed by Yemeni migrants, and put pressure on them to leave. By mid-October, between 30,000 and 40,000 Yemenis were reported to be crossing the border with Saudi Arabia every day. There was evidence of widespread arbitrary arrest, detention and torture of Yemenis since the Gulf crisis had erupted, and of widespread harassment by the Saudi authorities, both prior to the exodus and en route (Amnesty International, 1990). Such action no doubt induced many more Yemenis to leave, adding weight to the view that the exodus was more in the nature of a mass expulsion than a simple deportation of illegal immigrants.

Many of the Yemenis had been in Saudi Arabia for a decade or more, and some had been born in the kingdom. By the mid-November deadline for Yemeni migrants to regularise their status under the new rules, 650,000 were said to have left. By the end of 1990 it was estimated that 850,000 of them may have returned to Yemen (CAFOD *et al.*, 1991; ODI, 1991; UNDP, 1991a).

These two episodes of mass exodus were different in form. The mass exodus of Yemenis from Saudi Arabia was arguably an expulsion, since the Saudi authorities suddenly changed the rules governing the migrants' right to stay, as well as allegedly harassing, detaining and torturing some of them, and thereby induced them to leave. By contrast, although there was harassment and abuse of the foreign workforce while Kuwait was under Iraqi occupation, the principal reason for the flight of Arab and Asian expatriates seems to have been fear of the new regime and of the war that the occupation might provoke. In both cases, however, much of the flight was in anticipation of persecution, harassment or intimidation, or of instability, civil conflict or war. Like many involuntary migrations, flight was predicated on the calculation that a tolerable life was no longer possible under such conditions.

Second period: the war-time exodus

At the end of 1990 it was estimated that there were still more than a million foreign nationals remaining in Iraq and Kuwait. During the first wave of mass exodus to Jordan and other neighbouring countries, international agencies formulated a programme to deal with further flight expected during and after the outbreak of impending hostilities. The programme – the Regional Humanitarian Plan of Action – was revised and updated in January 1991, just before the outbreak of the war. Further out-movement of expatriates was anticipated, accompanied this time by substantial numbers of Iraqi refugees from the conflict (UN Office, 1991a).

After the war started there was movement to the four main destination countries anticipated – Jordan, Iran, Turkey and Syria – but it was on a much smaller scale than the 100,000 arrivals expected in each country under the contingency plan. Between the start of the war and the end of March, before the mass exodus of Kurds and Shias into Turkey and Iran, probably no more than 65,000 people in all left Iraq and Kuwait. Among the reasons for the lack of out-movement during the war were the closure by the Iraqi authorities of the borders with Turkey and Syria, and restrictions on movement to Jordan and Iran. Movement was in any case difficult and dangerous because of allied bombing. Nevertheless, unknown numbers of displaced people must have been moving within Iraq. The fate of some of them is discussed in the section on stranded people and *de facto* refugees, below. In view of the relatively small number of new arrivals from the war zone, it was decided to wind down the reception and relief facilities that were being developed in Jordan, Iran, Turkey and Syria (UN Office, 1991a).

Third period: the mass flight of Kurds and Shias towards Turkey and Iran

Just as the international agencies were running down their preparations for a wartime mass exodus that never materialised, the largest mass flight since the inception of the crisis erupted, in the wake of the suppression of the Kurdish rebellion in northern Iraq and that of the Shia population in the south. By mid-April 1991, up to two million Kurds, about half the population of Iraqi Kurdistan, were said to be on the move as they fled the Iraqi military and made for the Turkish or Iranian borders or for the relative security of mountains away from the main towns. Up to 500,000 Kurds were said to have crossed the border into Turkey, and more than a million Kurds and Shias were reported to have moved into Iran. Many more massed on the borders in miserable conditions awaiting entry into these two countries. Between 2,000 and 3,000 people were said to be dying daily from exposure, disease and starvation (McHugh and Epstein, 1991; USCR, 1991; UNHCR, 1991; De Almeida e Silva, 1991).

Stung by public pressure over the abandonment of the Kurdish and Shia rebellions and widespread media coverage of the suffering of Kurdish refugees, the US, British and other European governments launched a military intervention, 'Operation Provide Comfort', to relieve the crisis on the Turkish border (McHugh and Epstein, 1991). Having resisted the entry of refugees into its territory, the Turkish authorities also eventually succumbed to pressure to allow some of the Kurdish refugees to move down from the mountains to more accessible sites within Turkey's borders.

The much larger movement of refugees to Iran received far less attention. Even though it already hosted some 2.35 million Afghan refugees, Iran opened its borders and accommodated around 1.3 million displaced Kurds and Shias; this meant that, at the peak of the crisis, Iran hosted the largest refugee population in the world. Nonetheless the international community allocated Iran less than half the funds designated for Turkey, which adopted a largely hostile stance towards the refugees (USCR, 1991). As deaths continued to mount, international pressure grew to move all of the refugees from the perilous conditions on the mountainous border with Turkey. Refugees' security then became as important an issue as immediate, life-saving relief. However, conflicting visions of this security subsequently emerged.

The US government initially resisted Turkish, French and British government proposals for the establishment of secure enclaves within Iraq so that refugees could return. But in mid-April, in a startling reversal of policy, 'Operation Haven' was launched to establish an enclave in northern Iraq under the protection of US and European troops (McHugh and Epstein, 1991). It was accompanied by a US declaration restricting Iraqi military activity north of the 36th parallel. Meanwhile another initiative was under way under the auspices of the UN Secretary-General's executive delegate, Sadruddin Aga Khan. In mid-April a memorandum of understanding was signed with the Iraqi government, governing the conditions for humanitarian assistance and allowing for the establishment of UN 'humanitarian centres' throughout the country, through which relief would be channelled (UN Office, 1991b).

Most crucially, however, the issue of security for returnees was left unresolved. The hope that a UN civilian presence and the later deployment of UN guards to the area would ensure returnees' safety were unconvincing. Amid considerable Kurdish scepticism, difficult and protracted negotiations were under way between the Iraqi government and Kurdish political leaders for an agreement that would give the Kurds a degree of autonomy and security within Iraq. However, much of the Kurdish population believed that the presence of allied troops was the only guarantee of security.

The Shia population of southern Iraq – said to constitute 55 per cent of the country's population – had good cause to feel aggrieved at their neglect by the international community. Proposals to match the havens emerging in the north with safe areas for the Shias came to nothing, although late in May the UN undertook to deploy its guards in southern Iraq. Those who could had fled to the southern zone controlled by allied forces, or to Iran or its borders. Several hundred thousand others were reported to have fled to the marshlands of southern Iraq where they were living in pitiful conditions, and under the threat of new attacks by the Iraqi military. Information about these displaced people was sketchy and often contradictory, but late in April 1991 it was estimated that they numbered between 400,000 and 600,000, with several hundred crossing into Iran each day (USCR, 1991). Areas of operation of UNHCR in the region as a whole are outlined in Figure 5.2.

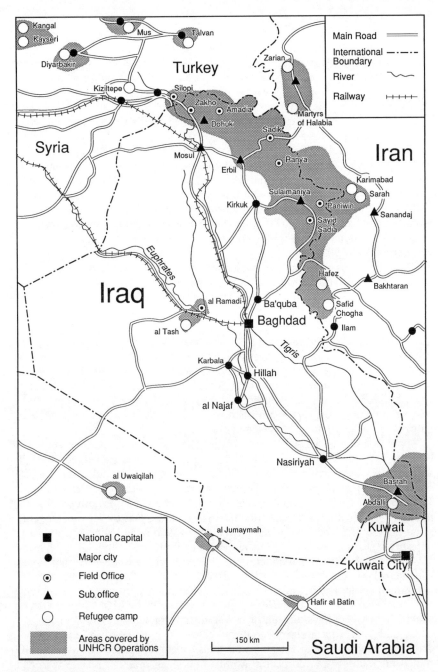

Figure 5.2 Areas in the Middle East covered by UNHCR operations, 1991

Fourth period: mass return

Mass return from Turkey and Iran

As the provision of assistance and security appeared to improve, refugees began to return to Iraq. If the mass exodus of Iraqi Kurds and Shias was 'the fastest refugee movement in the 40-year history of UNHCR (De Almeida e Silva, 1991), the rapidity of the mass return was equally remarkable. It was all the more so for the fact that still no one was in a position to deliver sustained security for returnees and displaced people – what one commentator called 'the single most important relief commodity' (Rogge, 1991, p. 11).

Towards the end of May 1991 a substantial return from Turkey and Iran was under way. By early June the camps in Turkey were reported to have emptied. At the end of May, those still in Iran were said to number 788,000. The UNHCR anticipated that the populations requiring winter accommodation might number 600,000 in Iran; but by the end of August all but about 70,000 people were said to have returned inside Iraq (De Almeida e Silva, 1991), and the movement was reported to be continuing despite periodic clashes between the Iraqi military and Kurdish guerrillas.

The return was based on a combination of tenuous sources of security: the establishment by western military forces of the controversial 'safe haven' for the Kurdish population in northern Iraq and the restriction of Iraqi military activity by the allied forces; world public attention on events in the region; the conclusion between the government of Iraq and the UN of the memorandum of understanding governing humanitarian assistance and the beginnings of UN intervention; the resurgence of Kurdish guerilla groups and their control of substantial swathes of territory; and apparent progress in negotiations between the Iraqi regime and Kurdish leaders. Also reflected in the refugees' decision about whether to return were the inhospitable conditions encountered particularly in Turkey, but also in Iran or on the borders of these countries; indeed the refugees in Turkey in particular arguably had little choice but to return.

These sources of security were volatile and likely to evaporate. The talks between Kurdish leaders and the Baghdad regime remained stalled, and were in any case of questionable value in the eyes of the Kurdish population. The UN conceded that it could not guarantee returnees' safety (UN Office, 1991b). In mid-July the allied forces – the most credible source of security from the refugees' point of view – withdrew from northern Iraq to southern Turkey, leaving the relief effort to the UN and non-governmental organisations and the security issue unresolved. However, the withdrawal did not precipitate the immediate renewed mass exodus that some had anticipated. Following clashes between Iraqi forces and guerrillas in the north-east in July, 40,000 people were said to be heading for the Iranian border again; but no other large-scale movements were reported until late in the year when the UNHCR reported the mass flight within northern Iraq of some 200,000 people as a result of Iraqi military attacks.

By mid-1991, four groups were identifiable among the Kurdish returnees and displaced people: people remaining in transit camps; 'spontaneously' or self-settled internally displaced people who had not been in exile; people who had returned to their former villages or towns, often destroyed in the course of the Iraqi regime's previous campaigns of depopulation and forced relocation; and those who had gone back to the collective villages or towns to which they had been forcibly relocated in previous years (Rogge, 1991, p. 12). The issue of assistance to all but the last category of returnees and displaced people remained unresolved, for the Iraqi government maintained that refugees should return to the status quo, that is, their homes as of early 1991. As winter approached and no political resolution became apparent, the prospects for these returnees gave cause for much concern, particularly the estimated 640,000 people along the northeastern border with Iran, who were receiving some assistance from the UNHCR and NGOs (UNHCR, 1991; De Almeida e Silva, 1991).

The impasse continued, although late in the year the memorandum of understanding between the UN and the Iraqi government, which laid down the conditions for humanitarian assistance, was extended to June 1992. Towards the end of 1991 there were thought to be some 500,000 Kurds still displaced who were without adequate food and shelter. Many of these came under the UNHCR's 'winterisation' programme, which provided temporary accommodation and food supplies to see the displaced through the winter (UNHCR, 1991; De Almeida e Silva, 1991; Graham-Brown, 1991). More sustained resettlement and reconstruction awaited a resolution of the politico-military stalemate between the Baghdad regime and Kurdish forces. With the Baghdad regime's economic blockade of the north in the process of reinforcement at the end of 1991 by the construction of a military line along the 'border' with Kurdistan, that resolution looked as far away as ever. The prospects for the large numbers of internally displaced people in southern Iraq appeared equally bleak.

Would-be returnees and stranded people in Southern Iraq,
Kuwait and Saudi Arabia

While the pattern of displacement in northern and eastern Iraq was relatively clear, other involuntary displacements in southern Iraq during and after the war and the civil war made for a pattern that was rather more complex. One such movement was that of Asian and Arab migrant workers formerly in Kuwait, and of Palestinians, Jordanians, Iraqis and others who held professional or administrative posts in the emirate. After the restoration of the al-Sabah regime, many of these who had fled to southern Iraq attempted to return to the emirate, only to be turned back by the Kuwaiti authorities at the border amid government rhetoric that the country was to reduce its dependence on foreign labour. Some people of Kuwaiti origin who did not hold citizenship – known as the *bidoon* – and others who had lost their papers during the conflict found themselves denied entry and stuck in camps sharing the conditions of others refused readmission to Kuwait. Another stranded group were Iraqi civilians, disaffected soldiers and deserters who had fled the civil war to the zone in southern Iraq controlled by allied forces after the cease-fire. As allied forces withdrew, nearly 8,400 displaced people were airlifted to camps in northern Saudi Arabia. Here they joined some 10,000 Iraqi former prisoners of war who refused to return to Iraq and opted for refugee rather than prisoner-of-war status. Others sought refuge in Iran, which agreed to take some refugees with Iranian connections, and where movement was more free than in Saudi Arabia. As of mid-1991 there were said to be 23,000 Iraqi civilian refugees and some 13,000 Iraqi former prisoners of war in two camps in Saudi Arabia (UNHCR, 1991; De Almeida e Silva, 1991).

The position of some of these groups was slowly resolved. Some of the foreign workers and some stateless persons of Kuwaiti origin, the *bidoon*, were readmitted. They were issued with temporary papers by the restored Kuwaiti authorities, and some of those who had remained in the emirate were re-registered. The need to renew temporary documents was subsequently deferred. While this lifted the immediate threat of deportation from Kuwait for many foreign nationals, more stringent rules for working and residence were introduced early in 1992, leaving their longer-term future and security unresolved.

Fifth period: further flight from Kuwait

Flight of Palestinians from Kuwait continued after the al-Sabah restoration as a result of violence against the Palestinian community by Kuwaiti militia groups avenging alleged collaboration. Reports of killings and torture mounted despite the critical attention of human rights groups (Lawyers' Committee for Human Rights, 1992). Internationally criticised trials of alleged collaborators increased the insecurity of Jordanians, Palestinians and other foreign nationals still in the emirate and induced many to leave.

Palestinians in the emirate before August 1990 were thought to have numbered up to 400,000. Many had lived there all their lives, and constituted what might be termed an 'alien' resident community rather than a category of migrant workers. Large numbers of Palestinian residents – perhaps half the pre-August 1990 population – left before and during the war for Jordan, Syria, Lebanon and the Occupied Territories. However, in addition, there were substantial numbers of Palestinians long settled in Kuwait who could not make claims on these destinations for refuge. They may have numbered 60,000 and included those from the Gaza strip with Egyptian documents, but whom the Egyptian authorities would not allow to enter Egypt; they also included many whose documents had expired.

Movement from Kuwait to Jordan of large numbers of Jordanians and Palestinians gathered momentum in August 1991. More than 10,000 such people were reported to have arrived in Jordan by land and air in that month. While persecution of Palestinians in the emirate had abated, continuing denial of access to employment, education or health services precipitated this exodus, which took the total number of 'returnees' to Jordan since August 1990 up to 300,000 (Van Hear, 1991a; Graham-Brown, 1991). In addition, Jordan was obliged to accommodate growing numbers of Iraqis seeking refuge, largely from minority Christian communities.

The mass departure of Palestinians, Jordanians and others from Kuwait after the restoration of the al-Sabah regime was akin to an expulsion, since flight was induced by harassment and torture, or fear of these in the early stages, and by denial of access to work, education and health care later on. Many of those who had wished to stay in Kuwait after the al-Sabah restoration appear to have reached the conclusion that a reasonable life was no longer possible there. The Kuwaiti authorities were thought to wish to reduce the Palestinian population resident in the emirate to about 40,000, in line with their stated intention to reduce drastically Kuwait's foreign population (Van Hear, 1991a; Graham-Brown, 1991).

The impact of displacement, 1990–91

At the time of writing, the prospects for the Kurdish and Shia displaced populations awaited resolution of the politico-military situation in Iraq. This section therefore concentrates on the impact of the exodus of migrant workers, professionals, and foreign residents who were obliged to leave in the first and fifth waves of displacement identified above.

Table 5.2 Estimates of workers' remittances forgone as a result of the Gulf crisis, compared with worldwide remittances in 1989[1] (millions of dollars)

Country	Remittances from Kuwait/Iraq	Total worldwide remittances
Egypt	1,000	4,254
Yemen	400[2]	438
Jordan	150–1,400[3]	627
Lebanon	150–500[3]	–
Sudan	300[4]	417
Syria	–	355
Occupied Territories	80–146[5]	–
India	200	2,662
Bangladesh	100–160	758
Pakistan	100–200	2,010
Sri Lanka	100–120	356
Philippines	40–60	360
Vietnam	379[4]	–
Thailand	–	80

Sources: UNDP 1991b; ILO, 1991a; CAFOD *et al.*, 1991; ODI, 1991; Abdalla, 1991. 1989 world remittance totals are from IMF, 1990; World Bank, 1991.

Notes: 1. Some estimates of remittances are wildly at variance with one another and with estimates of worldwide remittances.
2. Remittances forgone from Saudi Arabia.
3. The higher figure includes other financial assets in Kuwait or Iraq.
4. Includes repatriation costs.
5. The higher figure includes remittances from Saudi Arabia, estimated at $44 million, and from other Gulf states, estimated at $29 million. Lost trade and subventions from other Gulf states was said to total $400 million.

Migrants and foreign residents sustained substantial losses as a result of their involuntary mass departure. Among the principal losses were unpaid wages; end-of-service benefits; remittances not transferred, a grievance particularly of Egyptian workers; savings lost as bank accounts were destroyed or rendered inaccessible; personal belongings stolen, lost or left behind; and property or assets which were inaccessible (ILO, 1991b; Saith, 1991b). Kin and communities receiving returnees found themselves doubly affected – first, by the sudden removal of remittances they routinely received, and second, because they now had also to support new arrivals. More widely, the exodus had a profound effect on the societies and economies of countries surrounding the arena of conflict and beyond. The impact is difficult to disentangle from other effects of the crisis (notably the volatility of oil prices), and from the severe straits that many countries were already in before the crisis broke. However, the remainder of this section attempts to draw together some estimates of the scale of the impact of the mass exodus and repatriation (Table 5.2).

Jordan's position was different in several respects from other countries that received displaced people during the crisis. As outlined above, it was obliged to be the country of transit for 'third country' displaced migrant workers and professionals en route to their home countries. In addition to accommodating these evacuees, Jordan had to cope with up to 300,000 of its own nationals or document-holders from Kuwait, Iraq, Saudi Arabia and other Gulf states. The returnees may have added 8 per cent to Jordan's population and 10 per cent to its labour force (ODI, 1991; CAFOD *et al.*, 1991; UNDP, 1991b; UN ESCWA, 1991; Abdalla, 1991). Their return meant a substantial loss in the remittances on which the Jordanian economy depended. The total is difficult to calculate, with estimates of the remittances forgone varying between $150 million and $769 million (CAFOD *et al.*, 1991; UNDP, 1991b). Even the lower estimate accounts for a substantial proportion of Jordan's total remittances, which were estimated at $627 million in 1989, when they represented 10 per cent of GNP (IMF, 1990; World Bank, 1991; UN ESCWA, 1991).

Without diminishing the serious impact of mass return on other countries of the region and beyond, the impact on Jordan of the new arrivals was particularly severe. First, unlike those returning to other countries, who were mainly of working age, the returnees to Jordan included a large proportion of dependents (see Table 5.1), putting strain on both private and public sources of welfare services: return of students in particular put severe pressure on Jordan's educational system (Hashemite Kingdom of Jordan, 1991). Second, many of the returnees, although carrying Jordanian documents, had been away for most of their lives or had even been born and brought up abroad; according to one estimate, 90 per cent of the returnees had been away for more then ten years, 43 per cent for more than twenty years, and nearly a quarter had migrated before the early 1960s (UN ESCWA, 1991). This meant that they had limited direct experience of, or links with Jordan, a position they shared with many of the returnees to Yemen. Indeed, the term returnee is a misnomer, since most of those displaced could not be said to be returning to a homeland that they knew. Third, unlike other countries, Jordan had to cope with several waves or surges of return: the two peaks were in the period after Iraq's invasion of Kuwait in 1990 and in the period after the al-Sabah regime's restoration in 1991. Finally, while Jordan was far from unique in being beset by economic difficulties before the mass return, it did already accommodate one of the highest ratios of refugees to indigenous population in the world – nearly one in four of Jordan's population of four million are recognised as refugees (USCR, 1992).

Yemen was also very severely affected by its mass return. If the estimate of 800,000 returnees was accurate, Yemen would have absorbed a 7 per cent increase to its population within three months. The return may have added 15 per cent to the labour force (ODI, 1991). The earnings of Yemeni workers abroad were thought to have accounted for more than half of Yemen's legal foreign receipts, as well as a large volume that did not pass through official channels. The remittances lost were estimated at $400 million yearly (CAFOD *et al.*, 1991; UNDP, 1991b); this represented 90 per cent of total remittances in 1989 and 5.5 per cent of GNP for that year (IMF, 1990; World Bank, 1991). It appears that most returnees were absorbed into their communities of origin, or into the homes of relatives. However, as with returnees to Jordan, a substantial number – perhaps 20 per cent – had been away for decades or had even been born abroad and had no such destinations to make for; they were reported to have squatted in makeshift shanty settlements concentrated particularly around the port of Hodeidah (Van Hear, 1991b).

Egypt received up to 700,000 returnees. Loss of remittances from Iraq and Kuwait were estimated by the Egyptian authorities at up to $1 billion for 1990–91 (*Africa Economic Digest*, 3 and 17 September 1990; ILO, 1991a); total remittances for 1989 were estimated at $4.25–4.5 billion (IMF, 1990; World Bank, 1991). Whilst this loss – perhaps 3 per cent of 1989 GNP – and the impact on unemployment would have been substantial, these effects may have been offset by new sources of employment abroad. Egyptian returnees were reported to have been finding work in Saudi Arabia, which began to reshape its foreign workforce of some 2.5 million, as Asian workers left and Yemeni, Jordanian, Sudanese and Palestinian workers and professionals were made unwelcome or expelled because of what was perceived as their leaders' support for Iraq. Some Egyptians were also reported to be returning to Kuwait in 1991 (Addleton, 1991).

Life for Palestinians in the territories occupied by Israel was made harder by the fallout of the Gulf conflict. About 54,000 Palestinians were reported to have returned from Gulf states to the Occupied Territories, or to have been stranded there; of these 26,000 were said to have been working in Kuwait (UNDP, 1991b). Many families in the Occupied Territories relied heavily on remittances from relatives working in Kuwait. Estimates of remittances and other contributions forgone varied greatly, from $80 million to $146 million a year (*The Economist*, 22 September 1990; CAFOD *et al.*, 1991; Abdalla, 1991; UNDP, 1991b). In addition, the curfew imposed in the Occupied Territories before, during and after the Gulf War further deprived Palestinian households of sources of income. Their position was further exacerbated by the replacement of Palestinian workers by newly-arrived Soviet Jews, who made up 90 per cent of the record 200,000 immigrants to Israel in 1990 (Cohen, 1990). Unemployment among the 300,000-strong workforce in the Occupied Territories was thought to have risen to about 30 per cent by early 1991 (UNDP, 1991b). Some Palestinians saw the latest uprooting as a 'third wave' of Palestinian displacement, equivalent in its personal and socio-economic impact to the displacements of 1948 and 1967; taking into account the total movements of Palestinians to the Occupied Territories, Jordan and other destinations, there may be some substance to this claim.

The Asian countries to which migrants returned were also hard hit. Whilst a number were assisted in the repatriation of their nationals, the loss of remittances from former migrants was keenly felt, particularly when set against the background of other economic difficulties. The Indian government claimed that annual remittances of $200 million could have been lost as a result of the exodus of its 200,000 nationals – the highest non-Arab total – from Iraq and Kuwait (ILO, 1991a; Abdalla, 1991). Set against total remittances, estimated for 1989 at $2.66 billion (IMF, 1990), and against GNP, the impact on the Indian economy as a whole was small. However, the impact was spread unevenly. Most of the returnees were from the two states of Gujerat and Kerala; in the latter, remittances may have accounted for 15 per cent of the state's income (ODI, 1991; Saith, 1991a). Sri Lanka was probably worst off among the south Asian countries as a result of its mass return. Its 100,000 nationals in Kuwait were thought to send home $100–120 million annually (ODI, 1991; IOM, 1991; Abdalla, 1991), up to one-third of total remittances, estimated at $356 million in 1989, and 1.6 per cent of GNP in that year (IMF, 1990; World Bank, 1991). Sri Lanka was already suffering from 30 per cent inflation before the impact of oil price increases resulting from the crisis, from 20 per cent unemployment, and from the displacement of a million people as a result of civil war (ODI, 1991; CAFOD *et al.*, 1991; IOM, 1991). Bangladesh, Pakistan, the Philippines, Thailand, Indonesia, South Korea and Vietnam were among the other Asian countries suffering substantial losses in remittances among the other consequences of the Gulf conflict (UNDP, 1991b; Abdalla, 1991; see Table 5.2).

The double impact of the loss of remittances from migrants and new calls on domestic resources to assist repatriates made measures to integrate them urgent. However, programmes set up to assist the reintegration of returnees had had limited impact by the end of 1991. Unsurprisingly, most returnees had to fend for themselves. A commonly expressed wish among returnees was for them to seek employment abroad once again, either in the Middle East or in new destinations; some, particularly south Asian migrants, were already doing so by the end of 1991 (Abella, 1991; IOM, 1991).

The governments of countries receiving large numbers of returnees approached the international community for assistance to offset the costs of the return of their nationals from the Gulf and pressed for compensation for losses their nationals had incurred (ILO, 1991a, 1991b). A programme to address returnees' needs was eventually drawn up by UNDP with the assistance of the ILO, IOM and other concerned agencies. It focused on measures to facilitate re-migration and on job creation programmes of various kinds. Most of the programme's proposals still awaited funding early in 1992, long after the mass returns they were designed to ameliorate.

Progress on the other main issue exercising countries receiving returnees – that of compensation for their returning nationals – was likewise slow. Under resolutions passed after Iraq's defeat, the UN Security Council undertook to set up a fund to pay compensation for loss, damage or injury resulting from Iraq's invasion and occupation of Kuwait. One year after the invasion, the UN Compensation Commission sat to develop mechanisms and guidelines for compensation (UN Security Council, 1991a; UNDP, 1991b). Part of the reparations programme in which Iraq was obliged to participate under UN resolutions, the compensation was to be financed by the proceeds from UN-supervised Iraqi oil sales. Up to two million claimants – among them many migrant workers – were anticipated in all, which it was thought could result in claims totalling $5 billion (UN Security Council, 1991a, 1991b).

Welcome though this might have been for migrants who had suffered losses, quick settlement was most unlikely. Since Iraq refused to comply with UN conditions for oil sales, as of the end of 1991 there were no means to finance any compensation. Settlement of this issue, together with the accelerated release of foreign nationals' assets held in Kuwait and Iraq, would have released substantial private funds to returnees. Such an injection of capital could have proved crucial for the beleaguered economies to which migrants returned and might well have assisted the recovery of those economies rather more effectively than the intervention proposed by the UNDP and other international agencies. In the same way, given the right conditions, the return of often skilled labour power could also have been turned to advantage.

The diversity of mass displacement, 1990–91

The mass displacement generated by the Gulf conflict appears unprecedented in its diversity, both in terms of the nationalities and countries involved and in terms of the forms of involuntary movement. It has involved substantial numbers of nationals of at least fifteen countries, and significant numbers of the nationals of many more. As well as refugees who crossed international boundaries, there were large numbers of migrant workers and professionals expelled or obliged to leave their countries of residence; others unable to return to their countries of residence; huge numbers of internally displaced people; and smaller though substantial numbers of stateless people, prisoners of war turned refugees, and environmental refugees.

Some of these people fled military activity. Others fled persecution or harassment by virtue of their alien status (migrant workers and professionals), their ethnicity, nationality or citizenship status (Yemenis, Kurds, Palestinians, *bidoon*), or their religion or minority status (Iraqi Shias and Christians). But the flight of most was precipitated by the fear of military activity or persecution rather than its actual perpetration, or simply by the calculation that a reasonable or tolerable life was no longer possible under the conditions that developed in 1990–91.

As has been shown above, some of these groups managed to return home or to their places of residence. But the term 'returnee' when applied to others was misleading. Many of the Kurdish refugees who returned from Turkey and Iran were not able to return to their homes but to temporary camps or settlements within Iraq. Many of the Palestinians who left Kuwait and many of the Yemeni expellees from Saudi Arabia were second or even third generation residents for whom the country of return was not home. This presented particular problems of integrating these arrivals.

More than half of those displaced were not refugees in the sense currently accepted internationally, and many of them fell outside the specific mandate of any international organisation. They received protection and assistance in an *ad hoc* way, some groups effectively, others not. Most in the first wave of flight from Iraq and Kuwait were migrant workers and professionals who fell outside the net of the 'refugee regime'. After the initial confusion precipitated by their sudden influx into Jordan, evacuation and relief for these people was nevertheless relatively well handled. In contrast, protection and assistance for other groups technically outside the refugee regime – those displaced within Iraq (particularly the Shias in the south); migrant workers and others attempting to return to Kuwait; people rendered stateless; and Palestinian, Jordanian and other communities persecuted in Kuwait – were often thin, ineffective or non-existent. With resources stretched to provide help for those, like the Kurds, who crossed international boundaries and were thus recognised as refugees, this was perhaps not surprising. However, the diversity of displacement once again highlighted the fact that most international agencies were constrained from effective intervention on behalf of many categories of forced migrant.

Protection and assistance for categories of involuntary migrants who fall outside internationally accepted definitions and mandates have for some time been a matter of debate. Discussion has included proposals to extend the mandate of UNHCR, to establish new organisations dealing with internally displaced people, migrant workers, expellees and other forced migrants, and for better coordination within and outside the UN to handle emergencies involving mass exodus.

Receptivity to such reform has recently increased. A Convention on the Protection of the Rights of All Migrant Workers and their Families, supplementing and extending existing ILO conventions, was passed by the UN General Assembly in December 1990 (UN General Assembly, 1990). If ratified and acted upon, this convention would represent a substantial advance in the principle of protection for migrant workers in relation to forced mass exodus. In addition, proposals have recently emerged from a protracted debate over the international community's response to humanitarian emergencies, a debate given added impetus by the Gulf crisis (Cuenod and ECOSOC, 1991; Childers and Urquhart, 1991). As a result, early in 1992 the UN appointed an emergency relief coordinator directly responsible to the Secretary-General and with substantial resources available for rapid disbursement in the event of a humanitarian crisis (UN General Assembly, 1991). If this impetus is sustained and some of the categories of forced migrant described in this chapter are brought within the fold of the international forced migration regime, some of the lessons of the Middle East's mass displacement of 1990–91 will have been learned.

References

Abdalla, N., 1991, *Impact of the Gulf crisis on developing countries*, United Nations Development Programme, New York.

Abella, M., 1991, 'Recent trends in Asian labour migration: A review of major issues', *Asian Migrant*, **4** (3): 72–77.

Addleton, J., 1991, 'The impact of the Gulf war on migration and remittances in Asia and the Middle East', *International Migration*, **29** (4): 509–26.

Amjad, R., ed., 1989, *To the Gulf and back: studies on the economic impact of Asian labour migration*, United Nations Development Programme/International Labour Office, New Delhi.

Amnesty International, 1990, *Saudi Arabia: torture, detention and arbitrary arrest*, AI International Secretariat, London.

Appleyard, R., ed., 1991, *International migration: challenge for the nineties*, International

Organization for Migration, Geneva.

Birks, J., Seccombe, I. and Sinclair, C., 1988, 'Labour migration in the Arab Gulf states: patterns, trends and prospects', *International Migration*, **26** (3): 267–86.

CAFOD (Catholic Fund for Overseas Development) et al., 1991, 'The economic impact of the Gulf crisis on third world countries', memorandum to the Foreign Affairs Select Committee, jointly submitted by CAFOD, Christian Aid, the Catholic Institute for International Relations, Oxfam, Save the Children Fund and World Development Movement, London, March 1991.

Childers, E. and Urquhart, B., 1991, *Strengthening international response to humanitarian emergencies*, Dag Hammarskjold Foundation/Ford Foundation, New York.

Cohen, R., 1990, *Soviet Jewish emigration to Israel*, Refugee Policy Group, Washington DC.

Cuenod, J. and ECOSOC (UN Economic and Social Council), 1991, Report on refugees, displaced persons and refugees by Mr Jacques Cuenod, Annex to Coordination Questions Note by the Secretary-General pursuant to ECOSOC resolution 1990/78, E/1991/109/ Add.1, ECOSOC, Geneva, June 1991.

De Almeida e Silva, M., 1991, 'Persian Gulf exodus stretched resources', *Refugees*, **87**: 12– 15.

FAO (Food and Agricultural Organization), 1990, *Intraregional labour mobility and agricultural development in the Near East: phenomenon, impact and policy implications*, FAO Economic and Social Development Paper no. 94, Rome.

Findlay, A., 1987, *The role of international labour migration in the transformation of the national economy: the case of the Yemen Arab Republic*, International Migration for Employment Working paper, International Labour Organization, Geneva.

Graham-Brown, S., 1991, 'Refugees and displaced people: the aftermath of the Gulf crisis', *Gulf Newsletter*, British Refugee Council, Gulf Information Project, no. 1.

Hashemite Kingdom of Jordan, 1991, *The socio-economic characteristics of Jordanian returnees*, National Centre for Educational Research and Development, Amman.

ILO (International Labour Office), 1991a, Inter-regional tripartite round table on international migration (Arab and Asian countries), Bangkok, 11–12 December 1990, Informal summary record, ILO, Geneva.

ILO, 1991b, *Migrant workers affected by the Gulf crisis, Report of the Director-General, Third Supplementary Report*, GB.249/15/7, ILO, Geneva.

IMF (International Monetary Fund), 1990, *Balance of Payments Statistics Yearbook 1990*, IMF, Washington DC.

IOM (International Organization for Migration), 1990, *Plan of action: update of operations*, IOM, Geneva.

IOM, 1991, *Labour migration and returnees from Kuwait and Iraq: IOM assessment mission to Bangladesh, the Philippines and Sri Lanka, April–May 1991*, IOM, Geneva.

Lawyers' Committee for Human Rights, 1992, *Kuwait: building the rule of law. Human rights in Kuwait after occupation*, Lawyers' Committee for Human Rights, New York.

McHugh, L. and Epstein, S., 1991, *Kurdish refugee relief and other humanitarian aid issues in Iraq, Congressional Research Service Issue Brief*, Library of Congress, Washington.

ODI (Overseas Development Institute), 1991, *The impact of the Gulf crisis on developing countries*, ODI briefing paper, London, March 1991.

Owen, R., 1985, *Migrant workers in the Gulf*, Minority Rights Group, Report no. 68, London.

Rogge, J.R., 1991, *Report on the medium and longer term resettlement and reintegration of displaced persons and returning refugees in the proposed Kurdish autonomous region of Iraq, prepared for the UN Development Programme (UNDP)*, Disaster Research Unit, University of Manitoba, Winnipeg, Canada.

Saith, A., 1991a, *Absorbing external shocks: the Gulf crisis, international migration linkages, and the Indian economy 1990 (with special reference to the impact on Kerala)*, Institute of Social Studies, The Hague, Working paper no. 107.

Saith, A., 1991b, *Adding insult to injury: a first estimate of financial losses of Indian migrant workers fleeing the Gulf crisis*, Institute of Social Studies, The Hague, Working paper no. 108.

UNDP (United Nations Development Programme), 1991a, *Impact of the Gulf crisis on developing countries: needs and initiatives. Report of the administrator*, Governing Council of UNDP, DP/1991/60, New York.

UNDP, 1991b, 'Proposals for the socio-economic and environmental recovery of countries affected by the Gulf crisis of 1990–91'. Overview, draft for presentation to the International Community Funding strategy meeting scheduled for 16 December 1991, UNDP, DP/1992/4.

UNDRO (United Nations Disaster Relief Co-ordinator), 1990a, 'Iraq–Kuwait crisis: the plight of returnees', *UNDRO News: Special Supplement*, UNDRO, Geneva.

UNDRO, 1990b, *The Iraq/Kuwait Crisis International assistance to displaced people through Jordan (August–November 1990) Case Report*, UNDRO, Geneva.

UN ESCWA (United Nations Economic and Social Commission for Western Asia), 1991, *The return of Jordanian/Palestinian nationals from Kuwait: Economic and social implications for Jordan*, UN ESCWA, Amman.

UN General Assembly, 1990, International convention on the protection of the rights of all migrant workers and members of their families, UN General Assembly, A/Res/45/158, December 1990.

UN General Assembly, 1991, Strengthening of the coordination of humanitarian assistance of the United Nations, UN General Assembly Resolution 46/182, December 1991.

UNHCR (United Nations High Commissioner for Refugees), 1991, *Operations in the Persian Gulf Region: Information Bulletins*, UNHCR, Geneva.

UN Office, 1990, *Regional Humanitarian Plan of Action relating to the crisis between Iraq and Kuwait*, UN Office, Geneva, October 1990.

UN Office, 1991a, *Updates*, January, April, 1991.

UN Office, 1991b, *United Nations inter-agency programme for Iraq, Kuwait and the Iraq/Turkey and Iraq/Iran borders: updated and consolidated appeal for urgent humanitarian action*, May 1991.

UN Security Council, 1991a, 'Criteria for expedited processing of urgent claims', UN Doc S/AC.26/1991/1, August 1991.

UN Security Council, 1991b, 'Arrangements for ensuring payments to the compensation fund', UN Doc S/AC.26/1991/6, October 1991.

USCR (United States Committee for Refugees), 1991, *Mass exodus: Iraqi refugees in Iran*, USCR Issue Brief, Washington DC.

USCR, 1992, *World refugee survey, 1991*, USCR, Washington DC.

US General Accounting Office, 1991, 'Persian Gulf Crisis: Humanitarian Relief provided to evacuees from Kuwait and Iraq'. Report to the chairman, subcommittee on Europe and the Middle East, Committee on Foreign Affairs, House of Representatives, US General Accounting Office, Washington DC, GAO/NSIAD-91-160, March 1991.

Van Hear, N., 1991a, *Mass exodus and mass displacement in the Middle East, 1990–91*, Refugee Studies Programme working paper, University of Oxford, September 1991.

Van Hear, N., 1991b, 'Forced migration and the Gulf conflict, 1990–91', *The Oxford International Review*, 3 (1): 17–21.

World Bank, 1991, *World Development Report 1991*, Oxford University Press, Washington DC.

Further reading

Addleton, J., 1991, 'The impact of the Gulf war on migration and remittances in Asia and the Middle East', *International Migration*, 29 (4): 509–26.

Birks, J., Seccombe, I. and Sinclair, C., 1988, 'Labour migration in the Arab Gulf states: patterns, trends and prospects', *International Migration*, **26** (3): 267–86.

De Almeida e Silva, M., 1991, 'Persian Gulf exodus stretched resources', *Refugees*, **87**: 12–15.

Laizer, S., 1991, *Into Kurdistan: frontiers under fire*, Zed Books, London.

Van Hear, N., 1991, 'Forced migration and the Gulf conflict, 1990–91', *The Oxford International Review*, **3** (1): 17–21.

PART III

Refugees and asylum-seekers in the
Developed World

6 Refugees and asylum-seekers in Western Europe: new challenges

Richard Black

Introduction

In the period immediately after the Second World War, massive displacements of population from the east represented a major challenge in the reconstruction of Western Europe. With the establishment of UNHCR, permanent solutions were sought to what was regarded as a temporary problem, created by the legacy of war and Nazism, and the rise of state communism. Displaced people were resettled: many in North America, but many too in Western Europe itself, and over time they became integrated into the societies and economies into which they had moved. However, over time too, the world's 'refugee crisis' did not go away as expected, but intensified. New flows of refugees in the Middle East, Africa, South East Asia, Central America and elsewhere changed the geographical focus of UNHCR, and vastly increased its caseload. Still some 'permanent' solutions to refugees' plight were sought, through the resettlement of over one million South East Asians in the West (Rogge, 1985; see also Chapter 9), but in general, the temporary measures of containment in camps and settlements within refugee-producing regions became the goal of international refugee policy.

More recently still, a complex set of developments, ranging from improved international air travel, to renewed political upheaval in Eastern Europe, has once again brought displaced people to the heart of Western Europe. However, the response to this new challenge differs markedly from that of forty years ago. Rather than seeking permanent solutions, emphasis has increasingly shifted to ensure that in Europe too, the refugee's stay will be a temporary one. In Germany, after years of rhetoric directed towards the east, that political freedom must include the right to migrate, political debate has now shifted to removing the individual's right to asylum from the German constitution. Elsewhere in Western Europe, rising numbers of asylum claims, coupled with a reduction in the proportion of applicants accepted as refugees under the Geneva Convention, have formed the justification for even more restrictive asylum policies.

In the context of poor statistics, media hype, and political interests, which have combined to portray the growing number of asylum-seekers as a threat to host nations, description of the extent and pattern of asylum-seeking in Europe is particularly important. Ironically, the task of description is perhaps more complex and difficult in this well-monitored part of the developed world than in much of the Third World. It is to this task that the first part of this chapter is devoted. Available statistics on flows of refugees and asylum-seekers to Western Europe are placed in the context of a range of migration and demographic indicators in receiving countries. Difficulties of both a quantitative and a conceptual nature are highlighted, particularly concerning the relationship between 'political' and 'economic' migration.

Moving on from this, however, there has been considerable recent attention to changes in the right to asylum in Western Europe (JCWI, 1989; Loescher, 1989; Rudge, 1990; Hailbronner, 1990), but few studies have analysed the potential or consequences for Western Europe of allowing more refugees to stay. In contrast, the discussion here focuses on changing conditions for incorporation of refugees and asylum-seekers into host economies and societies within Western Europe. The significance of state policy towards refugees and asylum-seekers in this regard is highlighted.

Asylum-seekers in Europe: a new burden?

Figures from UNHCR suggest that during 1990, over 400,000 people sought asylum in the countries of Western Europe, representing a rise of 26 per cent over the previous year, and more than double the average number during the 1980s. Such figures perhaps underlie the nervousness of European governments in approaching the question of asylum. Nonetheless, the value of focusing exclusively on statistical data in this field, and the reliability of that data, are questionable. Rudge (1985), for example, commented that with respect to asylum-seekers in Europe, there was 'gross misrepresentation of the scale of the problem', and little has changed since in either the mechanics or the politics of data collection on asylum-seekers to change that view. At the same time, the number of refugees and asylum-seekers needs to be placed in the context not only of Europe's population, and its ability to absorb such migrants, but also of the other migratory movements within, to, and from Europe during the latter part of the 1980s.

Assessing either the total number of refugees, or indeed the total 'foreign' population in Western Europe, is a task fraught with difficulties. On the one hand, naturalisation, available to varying degrees and at varying speeds to migrants, refugees, and their immediate families allows a proportion of each group to disappear from official statistics in most countries each year. Similarly, comparison of flows is hindered by the variety of legal definitions and methods of counting across Europe, as well as a simple inability to keep track of the complex movements that are occurring. However, at the same time, it is unclear whether the total number of people seeking asylum in Europe has grown as a result of an increase in involuntary migration, or whether, as is alleged by some European governments, the closure of other legal channels for immigration to Western Europe is encouraging people to use the asylum route as an alternative.

Some initial problems with statistics on asylum can be identified at a very basic level, which call into question at least some of the pessimistic assessments of trends in the latter part of the 1980s. First, it is not clear whether the numbers of spontaneous arrivals of asylum-seekers issued by UNHCR include some whose application for asylum is still pending from previous years. It is also certainly true that some asylum applicants have been able, or indeed forced, to file applications in more than one European country. Both of these factors would tend to inflate the

overall figure, although recent moves to speed up asylum determination procedures, and the signing of the Dublin Convention, which amongst other things bans
multiple applications, may have reduced anomalies (Van Hear, 1991).

In addition, significant groups of asylum-seekers are not new arrivals at all, but
people who were already living legally in Europe when they claimed asylum.
Included here are some guest workers in West Germany, who applied for asylum
at the end of their work contracts, and certain groups of students, such as Iranians
in the UK who feared to return to Iran after the revolution and the initiation of the
Iran–Iraq war. Another 'new' group of asylum-seekers is composed of foreign
workers in countries of Eastern Europe, whose security has been undermined after
the collapse of communist regimes, but for whom repatriation is not necessarily
a viable option. For example, some 9,000 Vietnamese claimed asylum in Germany in 1990, out of an estimated 40,000 Vietnamese people working in East
Germany prior to reunification, and 135,000 in Eastern Europe as a whole (Grečic,
1990). In this sense, it would clearly be wrong to assume that asylum-seeking
necessarily increases a country's foreign population: indeed, in this case, with
some repatriation to Vietnam, the total may actually be decreasing.

Asylum-seekers also need to be placed in the context of other migratory flows
taking place in Europe at the present time, as well as the size of the population in
their host nation. For example, Rees *et al.* (1992), in a projection of migration in
the European Community (EC) for 1990–95 based on the maintenance of existing
rates, put net immigration from outside the Community at just over 700,000,
compared with 2.2 million migratory moves between countries of the Community,
and nearly 14 million between different regions. Meanwhile, according to UNHCR
figures, only four European countries received asylum applications in 1990 that
represented more than two per thousand of their own population (Switzerland,
Sweden, Austria, and Germany), whilst others had negligible rates (under 0.5 per
thousand in the UK, Spain, Italy, Portugal) or no official asylum-seekers at all
(Ireland, Luxembourg).

The two countries with the largest total numbers of asylum-seekers each year
throughout the 1980s, France and Germany, both saw significant additional migration not related to asylum during the decade. Thus although there was a
cumulative total of over 700,000 asylum requests in West Germany during the
1980s, this was overshadowed by the movement of ethnic Germans from Eastern
Europe in general, and East Germany in particular (*Aussiedler*, and *Übersiedler*
respectively, both of whom had the constitutional right to settle in West Germany). A total of nearly one million *Aussiedler* were received during the decade
(Hofmann and Heller, 1992), along with 345,000 *Übersiedler* in 1989 alone
(although these would now be regarded as 'internal migrants'). Meanwhile, of a
record net gain of population through migration of 1.2 million in the European
Community in 1989, some 700,000 was accounted for by ethnic Germans migrating legally from East Germany and Eastern Europe to West Germany.

No other country has come close to the level of migration into Germany in
recent years, where the combination of the fall of the Berlin Wall and the existence
of several million ethnic Germans outside the country's borders created a special
case. Nonetheless, elsewhere too, asylum-seekers are still outnumbered by other
kinds of migrants. For example, in France, the total of 58,000 asylum applicants
in 1989 can be compared with over 53,000 other foreign nationals who migrated

to the country that year, and a further 61,900 seasonal migrants who received work permits (SOPEMI, 1991). Similarly, Penninx and Muus (1991) criticise the selective perception that focuses on the 588,000 foreign residents in the Netherlands, most of whom are not asylum-seekers, when in 1987, some 644,000 Dutch nationals were living abroad.

Asylum-seekers and refugees: patterns and processes of change

Bearing in mind both the reliability of statistics and the context of refugee flows, it is possible to sketch out the extent and patterns of involuntary migration generated in recent years, as a precursor to discussing its effects. Broadly speaking, three categories of refugee and asylum-seeker can be identified in Western Europe since 1945 in terms of their origin. First, and most numerous, are those from Eastern Europe and the former Soviet Union; second are so-called 'quota' refugees, resettled mainly from South East Asia, but also in small numbers from South America and elsewhere; and third are non-Europeans who have claimed asylum independently and 'spontaneously' after their arrival, usually by air or sea.

The refugee flows from Eastern to Western Europe can be divided into two distinct phases: one in the period after 1945, until travel restrictions in the East and the construction of the Berlin Wall in 1961 made it increasingly impossible to move to the West, and a second phase after 1981, when first Poles and then other nationalities, including ethnic Germans and Greeks, began to leave again for the West. Two countries, Austria and Germany, have taken the bulk of these movements. Thus in the period since 1945, more than two million refugees have passed through Austria, with around 613,000 settling within the country (USCR, 1992). Of these, half were ethnic Germans. West Germany, meanwhile, took in an estimated eight million ethnic Germans expelled from the East before 1950, and has continued to top the European table in terms of the number of asylum requests. The relative weight of Eastern Europeans in the total number of asylum claims today remains higher in Austria and Germany than in any other European country, with the exception of Italy, which until 1990 did not in any case accept claims from non-Europeans (Table 6.1). Austria, Greece and Italy have all acted, meanwhile, as transit countries for East Europeans seeking to resettle in North America.

In contrast to the pattern of flow from Eastern Europe, the second category of refugees mentioned above – those brought in under international quotas – saw a rise in the 1970s, but has become relatively insignificant in the 1980s. In the decade after 1975, some 150,000 South East Asian refugees were accepted into European Community countries as part of an international agreement to find permanent solutions for Vietnamese and others stranded in camps in Hong Kong, Thailand and elsewhere. This flow was particularly important in France, which took nearly two-thirds of the total between 1975 and 1985, and unlike other European countries, accepted both the 'boat people' from camps in Hong Kong, and Laotian and Cambodian refugees from camps in Thailand (Yen, 1986). Annual quotas for the resettlement of refugees remain in most countries of Western Europe, although seldom do these amount to more than a few thousand each year.

Table 6.1 Asylum-seekers in Western Europe, 1990

	Total	% Eastern Europeans
Austria	22,800	67
Belgium	12,950	30
Denmark	5,300	19
Finland	2,750	30
France	49,650	11
Germany	193,050	41
Greece	6,200	21
Italy	3,400	93
Netherlands	21,200	23
Norway	3,950	32
Portugal	100	26
Spain	6,850	44
Sweden	29,350	24
Switzerland	35,850	26
United Kingdom	25,000	1

Source: UNHCR

The third category of refugees highlighted above comprises mainly those from the Middle East, Africa, and the Indian subcontinent, and has grown in numbers principally during the 1980s. Over 70 per cent of the one million or more asylum-seekers in Europe over the decade originated from the Third World, with Sri Lanka, Iran, Lebanon, and Ethiopia generating particularly high flows (Loescher, 1989). These flows stabilised or declined towards the end of the decade, although several new countries of origin contributed to an overall increase in the number of Third World asylum-seekers. The countries in Europe most affected by these flows, in terms of the size of their own populations, are Switzerland, Sweden, Germany, and the Netherlands although, clearly, the vast majority of Third World refugees are still living in neighbouring countries of the Third World itself.

When considering the figures presented above, an important point to note is that in no case does the cumulative total of asylum applicants equal the total number of 'refugees' who remained in those countries in the medium term. In Germany, for example, by the end of the 1980s, only 151,000 people had been granted full refugee status under the Geneva Convention, and of those, 45 per cent were 'quota refugees'. With an estimated 300,000 further asylum-seekers allowed to remain in Germany on humanitarian grounds, under half of the total registered during the decade had remained in the country.

In Europe as a whole, this is partly explained by some voluntary repatriation of refugees and asylum-seekers: for example, there are currently European government programmes to help a proportion of the 60,000 Chileans in Western Europe to return to their country after the return to democracy (Council of Europe, 1991a), whilst others return voluntarily or are deported after the failure of their asylum claim. At the same time, a proportion is also accounted for by the phenomenon of 'refugees in orbit' – refugees who are passed from one European country to another, without any individual country granting the right to asylum.

Some definitional problems

Whilst some of the difficulties in estimating both absolute numbers and flows of refugees noted above reflect technical enumeration problems, the matter is complicated by definitional issues, in the domains of public policy and academic debate. Putting the institutional view of UNHCR, Widgren (1989) echoed European governments when he suggested that a 'major threat' is posed to the refugee regime by the growth of asylum-seekers with weak or no genuine claim at all for refugee status, especially from Eastern Europe. A growth in migrants with mainly economic motives can be seen to inflate the figures for asylum-seekers. In addition, the existence of such 'bogus' claims is being used by governments to justify their own moves to tighten up on 'abuses' in the asylum procedure, and indeed, most European countries can point to a decrease in the proportion of asylum claims that achieve the outcome of refugee status as evidence on this point. Thus although an increase in the number of 'true' refugees does not represent a problem for Europe, use of the asylum route by 'economic' migrants is seen as creating a problem that warrants a crackdown on asylum-seekers.

Such a perspective, however, begs a number of important questions. First, although it is true that the rate of acceptance of asylum claims decreased dramatically over the 1980s, there are several possible interpretations of this trend. In practice, the recognition rate for refugees may reflect more the decision-making characteristics of the host country, rather than the nature of applications (Avery, 1983). Thus a lower rate of acceptances could be taken as reflecting a more harsh determination procedure, which has begun to exclude 'political' refugees as well as 'economic migrants'. Evidence for this is provided by a number of recent deportation cases (see, for example, *Refugees*, March 1990, p. 24). Certainly the asylum-determination procedure is far from perfect in most countries of Western Europe, and considerable scope exists for governments to reduce the numbers granted asylum regardless of the 'quality' of the claims.

Perhaps a more reliable indicator of refugee status in the broader sense is not the number offered asylum, but the proportion whose right to remain in Western Europe is actively refused. In several countries of Europe, for example, a number of asylum-seekers are given residence permits without being granted asylum. Such groups include those with 'exceptional leave to remain' in the UK, B or C status refugees in Scandinavia, the categories of '*assimilé à refugié*' in Belgium, and '*asilo*' in Spain, and those granted temporary residence permits on 'humanitarian grounds' in Germany (Joly and Nettleton, 1990). Taking the UK as an example, although the recognition rate fell from 64 per cent in 1980 to just 14 per cent in 1986, rising again to 32 per cent in 1989, the proportion granted exceptional leave to remain rose steadily over the decade from just 13 per cent in 1980 to 59 per cent in 1989. Overall, the result was a decline in refusals of the right to remain from over a quarter of all applicants, to just 10 per cent in 1989.

Refugees in Europe: incorporation or marginalisation?

The mass and individual movements of refugees to Western Europe since the Second World War have placed a range of pressures on European economies, populations and states. In particular, regardless of the individual causes of migration, the recent increase in the number of asylum-seekers in Western Europe has led to a significant increase in restrictions on further flows of asylum-seekers, including new legislation, or proposals of new legislation in all the major countries of Western Europe. Discussion about the harmonisation of European policy on asylum, for example, has focused on the potential for cracking down on those 'abusing' current procedures, and has been conducted in an atmosphere of secrecy alongside discussion of terrorism and drug smuggling (Rudge, 1990). Meanwhile, European policy makers and commentators alike have looked anxiously to the east and the south, fearing future influxes, and seeking to construct a 'Fortress Europe' to protect the continent from a wave of future immigrants (Van Hear, 1991).

In the midst of this concern with asylum procedures, there has been minimal academic interest in the integration of refugees and asylum-seekers already admitted to the countries of Western Europe. There are several reasons for this. First, concern with the mechanics of asylum procedure has clearly been important to those in opposition to state policy, as much as to the policy-makers themselves, and has tended to dominate discussion on refugees in Europe (Lundström, 1991). Meanwhile, in the academic community, doubts about the notion of 'integration' as a concept have led to a period of reflection rather than action. For example, Wong (1991) has argued that integration represents an inappropriate model, since it takes the receiving society for granted, and assumes a normative and linear 'trajectory' for refugees once they arrive in that society. Instead, she focuses on the condition of 'otherness' that characterises the refugee experience, in both flight and exile.

However, an additional and important factor that has prevented those in the refugee field from considering seriously the issue of integration has been the segregation of refugee research from the field of migration studies as a whole (Robinson, 1990a). Such a distinction is not without its merits. For example, for those involved in refugee policy, if it is accepted that economic migration should be, or at least is likely to be, promoted or restricted according to prevailing economic conditions in Europe, then there is clearly a benefit to refugees if they are regarded as a separate category, which European governments have an underlying duty to accept regardless of economic conditions. Aside from this humanitarian concern, emphasised by other contributors to this volume, various writers in the US in particular have also pointed out objective differences between refugee and migrant populations, in terms of their original motivations for migration, and their characteristics on arrival (Desbarats, 1985; Portes and Böröcz, 1989; Hammar, 1989).

Also contained, however, within the argument that refugees must be given unique or preferential status in government policy is the implicit assumption that refugees are a burden to host societies, an image that is challenged below. A major problem in this regard concerns the lack of research carried out on the economic impact of refugees on host societies, or indeed on the economic contexts of refugee movements. An insistence on distinguishing 'economic' migrants from 'political' refugees may have a role to play in focusing on the specific human rights issues surrounding refugee movement, but it also risks a distortion in refugee studies whereby the application of economic principles is seen as inappropriate, even when asylum has already been granted (Kutch, 1988).

By drawing on the wider field of migration studies, it becomes possible to make some broader comments or suggestions about the integration of refugees, in spite of the fact that remarkably little work has been carried out by geographers or indeed by other social scientists on this subject in Western Europe. Such comparison is not intended to imply that there is no distinction between refugee migration and other, more voluntary forms of migration, but rather that there are fruitful grounds for cross-reference between the two fields.

Refugees, discrimination, and the cost of assistance

One of the first things to note about the process of adaptation and integration of refugees and asylum-seekers is that, notwithstanding the fact that many do not wish to become integrated into host societies and economies, those who do often face considerable discrimination and exclusion. These processes can be observed at a variety of levels across Western Europe, in fields as diverse as housing, education and employment (JCWI, 1989). Most clearly there is a distinction to be made between the treatment of asylum-seekers, who have been the subject of a number of 'deterrence' measures on the part of governments, and those granted refugee status, who are generally treated rather more favourably (Bruun *et al.*, 1990). However, given the increasing tendency towards the granting of residence permits without full asylum, the category of '*de facto*' refugees also merits attention.

In the housing field, the situation of asylum-seekers is often very poor. At its most extreme, a number of asylum-seekers are currently held at detention centres, notably in the UK, Denmark and Finland, as well as in Sweden, where ships offshore in Malmö and Göteberg have been used for this purpose (Joly and Nettleton, 1990). In France, asylum-seekers are excluded from social housing, whilst in the UK, the Asylum Bill before parliament at the time of writing seeks to do the same thing. At the same time, however, there is considerable evidence of discrimination against immigrants in general, and refugees in particular. Gans (1990), for example, argues that Turks in the city of Kiel operate within housing submarkets, which are distinguished by lower social status and poorer living quality. Access to such markets is dictated by the policy of local government and private landlords. Elsewhere, in France, refugees have been seen to congregate in certain areas because of the concentration of particular types of housing (White *et al.*, 1987), and especially social housing (Mignot, 1983). Meanwhile, in Greece, reluctance by Greek landlords to rent houses to refugees has led to their concentration in low-quality, relatively high-price apartments (Black, 1992), although a process of self-selection may also operate in some instances (see for example, Robinson and Hale, 1989). Of significance is the role of social housing: in some countries, such as the Netherlands, social housing is set aside for refugees (Sayers, 1987), whereas in others, such as Belgium and Greece, there is more or less complete reliance on the private sector (Joly and Nettleton, 1990).

Access to employment for asylum-seekers and refugees also varies across Europe, and is heavily dependent both on state legislation, and on the level of enforcement of that legislation. For example, in Germany, asylum-seekers are prevented from working during the first five years, but several *Länder* do not enforce the law. Elsewhere, asylum-seekers are allowed to work after a short period, as for example in the UK and France, but not (until they are granted refugee status) in Denmark, Italy, Spain or the Netherlands (Vetter, 1987). Martin *et al.* (1990) comment that most asylum-seekers in Europe are able to find employment, but that this exists in the grey area between lawful and unlawful, since they are usually allowed to earn 'pocket money' but no more. In some cases, refugees are not allowed to work even when recognised under the UN convention: for example, in Greece, this right is excluded by law, with the exception of some 200 Vietnamese, and an even smaller group of Kurdish refugees from Turkey (Labreveux, 1989).

At a more general level, Gordon (1991) notes that 'migrant populations have tended to enjoy, and were expected to enjoy, fewer of the fruits of the full employment and state welfare which, at least up to the late 1970s governments ... undertook to provide for their citizen electors', commenting that with an increased variety of potential immigrants, 'new gradations of such citizenship rights' are emerging (p. 2). Such distinctions can operate at the level of ideology as well as in simply legal terms: thus, for example, in Germany, the term 'refugee' (*Flüchtling*) is reserved for those of German descent who fled to the West after the Second World War, whereas the more pejorative term 'asylant' (*Asylant*) is used for refugees and asylum-seekers alike. The role of the state in categorisation, thereby controlling access to rights and resources, is crucial in this regard.

It is in the context of the discrimination described above that some of the more depressing figures about the cost of receiving asylum-seekers and refugees in Western Europe must be placed. For example, Widgren (1990, p. 24) estimates that the 'cost of providing assistance for asylum-seekers in the industrialised states now amounts to ten times the total budget of UNHCR', or some $5 billion annually. Such a figure is inevitably inflated when asylum-seekers are not allowed to seek work, and must therefore be reliant on public assistance. Similarly, there are now many complaints in the press in European countries of increases in crime associated with asylum-seekers. However, the most common crimes are those of staying or working illegally in Europe, both offences directly related to the asylum-determination procedure itself. Equally, the asylum-determination procedure itself is extremely expensive, with Loescher (1989, p. 622) estimating that total cost to Western Europe at a further $4 billion annually.

An interesting study by the IOE Group (1990) in Spain estimated that there are 135,000 immigrants from the Third World working in the black economy of Spain, a sector which, far from inhibiting development, contributes as much as 5 per cent of GNP. They comment that the 'illegal immigrant worker bolsters our new model of economic development based on minimal government intervention in the supply and demand for labour', and argue that such illegal labour represents a privileged source of profit for employers (IOE Group, 1991, p. 134). Meanwhile, they reject the view that there is substantial criminal activity amongst such immigrants, noting that whilst there is some petty crime, most of the organised crime concerns immigrants from other EC countries, 'such as Italy, France and Germany'.

Discrimination against refugees and asylum-seekers is clearly a problem of the host society rather than of refugees themselves. At the same time, it is not universal: for example, incidents where local authorities have refused to rehouse refugees in Belgium (Cels and Loescher, 1988; Joly and Nettleton, 1990) can be contrasted with examples such as the city of Leiden, in the Netherlands, where a 'City of Refugees' campaign was launched both to provide legal, social and housing support to refugees, and to raise awareness of refugee issues amongst the local community (Muller, 1990). However, where there is discrimination, refugees will remain at the bottom of the economic ladder, and will be less able to contribute to economic development.

Refugees and the labour market: self-employment

Where refugees and asylum-seekers are allowed to enter the labour market legally, there is some evidence that this can represent a bonus for receiving countries. One particular area of absorption of refugees into labour markets involves their self-employment, or employment within ethnic businesses. There is now a considerable literature on ethnic businesses and 'ethnic enclaves' in the US economy, some of which has focused specifically on refugee groups, such as Cubans in Miami (Wilson and Portes, 1980). In Europe once again, such research has tended to be limited to migrant groups other than refugees (Zimmer and Aldrich, 1987), with some exceptions (Robinson, 1990b). Nonetheless, a number of conclusions of existing research are of relevance to the question of integration of refugees.

In a study of the self-employment of immigrant and minority women in five European states, Morokvasic (1991) argues that self-employment can be a successful strategy which contributes to the overall economy. Importantly, the small businesses that are created do not represent an 'enclave economy', in the sense that they cater for the specific needs of a minority community, but are most successful where orientated to a wider market, and where ethnicity can be used as a marketing tool, or family or kin support networks can be utilised to provide labour. Meanwhile, success was seen to be most commonly associated with an earlier period of salaried employment in the sector, or even some parallel work as a back-up strategy, rather than with situations where establishing a business was a response to unemployment. Similar findings have arisen from British studies of South Asian entrepreneurship (Robinson and Flintoff, 1982) and from Sen's (1991) study of Turkish small businesses in Germany. Turkish firms were found to be operating in fifty-five different sectors, with some 33,000 firms employing between 105,000 to 110,000 people. There was a concentration of firms which exploited links with Turkey, whilst some 40 per cent were in the catering business, often specialising in Turkish food. However, two-thirds of custom was estimated to be German rather than Turkish.

Although businesses that mobilise ethnic identity or social support networks can be successful, a number of caveats must be introduced. For example, Morokvasic warns against the American image of the 'self-made man' as a role model, arguing that self-employment for immigrant women in Europe masks a lack of real choice faced by such women for alternative employment, and in any case represents only a tiny fraction of total employment. Pohjola (1991) comments too that whilst social networks can convey support, they also automatically separate migrants and socialise them into narrow, pre-existing networks, a factor that may work against the integration of refugees in the longer term.

What is perhaps the most interesting aspect of the emergence of ethnic businesses involves a consideration of the conditions under which 'successful' businesses, rather than 'unsuccessful' incorporation into manual labour with low pay and conditions, might occur. Within the US, there has been some discussion that focuses on the relative success of different ethnic groups. Portes and Böröcz (1989) point to three important factors in the integration of migrant groups, namely conditions of exit (from the sending country), social class, and the context of reception. Using the latter two factors, they construct a matrix of 'modes of incorporation', in which migrants may be of lower social class, professionals, or entrepreneurs, and at the same time may be handicapped, received neutrally, or welcomed by the host population. Each of the nine points on this matrix defines a different labour market outcome for the migrants concerned.

Such a schema is useful, but it omits some issues of particular importance in considering the incorporation of refugees into host societies. For example, although 'conditions of exit' are identified as a factor, and refugees noted as a separate group, questions relating to the cause of migration are not incorporated into Portes and Böröcz' model. Moreover, they suggest that the distinctive features of refugee migration are that on the one hand, welfare assistance is available, and on the other, the possibility of return to the country of origin is precluded. Whilst this may be true for refugees permanently resettled in the US, it certainly does not hold for spontaneous asylum-seekers, who often do not qualify for full welfare assistance, and for whom repatriation may remain a long-term goal. Meanwhile, other characteristic features of the refugee experience, such as their differentiation on the basis of legal status, are not considered, except with regard to rather vague categories of 'handicapped', 'neutral' and 'advantaged'. Nonetheless, this perspective does emphasise the need to consider integration of all kinds of migrants as part of a continuum, whilst also stressing the links between 'ethnic enclaves' and other sectors of the economy.

Refugees and the labour market: labour shortages

It is also important to consider refugees in the context of more general labour market changes in Europe. In the immediate post-war period, displaced persons were significant in filling labour shortages and stimulating economic growth. Meanwhile, it has been argued that the labour migration of the 1960s played a crucial role in the 'Golden Age' of Western European capitalism (Castles and Kosack, 1973), although others have stressed the conflicting effects of immigration on local economies as a whole (Reubens, 1986). Recent studies show indigenous populations, and with them the supply of indigenous labour, falling again in several of the EC countries most affected by asylum-seekers, notably Germany, Belgium and Denmark, although population growth elsewhere, and especially in

Ireland, Portugal, Spain and Italy contributes to a predicted rise in the labour supply of 0.1 per cent per year up to 2000 (Commission of the European Community, 1991).

Even in the southern countries of the Community, where internal labour markets may grow to the end of the century, there is already demand for labour that has led to the growth of substantial clandestine migration. Golini *et al.* (1991) suggest that such demand is generated despite continued youth unemployment in those countries, and is due in part to a growth in household incomes, the development of social security systems, and increased education of the young, all of which leave a segment of the labour market uncontested by nationals. Meanwhile, completion of the Single European Market was predicted by Cecchini (1988) to lead to the creation of between 1.8 and 5.7 million new jobs in the medium term, despite some initial job losses. Martin *et al.* (1990) suggest that with investment already occurring in advance of completion of the market, new jobs were already appearing. They cite the case of Belgium, where there was a net gain of 100,000 jobs, as well as a rise in GDP of 4.5 per cent in 1989, compared with a predicted rate of just 2 per cent.

There is some debate as to whether the nature of labour demand generated is one that is able to be filled by immigrant labour. For example, a survey by Prognos (1989) suggests that despite a growth in employment in the EC of 2.2 million by 2000, the demand for unskilled workers will decline, so that immigrants represent an unsuitable source of extra labour power. However, Golini *et al.* (1991) point out that with strong economic growth, demand may indeed be for lower-qualified workers, especially for manual services such as cleaning, hotel, restaurant and health services. In any case, the evidence of Mignot (1981) that Vietnamese refugees in France are employed below their existing skill levels, as well as that there is a readiness, especially amongst the young, to improve their education as quickly as possible, contradicts the notion that asylum-seekers are inevitably low-skilled people of little 'use' to the European economy. Moreover, a recent survey of asylum-seekers in Greece showed that one in five had a university education (Mestheneos, 1988).

Not all countries continue to view immigration as negative, and indeed, since 1988, some European employers have begun to press for renewed recruitment of foreign labour (Hammar, 1989). For example, labour shortages were identified by the OECD in 1990 in Austria, Germany, the Netherlands and Switzerland (SOPEMI, 1991), whilst Spain, Italy, Greece and Portugal have all seen significant influxes of foreign labour generated by local demand, notably in the construction industry. Meanwhile, a recent report by the Institute of the German Economy estimated that Germany may need as many as 300,000 new migrants each year in the next decade to compensate for a decline in the indigenous labour force (*Guardian*, 4 February 1992). In this context, categorisation of immigrant groups can be seen not as an attempt to keep them out, but as a renewed attempt to make them more pliable to the needs of capital.

What is required is a move to more positive thinking on immigration, which could extend to asylum seekers in a context where their incorporation was not on disadvantaged terms. Two examples of such a positive outlook can be identified in Europe, although these represent exceptions rather than the rule. In Germany, government sources estimate that the benefits of migration of *Aussiedler* from

Central and Eastern Europe may amount to the equivalent of 4 per cent on GNP by the end of the century, reflecting the fact that these migrants are young, well-trained, and mobile (Council of Europe, 1991b). Similar thinking has led the Greek government to welcome ethnic Greeks from the Soviet Union (Voutira, 1991). Meanwhile another example demonstrates how it is useful to view refugees and asylum-seekers not only as potential producers, but also as consumers who could help to stimulate demand-led growth of the economy. Thus the integration of refugees into national economic planning in Cyprus after 1974, and the recognition of demand for housing, helped to fuel a construction boom which benefited both the refugees themselves, and the southern part of Cyprus as a whole (Zetter, 1992).

Conclusion

In tackling the question of the potential for integration of refugees and asylum-seekers in Western Europe, and more particularly in developing a comparative study of European practice, it is important to begin from a sound theoretical position. However, Bovenkerk *et al.* (1991), in examining approaches to the comparative study of immigration in Europe, have criticised existing studies, which they argue have tended either to seek 'good practice' or negative examples around Europe as a model for a particular nation, resulting in ethnocentric misunderstandings, or have been mere 'inventories', which involve comparison but do not make it clear on what basis variables are selected for comparison. In preference to such 'inductivist' approaches, they call for an 'embedding [of] comparative endeavour in a theoretical framework on a more abstract level than the phenomena under study' (Bovenkerk *et al.*, 1991, p. 387). Starting from a concern with the political economy of scarcity, they suggest that processes of signification and categorisation of migrants lead to their differentiation, and argue that these processes are 'structured by direct and active state involvement' (p. 389).

Such a focus on the role of the state in categorisation would appear to be particularly pertinent in the case of refugees, where there is a great variety in legal status between different groups and different states. Meanwhile, the issue is perhaps especially relevant in Europe, where emphasis on temporary immigration in general has led to a much greater differentiation of migrants than, for example, in North America, where permanent immigration has usually aimed at future full citizenship (Hammar, 1989). The state's control over the legal status of refugees and asylum-seekers can be used as a means of determining access to labour markets, education, and housing, as well as political rights. It also controls the overall framework within which migrant groups, including refugees, are incorporated into the host economy, if at all.

However, it is important at the same time not to overemphasise the role of the state – a particular risk in comparative work where differences in individual states' policies form the most obvious basis for comparison – or indeed to fall into the trap of assuming that state action has an unshakeable logic, directly explicable in terms of its outcome. State action may, for example, have unintended consequences, as in the case of Germany's introduction of restrictions on Turkish migration in the 1970s, which led to thousands of Turks bringing their children to

Germany because of fears of further restrictions. At the same time, refugees themselves may be involved in strategies to improve their socio-economic status, strategies that have successfully by-passed state initiatives in certain cases (Mignot, 1981).

Overall, this chapter aims to refocus attention away from speculation about future numbers of refugees, to a concern with the survival and incorporation into the host economy of those who stay. In doing so, a number of new questions are raised. For example, restrictive immigration and asylum policies are usually portrayed as a response to rising numbers of immigrants and asylum-seekers, but can also be seen as a mechanism to differentiate migrant groups already resident in the host country, thus increasing their economic vulnerability, reinforcing their temporary status, and at the same time increasing the possibility for exploitation.

In an era of Euromania amongst academics, it is perhaps ironic to have to call for more research to be done at the European level. Nonetheless, a need clearly exists for further comparative studies at this level to examine the economic potential for integration of refugees and asylum-seekers, and to identify the structural conditions, as well as the conditions within refugee communities and households, in which this process could be beneficial to both refugees and their hosts. Such work cannot be carried out in isolation, but must examine refugees in the context of migration as a wider process.

References

Avery, C., 1983, 'Refugee status decision-making: the systems of ten countries', *Stanford Journal of International Law*, **19** (2): 235–356.

Bovenkerk, F., Miles, R. and Verbunt, G., 1991, 'Comparative studies of migration and exclusion on the grounds of "race" and ethnic background in Western Europe: a critical appraisal', *International Migration Review*, **25** (2): 375–91.

Black, R., 1992, *Sources of livelihood and vulnerability of foreign refugees in Greece*, Occasional Paper no. 34, Department of Geography, King's College London.

Bruun, B., *et al.*, 1990, *Legal and social conditions for asylum-seekers and refugees in selected European countries*, Danish Refugee Council, Copenhagen.

Castles, S. and Kosack, G., 1973, *Immigrant workers and class structure in Western Europe*, Oxford University Press, London.

Cecchini, P., 1988, *The European challenge: 1992*, Wildwood House, Aldershot.

Cels, J. and Loescher, G., 1988, 'The refugee determination procedure in Belgium and the role of UNHCR', in A. Bramwell, ed., *Refugees in the age of total war*, Unwin Hyman, London.

Commission of the European Community, 1991, *The regions in the 1990s: fourth periodic report on the social and economic situation and development of the regions of the Community*, Office of Official Publications of the European Communities, Luxembourg.

Council of Europe, 1991a, *The return of Chilean exiles*, Parliamentary Assembly Document no. 6111.

Council of Europe, 1991b, *Refugees from the countries of Central and Eastern Europe*, Parliamentary Assembly Document no. 6167.

Desbarats, J., 1985, 'Indochinese resettlement in the US', *Annals, Association of American Geographers*, **75** (4): 522–38.

Gans, P., 1990, 'Changes in the structure of the foreign population of West Germany since 1980', *Migration*, **7** (1): 25–49.

Golini, A., Gerano, G. and Heins, F., 1991, 'South–north migration with special reference to Europe', *International Migration,* **19** (2): 253–79.

Gordon, I., 1991, *The impact of economic change on minorities and migrants in Western Europe*, Discussion Paper, no.2, Department of Geography, University of Reading, UK.

Grečic, V., 1991, 'East–west migration and its possible influence on north–south migration', *International Migration,* **19** (2): 241–52.

Hailbronner, K., 1990, 'The right to asylum and the future of asylum procedure in the European Community', *International Journal of Refugee Law,* **2** (3): 341–60.

Hammar, T., 1989, 'Comparing European and North American international migration', *International Migration Review,* **23** (3): 631–37.

Hofmann, H.J. and Heller, W., 1992, *Social and economic dimensions of the migration of Aussiedler into the former West Germany*, Migration Unit Research Paper no. 2, Department of Geography, University College, Swansea, UK.

IOE Group, 1990, 'Spain's illegal immigrants', *Contemporary European Affairs,* **3** (3): 117–39.

JCWI (Joint Council for the Welfare of Immigrants), 1989, *Unequal migrants: the European Community's unequal treatment of migrants and refugees*, JCWI, London.

Joly, D. and Nettleton, C., 1990, *Refugees in Europe*, Minority Rights Group, London.

Kutch, K., 1988, 'The economics of refugee movements: a framework for analysis', paper for EADI Working Group on Migration and Development, Geneva.

Labreveux, P., 1989, 'Greece: adapting to the force of circumstance', *Refugees,* **60**: 17–18.

Loescher, G., 1989, 'The European Community and refugees', *International Affairs,* **65** (4): 617–636.

Lundström, S., 1991, 'Bilateral municipal cooperation on migrants. Return ticket, Kulu–Stockholm', *International Migration,* **29** (1): 119–23.

Martin, P.L., Hönekopp, E. and Ullman, H., 1990, 'Europe 1992: effects on labour migration', *International Migration Review,* **24** (3): 591–603.

Mestheneos, L., 1988, 'The education, employment and living conditions of refugees in Greece and possibilities for (self-) employment', report for UNHCR Branch Office, Athens.

Mignot, M., 1981, 'Insertion en France des réfugiés du Sud-Est asiatique', *AWR Bulletin,* **19** (4): 188–95.

Mignot, M., 1983, 'L'influence de l'accueil des réfugiés en provenance du Cambodge, du Laos, du Vietnam sur le paysage communal français', *AWR Bulletin,* **21** (2/3): 96–99.

Morokvasic, M., 1991, 'Roads to independence. Self employed immigrant and minority women in five European states', *International Migration,* **29** (4): 407–17.

Muller, S., 1990, 'City of refugees', *Refugees,* **73**: p. 30.

Penninx, R. and Muus, P., 1991, 'No limits for migration after 1992? The lessons of the past, and a reconnaissance of the future', *International Migration,* **29** (3): 373–87.

Pohjola, A., 1991, 'Social networks: help or hindrance to the migrant?', *International Migration,* **29** (3): 435–43.

Portes, A. and Böröcz, J., 1989, 'Contemporary immigration: theoretical perspectives on its determinants and modes of incorporation', *International Migration Review,* **23** (3): 606–30.

Prognos, 1989, *The development of European Community labour markets up to 2000*, Prognos, Basel, Switzerland.

Rees, P., Stillwell, J. and Convey, A., 1992, *Intra-Community migration and its impact on the demographic structure at the regional level*, Working Paper no. 92/1, School of Geography, University of Leeds, UK.

Reubens, E.P., 1986, 'Benefits and costs of migration', in S. Klein, ed., *The economics of mass migration in the twentieth century*, Paragon House, New York.

Robinson, V., 1990a, 'Into the next millennium: an agenda for refugee studies. A report of the 1st annual meeting of the International Advisory Panel, January 1990', *Journal of Refugee Studies*, **3** (1): 3–15.

Robinson, V., 1990b, 'Boom and gloom: the success and failure of South Asians in Britain', in C. Clarke, C. Peach and S. Vertovec, eds, *South Asians overseas: migration and ethnicity*, Cambridge University Press, Cambridge, UK.

Robinson, V. and Flintoff, I., 1982, 'Asian retailing in Coventry', *New Community*, **10**: 251–9.

Robinson, V. and Hale, S., 1989, *The geography of Vietnamese secondary migration in the United Kingdom*, Centre for Research in Ethnic Relations, University of Warwick, UK.

Rogge, J.R., 1985, 'The Indochinese diaspora: where have all the refugees gone?', *Canadian Geographer*, **29** (1): 62–72.

Rudge, P., 1985, 'Fortress Europe', in *World refugee survey*, United States Committee for Refugees, Washington, DC.

Rudge, P., 1990, 'Europe in the 1990s: the Berlin Walls of the mind', in *World refugee survey*, United States Committee for Refugees, Washington DC.

Sayers, R., 1987, 'Resettling refugees: the Dutch model', in D. Joly and R. Cohen, eds, *Reluctant hosts: Europe and its refugees*, Gower, Aldershot, UK.

Sen, F., 1991, 'Turkish self-employment in the Federal Republic of Germany with special regard to Northrhine-Westphalia', *International Migration*, **29** (1): 124–29.

SOPEMI, 1991, *Continuous reporting system on migration*, Organization for Economic Cooperation and Development, Paris.

USCR (United States Committee for Refugees), 1992, *World refugee survey, 1991*, USCR, Washington, DC.

Van Hear, N., 1991, 'Some implications for Europe of recent trends in migration', paper presented at conference on 'The new Europe: integration versus disintegration', University of Southampton, UK, September 1991.

Vetter, H.O., 1987, *Report on the right of asylum*, European Parliament, 23 February 1987, p. 9.

Voutira, E., 1991, 'Pontic Greeks today: migrants or returnees?', *Journal of Refugee Studies*, **4** (4): 400–20.

White, P., Winchester, H. and Guillon, M., 1987, 'South-East Asian refugees in Paris: the evolution of a minority community', *Ethnic and Racial Studies*, **10** (1): 48–61.

Widgren, J., 1989, 'Asylum-seekers in Europe in the context of south–north movements', *International Migration Review*, **23** (3): 599–605.

Widgren, J., 1990, 'Asylum policy at a turning point', *Refugees*, **73**: 22–25.

Wilson, K.L. and Portes, A., 1980, 'Immigrant enclaves: an analysis of the labor market experiences of Cubans in Miami', *American Journal of Sociology*, **86** (2): 295–319.

Wong, D., 1991, 'Asylum as a relationship of otherness: a study of asylum holders in Nuremberg, Germany', *Journal of Refugee Studies*, **4** (2): 150–63.

Yen, V.N., 1986, 'Indochinese refugees in the European Community', *Migration News*, **35** (1): 37–40.

Zetter, R., 1992, 'Refugees and forced migrants as development resources: the Greek Cypriot refugees from 1974', paper presented to 3rd International Research and Advisory Panel on Refugees and Displaced Persons, University of Oxford, January 1992.

Zimmer, C. and Aldrich, H., 1987, 'Resource mobilization through ethnic networks: kinship and friendship ties of shopkeepers in England', *Sociological Perspectives*, **30** (4): 422–45.

Further reading

Bovenkerk, F., Miles, R. and Verbunt, G., 1991, 'Comparative studies of migration and exclusion on the grounds of "race" and ethnic background in Western Europe: a critical appraisal', *International Migration Review*, **25** (2), 375–91.
Joint Council for the Welfare of Immigrants, 1989, *Unequal migrants: the European Community's unequal treatment of migrants and refugees*, JCWI, London.
Joly, D., Nettleton, C. and Poulton, H., 1992, *Refugees: asylum in Europe*, Minority Rights Publications, London.
Loescher, G., 1989, 'The European Community and refugees', *International Affairs*, **65** (4): 617–636.
Refugees, **93**, Special issue on 'European Community: asylum and assistance issues'.

7 The 'Sweden-wide strategy' of refugee dispersal

Tomas Hammar

Introduction

On 13 December 1989, Sweden temporarily suspended its generous refugee policy, giving asylum only to applicants who met the requirements of the Geneva Convention or to a few others who were exceptional cases. In the previous four to five years a growing number of 'new refugees' had started to come to Sweden from the Middle East and from Asian regions as well as from some African states, mainly Somalia and Ethiopia. They were mostly spontaneous arrivals who came without warning, and without passports, other identification documents, or travel tickets. The examination of their claims had therefore often been extremely difficult and time consuming. However, the major change compared to the previous years – those before 1984–85 – was the increase in numbers.

Since 1950 Sweden had taken quotas of 1,250 refugees per year, selected from amongst those staying in international refugee camps, organised by the UNHCR or others. On top of this collectively organised inflow of refugees, Sweden had granted asylum to between 2,000 and 3,000 asylum-seekers per year. Statistics for earlier years do not distinguish between refugees and other immigrants, and the available figures shown in Table 7.1 are therefore only approximations. They show, however, that Sweden granted asylum to about 90,000 refugees during the thirty-five years from 1950 but that roughly the same number were also accepted in the ensuing six years alone. Table 7.1 also shows how much of this rapid growth in refugee immigration consists of 'new refugees' from the South, and in particular the Middle East. It is important to note, in addition, that these figures represent only those persons actually admitted, not all asylum-seekers. In comparison to other European states, Sweden has followed a policy of generous examination of asylum claims (until recently, about 80 per cent have been accepted), combined with a rather strict policy of deporting those who have been refused.

In summary, it can be argued that not only has Sweden received more asylum-seekers than other European countries, considering the size of its population (8.4 million), but it has also shown a greater willingness to grant asylum. This policy changed in December 1989, however, and by 1991 less than half of all applicants were being granted asylum, while deportations were practised as strictly as before. Sweden has in this way come closer to the general restrictive pattern in Europe, and it has taken an active part in the efforts to harmonise refugee policies, which are now under way.

Table 7.1 Refugee immigration to Sweden 1950–90

Refugees from	1950–67	1968–77	1978–84	1985–90	Total
Eastern Europe	10,100	13,000	7,000	9,300	39,300
Other Europe	6,300	5,700	100	200	12,300
Turkey	–	4,700	1,400	2,400	8,500
Middle East	200	1,200	5,000	39,500	45,900
Vietnam	–	–	3,800	2,000	5,800
Latin America	–	6,500	8,100	12,800	27,400
Other regions	7,400	6,900	2,600	21,500	38,400
TOTAL	24,000	38,000	28,000	88,000	178,000
Average per year	1,300	3,800	4,000	14,600	4,300

Source: Ministry of Labour (1978); Swedish reports to SOPEMI, OECD; Statistics from the Swedish Board of Immigration (SIV)

Background: population

This chapter discusses the reform of refugee resettlement which took place in Sweden in 1984 and its consequences for the dispersal of asylum seekers and refugees throughout Sweden. Before this, it is important to mention some basic facts which may be relevant to the understanding of the account. First, Sweden is a highly industrialised welfare state, which is not only sparsely populated (nineteen persons per km^2), but whose population is also very unevenly distributed. One third (around 2.7 million) live in the three metropolitan areas of Stockholm, Göteborg and Malmö, all of which are located at least 500 km south of the geographical centre of the country. Fourteen per cent (1.2 million) live in the northern parts called 'Norrland', which covers 60 per cent of Sweden's total land area of 450,000 km^2 (compared with 244,000 km^2 for Great Britain, and 547,000 km^2 for France). Even if the climate is colder than on the European continent, the combined effects of the Gulf Stream and of modern building techniques make living comfortable even in the far north. Meanwhile, in some branches of the economy, satellites and telecommunications can overcome the problems caused by high transportation costs. In other words, the population could reasonably be allowed to increase, especially in the north.

In a world which will become more and more overpopulated, the Scandinavian countries now seem to be one of the few undiscovered corners of Europe, where the population is stagnant and ageing but where there is still a lot of space, fresh water and wilderness. There is of course a question as to how long this will last. At the same time, how high a level of immigration the five Nordic states will tolerate, or might have to tolerate in the future, from the South, or from the East, or from within the European Community, is also open to debate. These are two of the many basic issues which have given the author a strong motivation to study recent Swedish refugee policy and especially the dispersal of refugees, starting in 1985.

These were not the questions, however, which gave the initial impetus to a substantial research project on this subject in 1986. The incentive was a major policy change of the Swedish system for refugee resettlement. Together with a group of researchers at the Stockholm University Centre for Research in International Migration and Ethnic Relations, I have studied the implementation of this reform both from the perspectives of three different refugee groups (Kurds, Poles, and Chileans), and also from the perspectives of six different municipalities with varying ambitions, preconditions, and resources for the job. My own contribution has mainly been a historical and political study of the ideas behind the reform, the decision-making process, and the many policy adaptations necessitated by external factors, not least immigration pressure and the large number of asylum-seekers.

Immigration and immigration policy

Sweden has not experienced immigration from previous colonies, as have the UK and the Netherlands. Nor has it employed a guest-worker policy, as have West Germany and Switzerland. Sweden has invented its own model, an immigration policy based on efficient regulation and permanent settlement for immigrants once admitted. A common free Nordic labour market has remained open to all Nordic citizens. Since 1972, Sweden has not allowed any further labour migration but has, instead, allowed a substantial family immigration and a generous refugee immigration.

This model of strict regulation and of permanent settlement is protective of the social welfare system and has been promoted by the trade unions. Regulation has been combined with a policy furthering integration of immigrants into the labour market, into housing areas, into Swedish politics and through language instruction. Furthermore, in the mid-1970s, without much political debate, a policy of ethnic pluralism was also included in this model (Parliamentary Commission on Immigration Policy, 1982; Lithman-Lundberg, 1987).

There are several reasons for this policy of permanent immigration. First, it was in keeping with the trade unions' aim of protecting the domestic labour market. It was felt that immigrant workers should be unionised and should enjoy the same wages and working conditions as Swedish employees and the same social benefits, including unemployment compensation. If not, unfair competition would prevail in which immigrants might usurp the position of Swedes in the domestic labour market. As a consequence, policy-makers sought a high level of integration. Full equality soon became the proclaimed goal, and permanent residence and work permits were granted. What is remarkable is not the quick unionisation and the relatively good conditions enjoyed by migrant workers, but instead the fact that trade unions in the 1950s and 1960s tolerated a sizeable labour immigration.

The second reason for Sweden's permanent immigration policy is growing Nordic cooperation. Nordic immigrants were soon given full economic and social rights and from 1954 workers enjoyed a right to free movement within a Nordic labour market. This Nordic agreement facilitated a relatively large interchange of labour. In the 1970s, more than half of all labour immigration to Sweden was Nordic, with most workers coming from Finland. This immigration decreased, however, as differences in income and working conditions became less conspicuous. It was partly replaced by increasing inter-Nordic circulation in which people moved in all directions for short term employment, family reunion or studies. As a result, about half of all foreign citizens residing in Sweden in 1990 were citizens of a Nordic country, and the same was true for half of all foreign-born persons residing in Sweden. Only 20 per cent of those who migrated into Sweden in 1990 were Nordic citizens.

Refugees in Sweden

As long as foreign workers were recruited or granted labour permits after arrival in Sweden, refugee immigration was small and little noticed. When this changed at the beginning of the 1970s, only two major channels of entry were left open for those who wanted to settle in the country. One of these two channels was meant for close relatives (parents, young children or a spouse) either of Swedes or of immigrants already settled in the country. Political refugees could therefore only apply through the other channel. Nor were arrangements after entry ideal. Asylum-seekers were not allowed to work as long as their claims were under examination, and many had to wait for a year or more until their cases were finally decided upon. In the meantime they had to rely on social welfare benefits which the municipalities distributed and then reclaimed from central government. Whilst awaiting a decision on their application, the asylum-seekers could really only prepare themselves for life in Sweden by learning the Swedish language (Rystad, 1990).

Those who received permission to stay in Sweden because they were granted refugee status under the 1951 Geneva Convention immediately became eligible for support from the National Labour Market Board (AMS). They were given language training and vocational training, and as soon as possible were used to fill vacancies in occupations where there were labour shortages. Since many of the refugee arrivals during this period (before 1985) were coming from international refugee camps, the National Labour Market Board established a number of reception centres in which the refugees spent their first six months in Sweden. These centres did not escape criticism: they were thought to promote institutionalisation and place too great a stress on getting refugees into the labour market at the expense of other aspects of their future integration. Thus, when in 1981 the powerful National Labour Market Board wanted to be free of some of its more peripheral responsibilities, the Minister of Immigration initiated studies of how refugee integration could be incorporated into Sweden's general programme for immigrants.

The reform of 1984

In May 1984, the Riksdag announced the results of this deliberation. The reform was based on the following principles (Board of Immigration, 1984):

1. Refugees should enjoy the benefits of Sweden's integration policy in the

same way as other immigrants, and the same authority, the National Board of Immigration, should be responsible for all immigrants, including refugees.

2.   Asylum-seekers and refugees should as soon as possible, and not later than four weeks after arrival, be placed in a municipality where they would obtain an appropriate apartment of good standard, money to buy and cook their own meals, daycare for their children, Swedish language training and medical services. It was felt that if refugees could be placed directly in locations where they might resettle permanently, they would be integrated quicker and with fewer problems. There, they could experience everyday life in Sweden, meet neighbours and workmates and learn how the host society functioned in practice.

3.   Government should select fifty to sixty municipalities most suitable for integrated refugee resettlement out of the total of 284. They should have good housing facilities, a promising labour market, appropriate language services, and a corresponding cultural competence. They should neither be too small nor too big, for the largest cities had already taken a disproportionate share of refugees during previous years and were to be given some relief. The National Board of Immigration should negotiate agreements with these fifty to sixty local authorities about the annual number of asylum-seekers and refugees for which they could make arrangements, and the state should pay them for the job, both a set amount per asylum-seeker or refugee and compensation for the housing costs and social benefits incurred during the first three years.

Table 7.2 Asylum-seekers and persons granted refugee status in Sweden, 1983–90

Year	Asylum seekers	Refugee status	Local placements	
			persons	municipalities
1983	3,100	3,800	–	–
1984	11,900	4,600	–	–
1985	14,600	6,600	14,200	137
1986	14,600	12,200	14,800	197
1987	18,100	14,000	18,700	245
1988	19,600	16,100	17,900	265
1989	30,300	24,900	21,100	276
1990	29,400	12,800	22,200	280
TOTAL	141,600	95,000	108,900	280

Source: Swedish Board of Immigration

When the Riksdag unanimously approved these reforms in the early summer of 1984, no one had yet noticed the change in refugee immigration which had already started, nor did anyone anticipate that this new refugee immigration would immediately and completely change the system of refugee resettlement. Although the new scheme was a well planned piece of social engineering, with a capacity for 5,000 to 6,000 persons per year, it had already been overtaken by events by the autumn of 1984. By that time, the number of asylum-seekers had started to increase sharply, to such an extent that about 12,000 arrived in Sweden in the full calendar year of 1984. Moreover, as Table 7.2 demonstrates, this increase continued in the following years. As the figures reveal, the number of asylum-seekers is higher than the number of persons who have been granted refugee status. This is explained both by refusals and by the constant delays in the refugee determination process. Asylum-seekers arriving one year may get their residence permit one or two years later. In a period with increasing numbers of applicants the waiting periods are long, and in 1990 almost 30,000 were waiting in refugee centres either for a final decision or for a placement in one of the 280 municipalities which had, by then, been recruited for the resettlement programme.

Refugee resettlement in practice

The reform never functioned in the way it had been planned. The National Board of Immigration had to care for all those asylum-seekers who were not directly deported by the police in the airports and harbours. Temporary refugee centres had to be found quickly. More places were needed in the local programmes, and as the fifty to sixty municipalities which had initially been selected had already fixed the numbers they could take, new municipalities had to be approached. During the first three years, almost every one of Sweden's municipalities agreed to take what was soon called 'its share', calculated so that the number of refugees taken by a municipality would be proportional to the percentage of the national population contained within it. In 1987 this share was 2.8 new refugees per thousand inhabitants. The proportional system was legitimised by saying that every municipality should demonstrate its solidarity, not only with the refugees, but above all with the other municipalities (Hammar, 1991).

The number of refugees requiring immediate settlement meant that the idea of placing them only in localities which were particularly suitable was forgotten. Municipalities with depressed economies and population loss through internal migration were persuaded to rent their surplus housing to refugees. In some municipalities local groups even asked for refugee immigration in the hope that they could help preserve a local school with too few pupils or a neighbourhood shop which could hardly survive.

As shown by Table 7.2, the Swedish Board of Immigration managed to resettle a remarkably high number of people – more than 108,000 – in only six years. Yet, even this did not match the number in need: the number of persons waiting remained the same or even grew, and as a result further measures were taken to shorten the determination process and therefore the queues. The Aliens Act was not changed, but it was rewritten and simplified. The examination procedure was changed and the administration reorganised and regionalised. Even this was insufficient, for with increasing numbers of asylum-seekers arriving in Sweden, the Swedish government in December 1989 used its right to suspend some articles in the Aliens Act dealing with so called *de facto* refugees, and to declare that for the time being Sweden could not accept other refugees than those who met the requirements of the Geneva Convention. Exceptions could only be made for other asylum-seekers in cases where they strongly needed protection.

The resettlement system, which had been conceived on too small a scale even at the outset, was progressively extended, but it still failed to meet demand. As a result, the capacity of the system brought about a less generous and more restrictive refugee policy, even though the country had the capacity to provide reasonable conditions for long-term settlement for a much larger number of refugees. The plan for each of the 284 municipalities to take 2.8 persons per 1,000 inhabitants meant that Sweden, with a population of 8.4 million inhabitants, could receive no more than 23,500 refugees per year. A ceiling had thus been set for the refugee programme, as a result of a combination of *ad hoc* decisions taken by local and state administrations rather than by a conscious political decision or by study of the consequences of alternative strategies for the country and its people.

The new system was given a nickname. It was called the 'Sweden-wide strategy', signifying the dispersal of refugees to almost all municipalities in the country. In an effort to legitimate this strategy, the Board of Immigration maintained that this was the only way to care for so many refugees. Furthermore, the Sweden-wide strategy gave all Swedes an opportunity to meet refugees and to learn about their background and their situation in Sweden. Politicians throughout the country were forced to discuss refugee issues in a way they had never done before, and it was argued that this might produce a more favourable attitude towards refugees, and a climate more conducive to a generous refugee policy.

Compulsory dispersal of refugees

One aspect of the new strategy which was seldom noticed or discussed was the change in how dispersal was seen. The original idea had been that a local placement in a suitable neighbourhood would lead to permanent integration and settlement in dispersed localities. With the revised policy, this view was substituted so that dispersal was seen as a temporary arrangement for a period of three years. As a result, the characteristics of the locality were seen to be less important, and refugees could be resettled in less favourable areas which would act as places of temporary residence prior to secondary migration (Hammar, 1992).

Refugees were also dispersed in order to prevent them from over-burdening the major cities. Several attempts had shown that, once refugees had settled in a large city, it was difficult to persuade them to move to another. It was hoped that it would be easier to persuade those who had only recently arrived to go to places they did not know about. It had been officially stated that all placements would be voluntary, and that the wishes and demands of the refugees should be respected. But in practice, this could not be operationalised. Refugees who refused to accept their placements often had to stay in refugee centres and wait for another offer. Some could perhaps make their own arrangements, but the need to find both a job and an apartment meant that most could not. The system thus effectively developed into compulsory dispersal, with little consideration being given to the individual's personal interests. Where possible, however, refugees were usually sent to municipalities which already contained some of their fellow countrymen. This meant that local services could be provided in their own language and that an ethnic – and perhaps also religious – community could be formed.

Initially, secondary migration was regarded as an indication of unsuccessful integration and perhaps also of inadequate local services. Refugees left because they did not get the service they needed or hoped for, or because they disliked the place and its people. However, when the policy objective was no longer permanent dispersal, but only a temporary sojourn in the place of first settlement, this attitude should have changed. Secondary migration might then be seen as positive, indicating that individuals had the ability to act on their own behalf and to locate jobs and housing for themselves. However, in practice this change in attitude did not occur. The local refugee administrators had been asked to do their best to integrate refugees, and they were often, but not always, frustrated when 'their' refugees left.

Distribution of refugees

The mid-1980s saw not only a change in the number of refugees arriving in Sweden but also changes in their source countries. Europe declined in importance as a source, and the Third World became more important. As Table 7.3 indicates, a new era of refugee immigration from the Third World had started.

Table 7.3 Asylum-seekers in Sweden by geographic origin, 1983–90 (%)

	1983	1984	1985	1986	1987	1988	1989	1990
Eastern Europe	5	10	9	12	10	16	34	17
Africa	–	2	4	7	7	7	10	8
Latin America	13	6	12	14	23	17	–	–
Middle East	26	36	21	10	12	16	24	26
Iran	17	16	35	48	32	26	15	15
Others	39	30	19	10	16	16	17	22
TOTAL %	100	100	100	100	100	100	100	100
TOTAL ('000)	3.1	11.9	14.6	14.6	18.1	19.6	30.3	29.4

Source: Police statistics

In 1984 and 1985, when the new immigration started, many came from Syria, Lebanon and Iraq, and especially during 1985 from the country which would for some years provide the largest refugee group, Iran. During the end of the 1980s, 40 to 50 per cent of asylum seekers came from the Middle East and Iran. Relatively few came from Africa, mostly from Somalia and Ethiopia. Latin American immigration was large until 1989, when it was abruptly stopped by the introduction of a visa requirement for Chilean citizens. During the Cold War, a majority of asylum-seekers had come from Eastern Europe, but after a period of low immigration, this category again started to grow in the late 1980s.

When the Swedish Board of Immigration started to disperse asylum-seekers and refugees over the country, agreements about local refugee programmes were made, as mentioned, with an increasing number of municipalities. Table 7.4 classifies these municipalities into categories according to the date at which they made their first agreement to take part in the programme. These categories are used in subsequent tables to demonstrate some of the consequences of the new Sweden-wide strategy.

Table 7.4 Classification of Swedish municipalities according to time of agreement to participate in dispersal programme, by region

Cat.	Time period	Eastern Götaland	Western Götaland	Svealand	Norrland	Total
1	Before April 1985	18	8	22	2	50
2	April–June 1985	16	3	7	6	32
3	July–December 1985	9	5	8	7	29
4	January–December 1986	21	8	24	10	63
5	January–June 1987	6	22	15	5	48
6	After June 1987	13	10	15	24	62
TOTAL		83	56	91	54	284

Source: Field data

First, it is astonishing to note that included amongst the fifty municipalities in category 1 – the first to join the programme – were all the largest urban municipalities which had previously received most of the refugees and which were now promised relief. The explanation is that they were all well equipped for the task, and were also the favourite choice of many refugees, who would in any case have chosen to go there. To this first category of fifty municipalities belonged also the administrative centres of fourteen of Sweden's southern provinces plus a number of large industrial cities.

During the second quarter of 1985 another thirty-two municipalities joined the programme, and during the second half of the year another twenty-nine. One year after the start of the reform, the number of municipalities was 111. More than half of the eighty-three municipalities located in Eastern Götaland were now in the project, and about 40 per cent of those in Svealand. Because of administrative problems, Western Götaland had not yet been mobilised. The same was also true of Norrland but for different reasons: this part of the country which, as we have seen is the largest, was characterised by internal out-migration and also by high unemployment and underemployment. Only fifteen of Norrland's fifty-four municipalities belonged to the first three categories, fifteen more to categories 4 and 5, with the remaining twenty-four only being asked to participate after two and a half years had elapsed. As shown by Table 7.5, the average size of the population was very high in the first category of municipalities, but below the average for Sweden in all other categories, falling during each of the subsequent periods. Correspondingly, the percentage of foreigners in the population fell, as new municipalities were mobilised which had previously had little or no prior experience of immigration. This trend is very clear when only non-Nordic immigrants are included.

Table 7.5 Mean population and number of foreigners in Swedish municipalities within each category

	Category of municipality (Table 7.4)						
	1	2	3	4	5	6	Total
Average population in 1985 (thousands)	82	29	28	20	14	9	30
Foreign citizens (%)	6.7	3.2	2.6	2.7	2.4	2.4	4.7
Non-Nordic citizens (%)	3.8	1.6	1.1	1.0	0.8	0.5	2.3
Born in non-Nordic countries (%)	6.4	3.0	2.2	2.2	1.9	1.2	3.9
Number of municipalities	50	32	29	63	48	62	284

Source: Swedish Board of Immigration

Table 7.6 outlines the economic and social characteristics of the different categories of municipalities. The tax capacity of a municipality is calculated as the total of all self-declared incomes divided first by 100 and then by the number of inhabitants. This indicator, and the figures for average salaries, show that more affluent municipalities were among the first approached whilst the less affluent were among those saved for the last category. Meanwhile, the unemployment rate was much lower in the first category and much higher in the last, but about the same between these two extremes. The rate of female participation in the labour market was very much lower in municipalities belonging to the last categories. This is probably also a good indicator of the opportunities on offer within the labour market. On this basis, we might say that municipalities in the first categories were well selected and better suited for the purpose. However, importantly, and especially in the beginning in 1985, there was a higher proportion of available apartments in the municipalities where income was lower and employment opportunities rare.

Table 7.6 Swedish municipalities by average capacity to pay taxes, average income, unemployment rate, female labour activity rate and percent of apartments available.

| | Category of municipality (Table 7.4) | | | | | | |
	1	2	3	4	5	6	Total
Tax capacity	522	487	469	459	438	430	460
Income (thousand SEK)	79.2	73.6	72.7	71.3	67.6	66.9	75.5
Unemployment (%)	2.19	2.53	2.78	2.76	2.79	3.83	2.62
Women in labour force (%)	67.2	61.9	63.0	60.8	58.8	56.6	65.0
Available apartments (%)							
1985	2.4	4.5	2.1	3.4	3.6		2.8
1987	0.7	1.7	1.1	1.5	1.6		1.0

Source: Field data

As Table 7.7 reveals, the redistribution of refugees from the metropolitan areas of Stockholm, Göteborg and Malmö to other parts of the country has been effective and probably even stronger than was initially envisaged. During the first years, 1985–87, there was only a small reduction in the actual numbers in metropolitan municipalities, but this should be compared to the strong increase in other parts of the country. Meanwhile, the table covers only the reform period from 1985 onwards. If figures had also been available for previous years, the share of all refugees taken by the metropolitan regions would have been even higher.

Table 7.7 Refugees admitted to metropolitan and other municipalities in Sweden 1985–89

| Year | Metropolitan municipalities | | Other municipalities | | Total | |
	Number	(%)	Number	(%)	Number	(%)
1985	7,400	(52)	6,900	(48)	14,300	(100)
1986	6,302	(43)	8,330	(57)	14,632	(100)
1987	7,176	(39)	11,424	(61)	18,600	(100)
1988	6,026	(31)	13,090	(68)	19,116	(100)
1989	6,164	(28)	15,470	(71)	21,634	(100)
1985–89	33,068	(37)	55,214	(62)	88,282	(100)

Source: Swedish Board of Immigration

Before 1985 Stockholm provided a home to more refugees than any other municipality, both in relative and in absolute numbers. It was never explicitly stated how far redistribution should proceed, and in practice Stockholm was not exempt from further refugee settlement since the principle of distributing refugees in proportion to the population was also applied to that city. However, the impact of this was to bring about a very considerable reduction in the numbers of refugees moving to Stockholm (Table 7.8). During the first year, the city admitted almost 20 per cent of all Sweden's refugees. Four to five years later its share had fallen to only 5 to 6 per cent. The proportion taken by Stockholm county (which on the whole, but not in all details, corresponds to the metropolitan area of Stockholm) also fell drastically. A few prosperous and conservative municipalities to the north and east of Stockholm city which had little previous experience of refugee settlement remained reluctant to take their per capita share under the new model, while some others to the south-west of Stockholm city, which had asked for reduced numbers, continued to do more than they should according to the proportional principle.

Table 7.8 Refugees admitted to Stockholm county and city, 1985–89

Year	Sweden Number	Stockholm County Number	(%)	Stockholm City Number	(%)
1985	14,300	5,429	(38)	2,800	(20)
1986	14,632	4,180	(28)	1,813	(12)
1987	18,600	4,362	(23)	1,913	(10)
1988	19,116	3,285	(17)	1,211	(6)
1989	21,634	3,250	(15)	1,097	(5)

Source: Swedish Board of Immigration

Presented with data of this sort, representatives of the metropolitan areas responded that they had to keep their initial intake very low, for they would later gain sizeable numbers of refugees from secondary migration. If they continued to accept large numbers of primary settlers, they would benefit little, if at all, from the new programme.

A new policy?

Studies of dispersal policies elsewhere in Europe suggest that strategies such as that outlined in this chapter may not provide a long-term solution for the permanent settlement of refugees. For example, in the UK, Robinson and Hale (1989) show that many Vietnamese refugees dispersed as part of government policy to different parts of the country have opted to make secondary moves after a period of one or more years to urban centres, and especially London (see also Robinson, 1992; and Chapter 9 of this volume). A similar conclusion was drawn by Norro (1991) in the case of dispersal policies for refugees in Belgium.

Unfortunately, Swedish data on the secondary migration of refugees are very limited. Only minor studies have been undertaken. They seem to indicate that many refugees have in fact moved; that such movement is often to administrative centres in the same regions in which they were first placed; and that flows are also going to the three metropolitan areas, as might be expected, although there is little agreement over the size of such flows. Several local municipalities believe that secondary flows are relatively strong, while national authorities suggest they are only moderate. All seem to agree, however, that the dispersal programme will bring about some lasting results, in the sense that several thousands of people are likely to stay permanently outside the metropolitan areas. So far no one knows who will stay and who will not stay in the long run, and how many thousands are going to move to the greater cities, out of those 55,000 plus who have been placed elsewhere.

The dispersal programme may perhaps not be continued, and at the time of writing Sweden's refugee policy and resettlement programmes were again under review. The new government, formed after the election in September 1991 by a coalition of four non-socialist parties, has revoked the 1989 suspension of some articles in the Aliens Act, but the rate of refusal still seems to be about as high as before at around 50 per cent of all asylum applications. The new government has announced a new programme with less public and more voluntary assistance and with much more room for the refugees' own solutions and initiatives. It is still not known how these ideas will be implemented, but they are hardly compatible with proportional and obligatory dispersal, and they might therefore bring the Sweden-wide strategy to an end.

Like other European states, Sweden will face a period of high immigration pressure. Forecasters expect numerous asylum-seekers, who will be met by a strict and harmonised immigration control. In 1985, when the Swedish dispersal programme was suddenly launched in answer to a growing new refugee immigration, it was soon found that even small municipalities far away from the greater cities were willing and able to provide opportunities for integration, and that a programme of this sort could be used to lessen the burden on some metropolitan centres. However, with an annual distribution to all municipalities of 2.8 refugees per 1,000 inhabitants, Sweden fixed its total number of refugees at some 25,000 per year and the maximum intake was defined by the administrative resources of the refugee programme. When, in the following years, the number of asylum-seekers increased beyond this level, the quota of resettlement places was already taken. Sweden had to change its refugee policy, refuse and return more asylum-seekers and give signals to the world that the new policy was restrictive.

A refugee crisis can seldom be foreseen, but global trends in international migration can be recognised, and may be of great importance to future refugee flows. Like other European states, in the 1990s Sweden is facing a period of high immigration pressure and increasing numbers of asylum-seekers and, because of this, all states in Europe will defend themselves by building 'walls' or a strict and harmonised system of immigration control. Based on its recent experience of growing refugee immigration, dispersal all over the country, and a permanent crisis administration, many Swedes are beginning to ask critical questions: how many refugees will ask for asylum in Sweden? How many can the present administration cope with, and how many is the country of Sweden willing and capable of admitting per year? Finally, are there international solutions available?

References

Board of Immigration, 1984, *Att ta emot flyktingar*, Board of Immigration, Norrkoping.
Hammar, T., 1991, 'Cradle of freedom on earth: refugee immigration and ethnic pluralism', *West European Politics*, **14** (3): 182–97.
Hammar, T., 1992, 'A crisis in Swedish refugee policy', in A. Daun *et al.*, eds, *To make the world safe for diversity*, Ethnology Institute, Stockholm University, Stockholm.
Lithman-Lundberg, E., 1987, *Swedish immigration policy*, The Swedish Institute, Stockholm.
Ministry of Labour, 1978, *Sverige och flyktingarna*, Ministry of Labour, Stockholm.
Norro, P., 1991, 'Refugee policy in Belgium: a critical evaluation of the dispersal plan, 1986', paper presented to conference on 'The Refugee Crisis: Geographical Perspectives on Forced Migration', held at King's College London, September 1991.
Parliamentary Commission on Immigration Policy, 1982, *Invandringspolitiken*, Commission on Immigration Policy, Stockholm.
Rystad, G., 1990, *The uprooted: forced migration as an international problem in the postwar era*, Lund University Press, Lund.
Robinson, V., 1992, 'British policy towards the settlement patterns of ethnic groups', in V. Robinson, ed., *The international refugee crisis: British and Canadian responses*, Macmillan, Basingstoke, UK.
Robinson, V. and Hale, S., 1989, *The geography of Vietnamese secondary migration in the UK*, Warwick University Centre for Research in Ethnic Relations, Coventry, UK.

Further reading

Desbarats, J., 1985, 'Policy influences on refugee settlement patterns', *Kroeber Society Anthropological Papers*, **65/66**: 49–63.
Hammar, T., 1991, 'Cradle of freedom on earth: refugee immigration and ethnic pluralism', *West European Politics*, **14** (3): 182–97.
Lithman-Lundberg, E., 1987, *Swedish immigration policy*, The Swedish Institute, Stockholm.
Lundström, S., 1991, '"Welcome home" in Stockholm: receiving refugees in a big city', *International Migration*, **29** (4): 617–21.
Robinson, V., 1992, 'British policy towards the settlement patterns of ethnic groups', in V. Robinson, ed., *The international refugee crisis: British and Canadian responses*, Macmillan, Basingstoke, UK.

8 'Only the women know': powerlessness and marginality in three Hmong women's lives

Kristen L. Monzel

Introduction

In the last five years, there has been a proliferation of writings on refugee issues. Yet surprisingly few have been concerned with how it *feels* to be a refugee. My research gives the reader a glimpse of how warfare, forced migration, homelessness, detainment, and resettlement were experienced by a few. Here, I present the experiences of three Hmong women, selected primarily because of my access to them through friendships developed over two years of participant observation. I use a number of qualitative research methods including the construction of their oral histories. Each oral history represents ten to twenty hours of taping time, then much longer periods interpreting, editing, and checking interpretations back with the women. Although I am learning the Hmong language, I am not yet fluent, so I was assisted by an interpreter. This was awkward at first, but became more comfortable as the project progressed.

In effect, it became a collaborative effort. For me, it was an opportunity to gain glimpses into the lives of three Hmong that I knew, yet didn't know – our friendships had developed despite the language barrier. For the women, it seemed to take on the character of a testimonial sharing of often lonely and painful experiences that they had previously been unable to communicate. For the interpreter, a very Americanized Hmong college student, the project offered a chance to learn about her own cultural background and community.

In addition to the oral history texts, I also draw on information collected through participant observation with this family, through three years working with the Syracuse Hmong community and with local refugee resettlement agencies, as well as through living in the neighbourhood where most Hmong reside.

Schematically, the chapter has five sections. The first examines the context, or geography of their worlds. The second introduces the women, while in the third section I examine their narratives in relation to an overwhelmingly apparent theme of powerlessness and lack of control. The fourth section outlines some of the means by which the women have attempted to assert themselves – and to establish some modicum of control long absent from their personal worlds. Lastly, I comment on the significance of the project.

The geography of their worlds

In attempting to interpret an oral history narrative, it is critical to understand the socio-economic and political context that helped shape that person's life; to situate it within time and space. Understanding the intersection between the individual and those elements of the larger world that impinged upon her provides important insight into how her life took shape, and how she makes sense of it (see Personal Narratives Group, 1989). Over their lifetimes, the geography of these women included various settings, yet in each situation the Hmong literally lived on the periphery. Thus, a most evident theme that emerged from the narratives was that of marginality, stemming from being members of an ethnic minority, refugees and women. I must note that marginality is my interpretation, not a term used by the Hmong. In fact, it contrasts sharply with their sense of cultural identity as proud independent people.

The Hmong first migrated to remote highland areas in northern Laos from China at the end of the last century. Swidden farmers, their primary cash crop was opium. The Hmong became wealthy relative to neighbouring ethnic groups, which often totally encircled those Hmong villages located on the highest mountaintops. As swiddenists, they frequently had to clear new plots for farming, and occasionally found themselves in conflict for land with others. They eventually became embroiled in the armed struggle of various others – including the Thai, French, Lao, Japanese, and then Vietnamese – to control the opium trade. As early as the Second World War, the Hmong in Laos were forced to relocate by numerous opponents who destroyed their villages. Some remained because they knew that others occupied the surrounding land, and they knew of no place to go. Many Hmong were slaughtered. This pattern escalated during the warfare of the 1960s and 1970s.

Many Hmong villages became allied with covert US operations, after the Americans were drawn into the hostilities in the late 1950s. When the US withdrew in 1975, the Hmong were singled out for extermination by the Pathet Lao, the victorious communist government of Laos. Approximately one-half of the Laotian Hmong died during the war, in its lingering aftermath, or during attempts to escape (depicted by a Hmong artist in Figure 8.1). Today, many remain in border camps in Thailand. Others have been resettled in the United States, Australia, and France. Most of the US Hmong reside in California, Minnesota, and Wisconsin, but a small community of approximately 350 Hmong live in Syracuse, a metropolis of 500,000 in central New York State.

After surviving years of war, then homelessness in the rainforest of Laos, the women in this study eventually arrived in Thailand and became 'legal' refugees. Rather than finding relief, however, they discovered that they had even less control over their life courses than during wartime. They were forced to live in designated UN-funded refugee camps, segregated from the Thai and Hmong populations of Thailand; they were given what they believed to be inadequate food, shelter, sanitation, and medical attention; they were also pressed to mass-produce traditional needlework.

After seven years they were accepted for relocation to Syracuse. But once there, they discovered that they had no close relatives and were the only members of their particular clan. With no close family ties, a family can only be on the social fringe of an ethnic community where clan affiliation is the primary basis for interaction. So, to view the family as marginalized within an already peripheral group gives us some understanding of these women's perceptions of their experiences. It is hardly surprising that they typically portray their worlds as being beyond their control.

Figure 8.1 *Paj ntaub* emroidery depicting a raid on a Hmong village, and escape through the rainforest and across the Mekong River (artist, Shoua Xiong)

The three women

Because the Hmong in Laos were not much concerned with recording birthdates, Xai and Kue (pseudonyms they've chosen) do not know exactly when they were born. By piecing together various details, we've figured Xai is between sixty and seventy, and her daughter Kue is between thirty-five and forty. Kue's daughter Nib Yia is sixteen, although her legal age is eighteen: her father lied about her age in the refugee camps to receive a larger rice ration.

Xai

Even by Hmong standards, Xai is a short woman. Her dark wrinkled face and hands are those of a farmer. She usually wears a stocking cap or a cloth wrapped around her head turban-style, and men's black pants cut off just below the knee and secured by an elaborately embroidered Hmong sash. In the summer she goes barefoot. She actually looks rather 'exotic' in the largely Italian–American, immigrant neighbourhood where most of the Hmong in Syracuse reside. The most notable part of Xai's appearance, however, is her quick broad toothless grin.

Xai often describes her life in terms of hard work: 'When I was a child, life was very difficult. I saw other families starving and knew that hard work pays at the end ...'. Others not only describe her in the context of hard work, but also in terms of generosity. A Hmong woman from Minnesota described how Xai had been renowned during the war for her efforts to feed other hungry and homeless refugees.

Kue

Despite the hardships she's faced, Kue somehow manages to see humour in almost any situation. She is the quintessential mother, having reared two nephews and seven children of her own. Her days are now filled with parenting, working in her enormous garden, and attending English classes. Somehow she manages to find time to sew items to sell at craft fairs for a little extra income. Kue's husband was disabled during the war, so they are one of the few Hmong families in Syracuse to receive public assistance.

I first became aware of her family through my work at a resettlement agency, where they had been labelled 'The Sick Family'. Every family member appeared to have serious medical conditions, resulting mostly from chronic malnutrition. Although not at first apparent to me, Kue's medical problems, including migraines and ulcers, have been the most persistent and troubling for the family since she is so central to their well-being.

Nib Yia

Kue has a wonderfully close relationship with her oldest daughter Nib Yia. Nib Yia is a sophomore in high school, having been age-placed despite the fact that she had no formal education prior to her arrival in Syracuse three years ago. She is in English-as-a-second-language rather than mainstream classes, and studies long hours every evening to keep pace. She hopes to attend a community college and have a career in the health industry. The odds, however, are against her, since most Hmong girls marry at about her age, and drop out of school after having two or three children. But Nib Yia may just make her goals; like the other women in her family, she works hard to achieve them. She was recently recognized by induction into the National Honor Society, an honour that her parents cannot really comprehend. She has few Hmong friends and rarely socializes outside of school. She is also careful to avoid situations that might bring her to the attention of Hmong males: 'I don't want to talk to them'.

Like so many Hmong teenagers, Nib Yia is really caught between two worlds, neither of which she fully comprehends. Hmong culture makes little sense to her because she was raised in the refugee camps. American culture is even more foreign, made up mostly of what she sees in the corridors at school, on television, and on the streets in her somewhat disreputable neighbourhood. She is keenly aware of and disturbed by frequent racial slurs which she only partially under-stands, and which come predominantly from young white males.

This chapter focuses more on issues raised by Nib Yia's mother and grand-mother, since their narratives reflect a much broader spectrum of resettlement issues. Nib Yia's experiences and perceptions are certainly no less interesting, but must wait to be discussed in greater detail elsewhere.

Lack of control

I was overwhelmed by the frustrations of these women at having so very little power. As I read and re-read the narratives in the light of this 'theme' of lack of control, I perceived three overlapping facets. First, as women in a patriarchal society, they had very little control over their personal lives. Second, the war was quite beyond their understanding or ability to affect. As a result, third, these women have had little control over the establishment of their own residence: their homes in Laos were constantly threatened, then they were shuffled from place to place as refugees in Thailand and again in the United States. They've had little chance to make a 'home-ground', a 'place' of their own. In the following sections, I have assembled fractions of their narratives according to this framework.

No control over personal matters

Xai and Kue in particular devoted a considerable amount of their narratives to the powerlessness of women within Hmong culture. The four arenas of domesticity which they most often discussed were marriage, children, health, and food pro-duction. Both women felt they had virtually no control in their marriages. Their male elders decided whom and when they would marry, then their husbands and the male elders made decisions, rarely consulting the women.

Xai first married at sixteen. She now regrets having not appreciated her good fortune of marrying an attractive man who was devoted to her. That marriage lasted four and a half years, until her husband was 'bitten by an evil mountain spirit' and died. Xai lived for two more years with her in-laws. 'I wanted to stay with my in-laws and be their slave for the rest of my life. But they said I had to marry again'. There were several men who wanted to marry her, but she was not interested. Remaining single, however, was not an option. She was physically forced to marry one of the suitors, when the men in her first husband's family received three silver bars for her.

Xai describes her second husband and marriage as very difficult:

> My new husband was a shaman and very lazy and heavily used opium while I struggled with the farm and livelihood of the family. He did not contribute to the farm work and neither did my new parents-in-law.

After considerable prodding, Xai revealed:

> I found him physically repulsive. But because I was his wife, I could not say no to his advances. I never gave either of my husbands reason to abuse me.

Her daughter Kue also describes a forced marriage to a man she did not like:

> I did not want to marry him. I was forced to marry him two months after we started 'talking'. It took the elders two nights and two days to convince me to marry him. A group of elders would talk to me, then another would come, and another … My uncles, male cousins, and brothers made me feel guilty and pressed for me to marry him. They thought he was a nice guy. They said it was time for me to marry. They talked to me until I basically gave up. My mother didn't want me to marry but my brothers and other men had more of a say. They kept talking to me so that it made me cry. Then they said that because I was crying, I must want to marry … They received four silver bars for me.

When the women first told me of their marriages, their demeanours were very stoic. However, they did not defend the 'bride price' custom as educated Hmong men typically do. When I asked the women how they had felt about men making such important decisions for them, both initially stated that it was simply beyond their control. Later both admitted their anger. Xai: 'All women hate that men make the important decisions'. The words *neeg ua qhev*, or 'slaves', reoccurred throughout Xai and Kue's narratives when they were speaking of their roles as wives and daughters-in-law.

Children were another component of domestic life over which these women had little say. It was presumed they should bear the maximum number possible, and they did not seem to question this. However, they did remark on their lack of control over the timing of pregnancies, which were affected by various social and natural forces.

Kue's husband was a soldier and away for four or five months before he could return for a few days. This made it very difficult to produce the grandchildren her father-in-law wanted. After three years, Kue gave birth to a girl.

> It was a normal birth – there didn't seem to be any problems … Then she started crying, so I breast fed her. She would not eat but just cried harder. It seemed as though someone was trying to strangle her by the sounds of her cries. Then blood came out of her nose and her eyes rolled around before she died. There were four or five other similar cases in my village, but it was a small village.

> It was a while before I had another child. My husband almost bought me a Laotian baby. I didn't really want a Laotian baby, but it was his decision to make. There were others that had the same difficulty trying to conceive. I was scared to have another child after that first one, and a little depressed, but we still tried. Two years later, Nib Yia was born. My father-in-law and husband were very happy.

Not only did the war affect her efforts to conceive, but children in her village died for unexplainable reasons. After the first child died, she had no control over her husband's desire to buy a replacement, and no say in how long she would grieve. It's hardly surprising that she notes the men's happiness, rather than her own, when she did bear Nib Yia.

As the quotes above attest, disease, poor health and death were common occurrences, later compounded by food shortages during the war. Kue described years of constant hunger and continual diarrhoea that left her family extremely weak.

Once the women reached the 'safety' of the Thai refugee camps, their diet did not improve. Xai: 'We were so hungry in Thailand. I cried all the time'. Kue:

> Everything was distributed to us. Everything was controlled. Food was limited, so if we ran out, then we would have to wait until the next time it was distributed. We could buy things at the Thai market outside the camp, but usually we didn't have any money.

> I didn't think we would make it in the camps. They were as bad as being in the jungle. There were many mosquitoes, diseases, and malnutrition ... Some committed suicide. Many died of starvation. There were too many people with illnesses. The waiting line at the hospital was very long and sometimes it was too late.

At Ban Vinai refugee camp (see Figure 8.2), the refugees were allotted five gallons of water for every ten persons, twice daily. They saved it for drinking and cooking, and used polluted water from wells for bathing. In the dry season, camp wells would empty, and the refugees would have to walk quite far, begging Thai farmers for water. Once the family arrived in Syracuse, they finally felt that they received adequate medical care. Yet, not surprisingly, 'culturally appropriate' medical care was unavailable, and the family rarely understood the basis or directions for prescriptions and other treatments.

Once I asked Xai in what aspect of their lives did Hmong women have control. Her first response was 'in no aspect'. Later, she came back to the topic, and conceded that women did have primary control over food production. Although the men decided where new fields would be located, and cut and burned the trees, the women took over from there. The women finished clearing the fields, chose what to plant, and just where to plant it. Yet the war seriously disrupted the women's ability to engage in the very activity that gave them some measure of control and that made them central to the village economy.

When the Lao destroyed their village in 1975, the family was forced to leave the village and survive in the rainforest. The soldiers often confiscated any produce found in the fields, ambushing unsuspecting Hmong. If they could outwit the soldiers, they preferred to farm the same plot rather than risk detection burning a new field. Many survived only on what food they were able to find in the forest, usually potatoes or bamboo shoots. Xai: 'After a while, my farming provided rice for the family and our diets improved slightly. We remained in the jungle for eight years. Rice gave us the advantage we needed to survive'. One evening's session recording her life story ended with Xai in tears. As she was leaving the room, she explained,

> It makes me so sad to think of all that I left behind in Laos. All my hard work to grow rice and have livestock. Then we just left everything. Only the women know how much we left. The men did some farming, but mostly drank and played around. The women did most of the work and we left it all behind. It makes me so sad now when I think back.[1]

No control over war

Xai remembers first encountering war refugees retreating from northern Laos when she was a small girl, during the Second World War. Then, a few years later, after repeated warnings from Laotians friendly with the Hmong, the Laotians

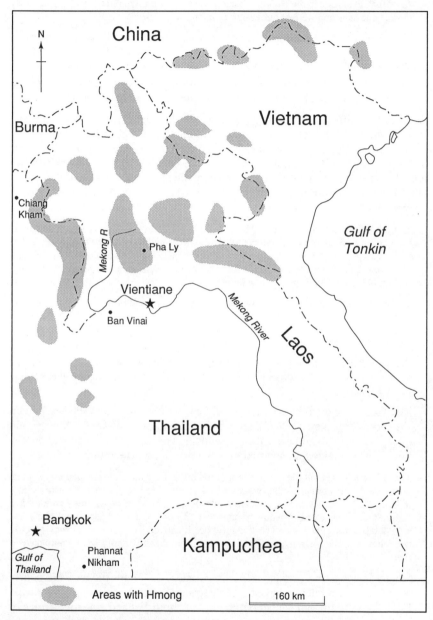

Figure 8.2 Source areas of Hmong refugees

invaded her village. Even after this assault, which left a number of Hmong dead, the villagers felt unable to leave, despite continued warnings from the Laotians that they would again be attacked:

After that, everyone in the Hmong village was very scared. We did not wake up so early to start our days and we lost our zest to farm and work hard ...

My parents could not really move from that village. We still had all our cows, chickens, horses, and everything. We knew of nowhere else to go. Most of our relatives were still there. We had no money, no other connections. We had only our farm to hold on to.

We thought all of the Hmong would be doomed because we had nowhere to go and no ammunition ... People had smoked opium before then, but now just about everybody did.[2]

Decades later, after Kue's marriage, Kue and Xai both lived in Pha Ly village, and its invasion in 1975 was an event still vivid in both of their minds. Throughout their narratives, both women repeatedly returned to this day, to add new details or insights to their description. Apparently, the Laotians again tried first to scare the Hmong into fleeing to Thailand by giving them advance notice of the attack, but the Hmong nevertheless felt they had nowhere to run. Kue describes what happened:

The day of the invasion, we heard dogs barking and knew something was wrong. The Laotians and Karen must have surrounded our village and waited until daybreak ... Half of the village was still in bed. But after that first gunshot, everyone was running around like crazy. There were some Hmong that did not find their belts in time and had to run, still grabbing onto their pants. [She laughed.]

There were grenades thrown near our house. It scared me and I ran out of the house and into the jungle. I left a pot of rice cooking. Nib Yia was only six months old and still sleeping in the bed. I didn't even think of her ... Nib Yia's father brought her to me in the jungle ...

Everyone fled from the village and into the jungle. Afterwards there was a hail storm. The sky became gloomy and the winds got very strong. After one hour, the weather became normal again.

I asked Kue if she thought the violence had caused the storm, and she was certain that it had. 'After the fighting, there were dead bodies all around. Children, old people, just anyone had been killed at random. The pigs surrounded and ate the bodies.' Kue explains the devastation and terror felt by the returning villagers:

The soldiers burned all the houses, farms, and everything down, and killed all the pigs, horses, and other animals. When we came back to the ruined village we did not know how to live. We had nowhere to go, so went into the jungle where the soldiers would have difficulty finding us and we would be more safe. We had no time to discuss our plans. We did not talk among the clan – everything was hectic and there was chaos ... I knew I would never have the chance to live in the village again and that my family and I would have to flee.

For many Hmong, and certainly for these women, the forces of war were poorly understood and completely beyond their capacity to act. Yet Hmong women and children faced additional dangers from the war. Both Xai and Kue told stories of women raped or forced into prostitution, and children taken prisoner. Kue naively explained that perhaps the Laotians wanted the children to raise as their own. Accounts by children taken prisoner indicate less humane motivations (see Moore, 1990).

Little control over a place called 'home'

In Hmong culture, residence reflects clan affiliation. After a woman marries, she no longer belongs to her father's clan, but to her husband's. Often, Hmong daughters-in-law were considered slaves to their fathers-in-law's households. Kue was more fortunate than her mother: she was welcomed by friendly in-laws who did not expect her to do all of the work.

After their village and fields were destroyed in 1975, these women and their extended family spent approximately seven years homeless in the rainforest. This phenomenon is not described in the literature: rather, the Hmong are typically depicted as immediately fleeing to Thailand after the attacks on their villages. Kue describes how they made shelter in the rainforest:

> We were always very cautious while walking in the jungle and made sure that we did not leave any trails. We stayed at least an afternoon's walk away from the village, and in a certain area only for one month at the most ... If one had a knife ... then banana leaves were chopped down to cover temporary huts that could fit three or four people.

Finally, the decision to migrate to Thailand also seemed beyond their control. Kue explains:

> We were tired of living in the jungle all the time, being very poor, always having to worry about food. The thought of going to Thailand had been in our minds for three years. We were not sure if we wanted to leave our country. We could not predict the outcome and we were unsure of where to turn next. We did not know yet of the United States. We knew only of the countries Laos, Thailand, and Vietnam. In the end, we did not know where to run, but that we had to run from the soldiers. We were not running to Thailand, as much as we were running from the war.

Both the preparations and the escape itself were arduous. Kue continued:

> We made the decision to leave with ten other families. We picked a Vang man to take charge and lead us to Thailand. He was educated and had a good head on his shoulders. He had been a soldier, and he had a map, so he knew all the routes ...

> Each carried whatever they needed. Besides rice, we carried knives, blankets, pots, and a bag of wild potatoes. We only brought one set of clothing each, that which we wore. We did not have any money. There were many of us by then, approximately one hundred families ...

> We were always on the move. We walked quickly and kept as quiet as possible. On the trail, we saw dead bodies, food and clothing left behind by those that went before us. We slept at two or three hour intervals and walked day and night.

> It took a month to reach Thailand, and we met up with many Hmong on the way. I saw soldiers far away. They killed the group ahead of us, and I remember seeing the bodies as I passed by ... It was not difficult to keep everyone quiet ...

Kue gave birth to her second child on the journey to Thailand, and by the time they reached and crossed the Mekong River, she was so exhausted that she remembers very little detail. She and her family were taken to Ban Vinai.

Xai and her sons were detained en route, remaining one day's walk from the Mekong in Laos at a segregated relocation centre for displaced Hmong. Xai's youngest son's new wife had not yet been paid for, and the wife's family wanted them to remain until the debt was paid. Soon afterwards, Hmong were not permitted to leave the country, and the family was eventually detained for eight years. An unfortunate misunderstanding leading to the murder of some Lao by some Hmong resulted in the centre's attack by the Lao. Many Hmong men were killed and tortured, and the rest told to leave the country immediately, resulting in a massive exodus of Hmong to Thailand.

Kue and her family spent five years at Ban Vinai. Xai spent one year at Ban Vinai – which she believed simply to be a large Hmong village – but arrived after Kue's family had been transferred to Chieng Kham camp. Both women and Nib Yia describe life in the camps as devastating. Kue remarked that at first sight, Ban Vinai '... looked so bad, I didn't know how we were going to survive there'. They described the living quarters as both alien and dangerous. All complained about inadequate food, medical treatment and sanitation, and about periodically being robbed by the Thai. Kue explained about the dangers of having to cook over open fires inside the unventilated bamboo and dried banana leaf buildings. Nib Yia pointed out that robbers could just walk into unlockable living quarters.

Kue explained how the family had to sew *paj ntaub* (traditional needlework) to earn extra money to supplement their diet:

> In the camp, everyone – men, women, and children – did needlework all day, every day ... Time seemed endless and very boring ... One person would get about twenty-five cents a week for the needlework, and you would have to work all the time to make that much ... I felt like a slave. It was frustrating, depressing, sad, and very maddening.

Kue's widowed mother-in-law wanted to relocate to China, and signed the family up for a relocation programme promoted by camp officials. Afterwards, they discovered that they had been tricked into signing paperwork transferring them to Chieng Kham camp, which all three described as much, much worse than Ban Vinai. It was more crowded and had no medical facilities and less food. Furthermore, it was completely enclosed by a metal fence. There were no trees, and no garden plots were allowed. Kue's family became very ill. 'I didn't have any feelings about our misfortune. I thought I was going to die soon ... I felt very much like a prisoner.'

They believed that they had to leave the camp or die. They saw others leaving in buses, bound for the United States, so in desperation they decided to apply. After what seemed like a long time, a sponsor was located in Syracuse. Kue's family was sent to Phannat Nikhom transit camp near Bangkok for six months of intensive language and cultural training. Living conditions were marginally better there, but the training was questionable. Kue: 'The Thai teachers said that Americans eat people. They taught things that totally confused me, like incorrect pronunciations and wrong phrases.' The only information Kue actually considered useful was instructions for an airplane seatbelt.

The trip itself was arduous, involving little sleep and much vomiting. No one had explained how long they would travel, and no one offered to feed them on the way. By the time they arrived at the airport in New York City, Nib Yia was very sick and they thought she would die. Kue:

> She couldn't stand up and threw up all the time. We tried to tell a black man that looked like he worked there that we and our children were hungry and thirsty. He brought some sandwiches and sodas for us.

Once the family was in Syracuse, they lived with another Hmong family for two months before an apartment was found for them. Kue describes the difficulties of that first winter:

> It was so cold! All the trees outside looked dead so I went out to collect firewood. Then I realized that the wood was green. My hair was still wet from the shower, and it turned to icicles at the ends. I thought that was very weird. I was afraid to touch the snow, afraid that something might happen to my hands. We didn't touch the snow until the next winter.

The family was extremely malnourished, and the youngest of Kue's six children spent four weeks in the hospital. Her husband also became very ill. Kue felt very isolated because she had no relatives or friends, and was therefore an outsider even in the Hmong community.

> When we first came, we were very sad because no one visited us. I knew everyone was busy, but I needed someone to talk to ... My husband became very sick, but no one came to help. He was sick for a whole month ... I was so sad, so lonely ... I didn't know what I would do if he died.

By summer, Kue's husband, mother-in-law, and two youngest children were diagnosed as having lead poisoning. Social Services threatened to place the children in a foster home if the family did not move to an approved apartment. It was this series of crises that brought the family to the attention of the refugee service agencies, and at last they began to receive much more personal attention. Kue:

> Now I have [*listed American names: all work at agencies*], and other good friends. I have more American friends than Hmong. I know that I can always count on my American friends to help me out as much as they can ... Life started getting better when we made friends with [*same American names*]. We are so thankful that we have friends like that. When I was in Laos, I never thought I would have such good friends as I have now.

Kue's caseworker's version of the family's resettlement experiences in Syracuse differs markedly from that of Kue. That is, her caseworker early on attributed the family's difficulties to material need due to the sponsoring church providing less than the 'bare necessities'. In Kue's version, the family was satisfied materially, but desperately isolated socially.

Re-establishing control

All three women are attempting to establish or re-establish some measure of control over their lives. All three, though, appear to use different methods. Xai actively distances herself from the past, and tries in her old age to live as much as possible in the present. She has developed a flexible optimism to deal with rapid change.

> I never dream about going back home ... My real ties are here in the United States and this is where I want to remain ... Living in Laos and Thailand were both equally hard times. But living in America now is like a breeze ... I can just hang out and not worry about starvation and poverty. If we desire money, we only need to work hard for wealth, and success will come to us.

> It doesn't matter that my children and grandchildren have lost the Hmong ways. I am happy that they have been given another chance. For myself, I am not saddened by adopting American culture. If I was back in Laos, there would be nothing for me.

Xai describes a turning point in her life, when she decided to make her own decisions. Immediately after the killings at the Lao relocation centre, *she* decided it was time to flee to Thailand – despite the wishes of the men in her family.

> All I know is that I did all the farming. No one helped me, and I was sick and tired from working so hard. Now, I don't really care what others think or do because I'll be doing my own things. If they don't take care of me, I could always live by myself. I can make it on my own.

For her daughter Kue, religion has played an important role in self-empowerment. She was first exposed to Christianity by Hmong missionaries when she was a teenager, 'but the elders forbade it'. After the death of her father-in-law, Kue and her husband converted.

> The Christian religion seems reasonable and logical to me. I like the aspect that it is less complicated than the Hmong shamanic beliefs. I don't have to beg or ask for someone to call my spirit back. I don't have to pay money for their work, which I think is ridiculous. I don't have to kill animals, and then not be allowed to keep but a small portion of the meat, then give the rest away. There is no obligation to call back one's spirit, or to have feasts on behalf of others when they are sick.

Her conversion, then, is clearly more of a rejection of a traditional belief system – one that, she explained, kept poor families in poverty – than the embrace of a new one. In fact through our two years discussing religion, it has become clear that she is unaware of even the most basic theology of Christianity. Yet adopting the label 'Christian' empowers her to shed the old beliefs, and to begin establishing a new worldview. Along with making American friends, her Christian identity appears to help her and her family circumvent their social marginalization within the ethnic community.

Nib Yia uses education as the means to gain some control. She avoids boys at all costs, and explains that she hopes to remain single until she is twenty-five; an 'old maid' by Hmong standards. By working towards a skilled career, she hopes to avoid the poverty she sees in her own family. More than anything, she seems to want to understand the world around her, which is still amazingly confusing.

Commentary

Compared to accounts of Hmong history based primarily on male experiences, these women's stories provide an important 'counter-narrative'. In traditional Hmong society, the division of labour prescribed that women were responsible for the everyday tasks of food and textile production, cooking, and cleaning – considerable work in a primarily subsistence economy. Childrearing was often shared with the men, who performed the heavy but occasional tasks of building houses and clearing fields, along with making important family decisions. Given these differences in gender roles, it is hardly surprising that Hmong men often romanticize their lives in Laos.

Figure 8.3 *Paj ntaub* (detail) of Hmong men reaping the bounty of the rainforest (artist, Lee Lo)

In doing so, however, they unwittingly support a Western romantic 'pastoral' vision of indigenous peoples of the rainforest. This is the vision of Hmong history most commonly portrayed in the popular and academic literature, most likely because male Hmong informants are usually more accessible to outsiders. This vision is also portrayed in *paj ntaub* tapestries such as that shown in Figure 8.3; these are, in fact, drawn by men before they are sewn by women. So, in the male version of Hmong history, the myth of return is quite strong and many – particularly those with little education who face a difficult adjustment to the United States – hope to return permanently. Conversely, the women's version is one of extreme hardship, and they rarely mention returning to Laos for anything other than a quick look around.

These narratives reflect a gendered experience often overlooked in mainstream refugee studies: an experience even more marginalized and powerless than that of a male refugee. Given that the large majority of the world's refugees are female, such insights are needed to correct our not only often Western-biased but also our *male*-biased assumptions.

Notes

Portions of this research were funded by the Roscoe Martin Fund of Syracuse University, the Otis P. Starkey Fund of the Association of American Geographers, and the American Association of University Women. Special thanks also to Dr John Western.

1. The women continue to 'farm', even in Syracuse. The family has converted much of their yards (Xai lives with her youngest son three houses away from Kue) into garden plots. Furthermore, they have a number of larger plots outside the city, scattered to the south and northeast, in a pattern not unlike traditional swidden farming. As in Laos and Thailand, the location of their 'farms' is dependent on the permission of non-Hmong.
2. Such statements draw into serious question assumptions that the Hmong in Laos practiced their traditional culture until disruptions from the so-called 'Second Indochinese War' of the 1960s and 1970s. Xai asserts that depression, widespread substance abuse, and fear of attack caused many to rethink the value of 'hard work', one of the fundamental components of Hmong ethnic identity, as early as the 1940s. Another basis of Hmong identity, independence (the word 'Hmong' meaning 'free men') was also already seriously in question, due to limitations on their ability to protect themselves, and real or imagined constraints on their migration.

References

Moore, D.L., 1990, *Dark sky, dark land: stories of the Hmong boy scouts of troop 100*, Tessera Publishing Inc., Eden Prairie, Minnesota.
Personal Narratives Group, 1989, *Interpreting women's lives: feminist theory and personal narratives*, Indiana University Press, Bloomington, Indiana.

Further reading

Downing, B.T. and Olney, D.P., 1982, *The Hmong in the West: observations and reports*, Center for Urban and Regional Affairs, University of Minnesota, Minneapolis.

Forbes Martin, S., 1992, *Refugee women*, Zed Books, London and New York

Hendricks, G.L., Downing, B.T. and Deinard, A.S., 1986, *The Hmong in transition*, Center for Migration Studies, New York.

Kelly, N., 1989, *Working with refugee women: a practical guide*, International NGO Working Group on Refugee Women, Geneva.

Quincy, K., 1988, *Hmong: history of a people*, Eastern Washington University Press, Cheney, Washington DC.

9 North and South: resettling Vietnamese refugees in Australia and the UK

Vaughan Robinson

Introduction

According to UNHCR, there are three 'durable solutions' to the refugee crisis facing many Third World countries. These are voluntary repatriation; permanent settlement in the country of first asylum; and permanent third country resettlement, usually in an advanced economy of the 'north'. At one time, the latter policy was seen as offering refugees the best prospects, and undoubtedly it was the most popular option amongst many of those in refugee camps. However, as the advanced economies slid into recession and xenophobia increased, options for long-distance resettlement withered. Countries in the north have progressively formalised and closed their borders to all but immigrants with skills in demand within the labour market (Dowty, 1987).

Permanent resettlement in the 'north' is unlikely to be a viable policy option for large numbers of Asian, Latin American or African refugees in the immediate future. Nevertheless, hundreds of thousands of people have been resettled throughout the 'north' in the past. Meanwhile, if the so-called demographic time-bomb does detonate, many 'northern' nations faced with ageing and declining populations and rising dependency ratios may be forced to turn to the 'south' for their manual and lower-paid service workers. It would therefore be premature to write off long-distance resettlement as an anachronistic option.

Given the recent hiatus in large-scale resettlement in the countries of the 'north', it is an appropriate time to assess what different governments have learned about resettling Third World refugees and to review the different policies they have employed to achieve this. In particular, this chapter looks at how two different countries – Britain and Australia – resettled the same group – the Vietnamese – and assesses their different policies and attitudes.

The two societies and their views and policies towards migration

Both Britain and Australia have traditionally been countries of immigration, this being particularly true of the two decades following the Second World War. During that period both countries required cheap and malleable labour to fuel their expanding economies. Australia, because of its climate, image and economic incentives, was able to choose its immigrants so that they were patterned in the image of the white Anglo-Saxon Christian pioneer. Indeed the White Australia Policy, introduced in 1901 and only rescinded in 1973, ensured the pre-eminence of white Europeans in the migration flows to Australia. From 1945 to 1975, the annual average net gain from migration never fell below 70,000 and for the period 1966–70 it was as high as 108,000 (Hugo, 1986). Yet less than 5 per cent of the immigrants arriving in 1966/67 were Asian (Jayasuriya and Sang, 1990) and by 1971, some 89 per cent of the Australian population had still been born in Australia, the UK, Ireland or New Zealand.

In contrast, post-war Britain had a population which shared many of the racial attitudes of its Australian counterparts (Robinson, 1987), but which no longer had the economic power or living conditions to attract those immigrants which it most desired. Indeed, it was losing population to America, Canada, South Africa and, of course, Australia. Britain tried to fill gaps in the labour market with Irish, Poles, Displaced Persons and European Volunteer Workers from the war-torn continent (Peach *et al.*, 1988), but these sources were insufficient. In desperation, employers turned to both the West Indies and the Indian subcontinent (Rose, 1969). By 1962, Britain had become a multiracial society and its immigration was dominated by black and brown groups.

As Britain became more demographically diverse, so many other facets of society – such as politics and the law and order issue – were racialised. The 1962 and 1967 Commonwealth Immigration Acts severely restricted further primary immigration of black settlers whilst still leaving white settlers largely free to enter the country. Further changes in legislation relating to immigration or nationality were enacted during the 1970s and 1980s to the point where black and Asian immigration has effectively been choked off. In 1990, for example, the net balance of migration between the West Indies and Britain was only 3,000.

Refugee policy within the UK has not been immune to similar pressures and has consequently been adjusted in the same direction, albeit more recently. After immigration policy became more restrictive, there remained some elasticity in refugee admission since the public still held long-established views of refugees as 'deserving', on humanitarian grounds. Indeed it was this traditional liberal notion (Panayi, 1992) which allowed government successfully to admit both the Ugandan Asians in 1972 and the Vietnamese in 1979. Since then, public perceptions have been muddied by the notion of economic refugees and the discussion of whether they deserve asylum in the same way as 'genuine' refugees. Weight has been lent to this view by the government's and UNHCR's refusal to accept many of the Vietnamese in Hong Kong as refugees; by their consequent decision forcibly to repatriate many of them to Vietnam; and by restrictive measures introduced in the Carriers' Liability Act and the forthcoming Asylum Bill which appear almost to criminalise certain forms of refugee status. The media, too, have played a role in reshaping public opinion. Headlines such as 'Nine out of ten "refugees" judged to be bogus' (*Daily Telegraph*, 26 June 1992) have legitimised racist and restrictive refugee policy which applies different rules and procedures to those from certain black African and Asian countries.

Many of the issues of visible minority immigration passed Australia by until the 1970s. It could still draw immigrants from its preferred pool, and awkward questions about developing policy specifically to exclude certain categories of applicant did not arise, since the White Australia Policy was still in place and since few visible minorities were, in any case, applying for entry. Black and Asian immigration did not really exist as a problem so long as cheap labour could still be attracted from Europe. Similarly, refugee policy was subjugated to the needs of the economy and humanitarian admission became an adjunct of immigration policy. Australia took some 170,000 Displaced Persons from central and east Europe in the period 1947–52 (Price, 1981) with the proviso that they spent two years in a designated job. As with migrant policy in general, single males were preferred and the scheme excluded the physically handicapped (Rivett, 1988). Other European refugees followed from Yugoslavia, Czechoslovakia and Hungary, but the criticism persisted that 'Australia was less interested in helping the unfortunate than in finding healthy and industrious "factory fodder" for its population and development programmes' (Price, 1981, p. 101).

By the end of the 1960s several developments conspired to force a shift in Australian immigration policy and to separate refugee admission from labour migration. Patterns of immigration from the 1950s until the early 1970s ensured that 'new immigrants, mostly non-British and almost wholly European, transformed Australia from a parochial monocultural society to a cosmopolitan, polyethnic, multicultural society, characterised by a marked degree of diversity and pluralism in all areas of social life' (Jayasuriya and Sang, 1990, p. 5). Britain made it clear by its decision to join the EC that the days of Commonwealth were at an end, and that Australia had to seek out an independent future rooted in its own locality and in partnership with its Asian neighbours. Liberal voices both within and outside Australia began more sharply to criticise racist immigration criteria. The response to these pressures unfolded over the next fifteen years, with first the relaxation of the White Australia Policy, and finally the rescinding of the 1901 Act in 1973, and its replacement by a non-discriminatory immigration policy. This introduced four criteria of admission: family reunion; ability to adapt to and contribute to Australian life; special eligibility; and refugees. The latter is further subdivided into two categories, those eligible as Convention refugees and those in refugee-like situations who are admitted under the Special Humanitarian Programme.

The effect of these changes has been dramatic. The proportion of immigration from Asian countries has increased sharply. Whereas it had stood at 12.5 per cent at the ending of the White Australia Policy, by 1976–77 it rose to 37 per cent. The family reunion category now constitutes around a half of all settler arrivals, with perhaps 45 per cent of these being Asians in 1988–89. The refugee intake has also been substantially expanded as a contribution to the solution of the problems of fellow ASEAN partners and as a symbol of Australia's growing world stature. From 1975, when the first annual quotas for refugee intake were announced, the importance of this category has grown to the point where around a fifth of all settler arrivals are now refugees. Governments have continued to commit themselves to annual quotas of 12–15,000 refugees, and resettled 168,000 refugees in total between 1975 and 1987 (DILGEA, 1989a).

In parallel to, and not unconnected with, changes in immigration, Australia also began to develop a formal policy of multiculturalism, with, for example, the creation of the Institute of Multicultural Affairs in 1979. Despite promising beginnings, there is no doubt that multiculturalism suffered a series of setbacks in the 1980s. The Blainey Affair[1] of 1984 involved much public discussion about the 'threat' posed by Asian immigration, and undoubtedly raised the spectre of racism and shifted public perceptions from immigrants as workers to immigrants as visible ethnic minority communities. The subsequent recession has forced multiculturalism down the political agenda (Liffman, 1988). Meanwhile, attempts to operationalise multiculturalism through non-specific government bodies and policies ('mainstreaming') is thought by some to threaten its immediate future. Nevertheless, it would still be fair to say that Australia is much more committed to multiculturalism than the UK.

The Vietnamese as refugees

Between 1975 and 1989 nearly two million refugees fled Indochina following the Vietnamese war and its aftermath in neighbouring countries. This represents one of the largest refugee movements of recent times. Those from Vietnam represent about half of this total, the remainder being Laotians and Kampucheans.

The exodus of Vietnamese has taken place in two waves, with a variety of migration vintages. The first wave comprised those who left Vietnam immediately before or after the fall of Saigon in May 1975. They numbered 135,000, were predominantly ethnic Vietnamese, came from the south of the reunited country, and left either for fear of their lives – due to their associations with the deposed regime or the Americans – or as opportunists (Viviani, 1984). Later vintages of this wave left illegally by boat over the next three years and numbered perhaps 30,000. The second wave began to leave Vietnam in mid-1978 and consisted of ethnic Chinese who were coming under increasing pressure from the government as relations between Vietnam and China deteriorated into the Third Indo-China War. The first vintage (around 230,000 people) left from the south and consisted of the large and small entrepreneurs whose livelihoods were being threatened by the government's decision to close down many private businesses. The second vintage fled from the north as conditions for ethnic Chinese deteriorated. The Hoa people were small traders, farmers and fishermen and, although it is unclear whether they were expelled by Vietnam or encouraged to leave by China (Godley, 1980), over a quarter of a million crossed into China through overland routes, whilst later departures again turned to the sea for their escape, ending their journeys in Hong Kong. During this time, ethnic Vietnamese were also leaving the country for economic reasons, largely unhindered by the government.

Neither Australia nor Britain got involved in the early resettlement efforts immediately following the end of the war. Indeed, as late as mid-1975 there were only 700 Vietnamese-born in Australia (Kelly, 1988) and the government accepted only two small quotas during 1976, amounting to 1,350 people (Price, 1981). Subsequently, two external factors precipitated more active Australian involvement in Vietnamese resettlement, namely the arrival direct by boat from Vietnam of 2,000 Vietnamese on its north coast beginning in April 1976 and peaking in mid-1978 (Viviani, 1980), and secondly the attitude of Australia's ASEAN partners who were under growing strain as the number of arrivals from Vietnam mushroomed. Their response was to put greater direct pressure on Australia to increase its own intake and also to refuel and resupply Vietnamese boats for onward transit to the Australian coast. Australia reacted by increasing its quota to 10,500 for 1978/79 and to 14,000 in 1979/80, in line with the Australian pledge given at the July 1979 Geneva conference. These admission levels made Australia the fourth most significant country for long-term resettlement and meant that by June 1985 Australia had resettled some 79,000 Vietnamese (Kelly, 1988), with a further 7,000 being accepted the following year. The peak years for admissions were 1979/80 and 1980/81 (BIR, 1990), as the Vietnamese-born population rose from 2,427 in 1976 to 41,096 in 1981, and 83,028 in 1986.

Prior to the Geneva conference of 1979, Britain had played little part in the resettlement of the Vietnamese, although by 1978 Britain was taking a small but increasing number of those rescued in the China Seas by British ships. By the beginning of 1979, the government was forced to take more urgent action by the plight of Hong Kong, its colony. The UK agreed to take an initial quota of 1,500 direct from there and also to resettle a further 1,400 who had been rescued at sea. This did not prove an adequate response to the problems of overcrowding and hostility which were beginning to surface in Hong Kong, and as a result Britain was the prime mover behind the 1979 UN Geneva conference, at which the government announced it would admit a further quota of 10,000 over the following two years. Since that time, Britain has continued to accept Vietnamese through three channels: the Orderly Departure Programme negotiated with the Vietnamese government; an additional two-year quota of 2,500 from Hong Kong announced in 1990; and family reunion. However, in reality, restrictions in Hong Kong and changes in UK legislation and practice have made it progressively harder for Vietnamese to gain entry to Britain. There are now thought to be between 22,000 and 24,000 Vietnamese in the UK, with perhaps two-thirds having arrived before the end of 1981.

The Vietnamese in Australia and the UK

Although the resettlement of the Vietnamese in both Australia and the UK was a humanitarian gesture, both countries were selective in the refugees they were willing to grant asylum.

In Australia the shape of the Vietnamese community has been formed both by deliberate selectivity on the part of government through its refugee entry criteria and by the timing of Australia's involvement in relation to the various waves and vintages of migrants. Even for refugees, there is an explicit bias in selection criteria towards those who are of most value in the labour market, namely young single men, young married couples with no children and those with skills. The elderly, those with dependants, those who are physically or mentally handicapped, widows and illiterates are less likely to gain admission (Viviani, 1984). Such overt selectivity did not go unnoticed, and criticism led the government in 1979 to agree to take 10 per cent of the refugee entry target on humanitarian grounds. Equally, from 1979 onwards, there was a deliberate attempt to correct the gender imbalance within the Vietnamese community in Australia by taking more women.

Australia's late entry into Vietnamese resettlement meant that few of the 1975 vintage of the first wave came to Australia, although some of the later boat escapees did: these very early 1975–77 arrivals would have been predominantly ethnic Vietnamese. By far the largest number of entrants in the first phase between 1975 and 1980 were, however, ethnic Chinese from the north. By 1981, the ethnic Chinese (of Vietnamese birth) in Australia outnumbered those of Vietnamese ethnicity by a ratio of 55:45. Since that time, 70 per cent of arrivals have been of Vietnamese ancestry, thereby shifting the balance between the two groups considerably, so that in the 1986 census 34 per cent of the community were Chinese and 65 per cent were Vietnamese.

Table 9.1 documents the socio-demographic characteristics of the Vietnamese in Australia. It indicates that they are, as expected, a youthful population with a median period of residence in Australia of 5.1 years, that they have few qualifications, and that 44 per cent have some difficulties speaking English.

The UK also received few of the first wave, although some of the late vintage did arrive from the camps of Hong Kong. Britain's main contribution came in two quota admissions from 1979 to 1982. Consequently, the peak of admissions coincided with the problems of the Hoa people, with Britain gaining an unbalanced Vietnamese community with almost three-quarters being ethnic Chinese, mainly from the north. Further bias was introduced by the tardiness of British selection procedures, which meant that many of the most skilled and adaptable candidates had already been made offers of settlement by other countries. Britain, too, was a rather unknown quantity for many Vietnamese who preferred to go elsewhere. Finally, it is widely reported, but not yet substantiated, that the British allowed humanitarian considerations greater weight in their selection procedures than other more economically orientated nations.

Britain did not hold a census in 1986 and the results of the 1991 census will not be made available until 1993. As a result there is no national data-set which can be used to indicate the socio-demographics of Britain's Vietnamese. Nevertheless, it is possible to piece together an interim statement of key demographic variables. As Table 9.1 reveals, the profile of Britain's Vietnamese is not markedly different to that of their Australian counterparts. They are young, have little formal education, do not yet speak English well and are predominantly Buddhist in belief. Unlike the Australian Vietnamese, they are much more likely to be ethnic Chinese. Those discrepancies which do exist between the characteristics of the Vietnamese in Britain and those in Australia would appear to stem from the greater selectivity of the latter country. Britain, for example, has taken more elderly, and a larger proportion of those without qualifications.

Reception policy

Britain and Australia have very different traditions of receiving immigrants and refugees. In the UK, provision for immigrants is usually made available through mainstreaming rather than through targeted policy instruments. The arrival of large refugee groups is a partial and temporally limited exception to this policy. In the case of the Poles, the Ugandan Asians and the Vietnamese, government did decide to intervene in the early stages of reception in order to ease adaptation. For the Vietnamese quota refugees, the government established an administrative framework (Robinson, 1985) and provided separate and additional funding. This was used to establish Reception Centres throughout the UK which would house

Table 9.1 Demographic characteristics of Vietnamese refugees in Australia and the UK (%)

	Australia 1986[1]		UK 1981/90
% male	55.0		53.0[2]
Age 0–15 yrs	21.3		36.5[2]
15–19 yrs	10.8		7.7
20–29 yrs	31.4		25.3
30–54 yrs	31.9		23.1
55–64 yrs	3.0		4.1
65+ yrs	1.7		3.3
Period of residence			
< 2 yrs	12.4		3.8[3]
2–4 yrs	30.6		7.0
5–9 yrs	51.4		40.1
10+ yrs	3.6		49.0
Qualifications			
Degree +	3.3	University	6.8[4]
Diploma	0.4	Teacher training	0.7
Trade Certificate	1.5	Technical college	6.8
Other Certificate	2.5	Secondary	48.3
None	74.1	Primary	23.1
		None	14.3
English proficiency			
Speak only English	2.2	Can shop	75.2[4]
Speak other langs & English:		Can hold conversation	54.8
very well	13.4	Needs help with forms	73.2
well	38.9	Speak English at home	5.7
not well	38.4		
not at all	5.9		
Religion			
Buddhist	36.7		59.2[4]
Christian	23.5		10.8
None	30.5		23.6
Ethnicity			
Chinese	34.1		60.0[4]
Vietnamese	65.2		38.0

Sources:

1. Bureau of Immigration Research, 1990
2. 11,300 records extracted from Charity records,1981
3. 1990 household survey of 739 Vietnamese in five cities
4. 1990 household survey, 157 household heads only

the Vietnamese for no more than three months, during which time permanent private accommodation would be located for them in the community. During their stay, they would be medically screened, taught survival English, and given orientation lessons on British society (Hale, 1992). Twenty-one million of the £23 million spent on the UK's Vietnamese programme was committed to the reception camps, following the American practice of front-end loading in which all available resources were focused on the reception phase in the hope that refugees could be made 'job-ready' and therefore relatively independent.

In Australia, the long tradition of recruiting foreign labour meant that a system already existed for receiving immigrants. Migrant Hostels had existed since the early post-war years and were used to housing individuals and families for relatively long periods of time: indeed it was quite normal for migrants to continue living in the hostels for many months after they got their first job, only leaving when they had the financial security to put down a bond on rented accommodation. The hostels were pressed into service in 1975 to accommodate the earliest arrivals, and have continued to host all non-CRSS arrivals ever since. In 1976 the Senate Standing Committee on Foreign Affairs and Defence was asked to assess their efficacy as part of a wider review of provisions for refugees (SSCFAD, 1976). They concluded that the hostels had not fully or successfully made the transition from servicing predominantly British or European settler migrants to handling non-English-speaking refugees. The absence of accurate information on the Vietnamese and their needs, and the government's failure to draw up an overall resettlement policy, meant that the hostels were forced to devise new forms of provision in an *ad hoc* fashion. To their credit, hostel staff had realised that the needs of these refugees were complex and some had been able to make innovative provision for these needs. Overall, however, the SSCFAD was critical of reception policy and of the assumption that existing practices and provision were appropriate. In 1978 the Galbally Committee was also asked to report on services for migrants, and recommended that there should be a new comprehensive initial settlement programme incorporating extensive language and orientation teaching; that greater attention should be given to the acquisition of English by migrants; that additional resources should be provided for programmes catering for non-English speakers; that migrant resource centres should be established; that more information should be made available to migrants about welfare service provision; and that special programmes and funding were necessary to stimulate multiculturalism. The hostels responded to these challenges and also to the rundown of sponsored and organised settler migration by reshaping their form and role. The Migrant Centres, as they are now known, are much smaller in number and are designed specifically to receive Australia's annual quota of refugees. They offer modern purpose-built single-family or shared houses. During their fifteen-week stay in the centre refugees have access to housing and employment officers as well as dental and medical care, counsellors, orientation classes and intensive language tuition. Research also shows that the Migrant Centres remain important to refugees after resettlement, and that three-quarters have made subsequent visits there.

Resettlement policy

As with initial settlement policy, the two countries had diverging traditions in the field of resettlement. Britain had a long history of direct intervention in the settlement patterns of both migrants and refugees. This usually took the form of managed dispersal, either across the country as a whole or within particular cities (see Robinson, 1992 for a more detailed discussion of the development of policy). In contrast, Australia more frequently allowed either labour market forces or migrant choice to determine the destination of individuals as they left the migrant hostels. These generalisations are also true of the initial quota phases of the two countries' responses to the Vietnamese crisis.

The British Home Office – through the Joint Committee for Refugees from Vietnam – decided early in the programme that it wanted the Vietnamese to be dispersed into small clusters of between four and ten families in any one locality. Dispersal was thought to have a number of advantages: these included the willingness of local authorities to offer housing if refugee numbers were small; the limited capacity of the local support groups which were established to assist in the early phases of resettlement; the implicit wish of government to see rapid assimilation; a desire to avoid ghettoisation; and the reduced likelihood of a local political backlash from extreme right-wing groups.

In practice, a fatal weakness of the dispersal policy was that it relied wholly upon local authorities coming forward with voluntary offers of public housing when they knew that they would receive no extra funds to replace these and no additional resources to service the ensuing Vietnamese community. As a result, the housing offers were neither abundant in number nor were they evenly spread around the country. The latter was also true, therefore, of the Vietnamese (Robinson, 1985; Robinson and Hale, 1989; Robinson, 1992), who found themselves distributed in a polarised pattern, with a minority located in remote and rural areas and a majority found in the inner areas of Britain's most deprived cities.

Because of front-end loading, the practicalities of local resettlement in the UK were delegated to volunteer support groups who took on the task of settling 'their' families in their new houses, helping furnish these, explaining the mechanics of everyday life in Britain, orientating them to the British way of life, assisting them with access to mainstream welfare benefits, and generally being supportive. None of the individuals was paid, so volunteers tended to be drawn from the middle class and from organisations which already had a well developed tradition of voluntary helping, such as local church groups. The support group concept and its efficacy have never been thoroughly reviewed in the UK in relation to the Vietnamese programme. Discussions with support group members in South Wales reveal them to have a negative attitude to the experience. They felt they had been left to their own devices too much, that the resettlement charities had failed to provide them with the basic equipment they needed (English–Vietnamese dictionaries were almost unobtainable in the UK in 1980), and that there had been an almost complete absence of information about the Vietnamese, their characteristics, their needs, and their beliefs. As one worker put it 'we never knew what to expect'. They also felt that they had gained at a personal level from the experience, but expressed feelings of having been 'used' by government and resettlement charities. It seemed unlikely that they would become involved in any similar project in the future, their skills and experience thereby effectively being lost. Finally it was clear from discussions that they had received no adequate training for their new roles and that they therefore had to rely upon personal qualities to get by: assistance would thus have varied considerably between different localities, different support groups and different individuals within those groups. To a certain extent, this basic weakness has been replicated in subsequent central government provision, where those Vietnamese living in areas of concentration have access to Vietnamese community workers funded through Section 11 or the Urban Programme, whilst the dispersed Vietnamese do not.

Australian policy for the early arrivals differed markedly from that of the UK. In line with the Australian view that refugees are effectively a sub-type of migrant and could therefore be accommodated within existing migrant and multiculturalist policies, the Vietnamese were allowed to make their own resettlement decisions after leaving the Migrant Centres. Each centre had its own housing officer who was responsible for housing advice, but refugees were free to live in whichever part of the country they wished and in whatever type of accommodation they felt they could afford. Unlike in Britain, where refugees were notionally given a choice between a small number of resettlement localities about which they really knew nothing, the presence of a larger and longer-established Vietnamese community within Australia meant that individuals leaving the Migrant Centres had access to a source of knowledge which could be used to guide them in their decision-making. As a result, surveys show that only 1–7 per cent (DIEA, 1982) and 5 per cent (Keys Young, 1980) of Vietnamese actually used the centre staff to help them locate suitable accommodation. Once relocated in the community, the very earliest arrivals were not well provided for. The SSCFAD report (1976) was very critical of resettlement efforts, commenting upon the inadequacy of language tuition and therefore the inability of the Vietnamese to access mainstream services, the failure to visit families after resettlement, confusion about the role of different commonwealth and state institutions, and competition between these different organs of government. Similar criticisms have been voiced by others (Viviani, 1980; 1984). The Galbally Report (1978) was, however, a turning point. It outlined a new and expanded role for voluntary ethnic organisations, recommended that funds should be made available to staff these with professional workers, and suggested the need for new Migrant Resource Centres.

After the Galbally Report, the Australian government pursued a dualistic policy towards refugee resettlement with the majority of new arrivals being resettled through Migrant Centres but with others being accommodated on the new Community Refugee Settlement Scheme (CRSS). The latter came into operation nationally in October 1979, and was an organised sponsorship scheme in which voluntary groups could 'adopt' one or more Indochinese families. The government would then arrange and pay for that family's transfer to Australia, where they would be passed to the voluntary group for immediate settlement without the need to spend time in a Migrant Centre. The sponsoring group would have to take full and financial responsibility for housing, furniture and clothing in the short term and also had long-term responsibility for helping the family gain its welfare entitlements, work and access to language classes. Sponsors were also expected to provide intensive and high quality emotional support for a period of at least six months to a year. The stated rationale of CRSS was to provide 'extra settlement support offered by the more personal approach' (DILGEA, 1989b) to those who had special settlement needs, such as large or single-parent families. By 1991, some 30,000 refugees had experienced the scheme and it had been widened to include groups other than the Indochinese (DILGEA, 1991).

At the time of its introduction, CRSS was designed to allow the community to become directly involved in refugee matters, provide an alternative method of resettlement which might be more suited to some individuals' needs, and to raise public awareness of the refugee issue. Commentators feel there was also a hidden agenda behind the scheme, namely to disperse refugees spatially to reduce the hostility being voiced against Asian immigration, and to reduce costs. The scheme has been officially monitored twice since its inception. A first report argued that CRSS was successfully building bridges between the Australian and Vietnamese communities, thereby reducing antipathy. In a second appraisal, Touche Ross (1987) reported that the recipients of CRSS praised the scheme and felt they had benefited from it even though, in statistical terms, they were no better off when measured against a range of resettlement variables. External researchers also evaluated the scheme. Viviani (1984) argued that the non-metropolitan CRSS candidates were disadvantaged in the labour market, that the scheme was inherently discriminatory in its application only to certain groups, that the ability to circumvent the Migrant Centres represented a public health risk, that refugees were being asked to choose between CRSS and conventional resettlement without having complete information, and that coercion was used in some cases. The scheme was revised in 1982 to give CRSS support groups an initial resettlement grant (worth $1.2 million in 1991, or $400 per person), and it was revised further in 1982 when it was decided to send CRSS candidates only to large towns and adjacent rural areas.

Resettlement outcomes

One of the most important factors affecting the opportunities offered to refugees by resettlement is the spatial distribution of that group. Although different regions, cities and neighbourhoods offer sharply contrasting economic and social prospects to their residents, this fact is too often ignored by those who devise resettlement policies. It is this spatial component of resettlement which will form the focus of the remainder of the chapter. It should be remembered, however, that spatial location forms an indirect surrogate for a range of more conventional resettlement measures such as access to employment, access to language tuition, access to housing, prospects for social mobility, and access to health and welfare services.

Australian geographers have been far more active than their British counterparts in the analysis of Vietnamese settlement, their work having been undertaken on a variety of spatial scales. As Table 9.2 demonstrates, the Vietnamese are highly spatially concentrated at the regional (state) level, with over 40 per cent of all Vietnamese resident in New South Wales, and a further 35 per cent located in Victoria. In addition, this pattern of concentration does not appear to have altered greatly between the two censuses of 1981 and 1986 (BIR, 1990) with 76 per cent of all intercensal growth being absorbed by these two states. What is also important is that the Vietnamese are under-represented in those states which are attracting the most rapid growth in Australian-born population, namely Western Australia and Queensland (Hugo, 1990a). Such a pattern indicates growing polarisation. Analysts suggest a variety of reasons for such sharp regional concentration. Hugo (1990b) argues that employment prospects are critical but not the sole determinant, although he also suggests the need for greater study of refugee decision-making processes. Coughlan (1989a) agrees about the importance of employment prospects but also draws attention to the significance of climate (Tasmania) and geographical isolation (Northern Territories) as negative factors discouraging settlement. Burnley (1982), however, sees the location of Migrant Centres as a pre-eminent causal variable.

Table 9.2 Regional distribution of Vietnamese in Australia, 1981 and 1986 (%)

	1981	1986
New South Wales	41.2	40.9
Victoria	31.2	33.6
Queensland	8.5	7.5
South Australia	9.4	8.4
Western Australia	6.8	7.1
Tasmania	0.5	0.3
Northern Territory	0.5	0.5
Australian Capital Territory	1.9	1.6

Source: Bureau of Immigration Research, 1990

Vietnamese are also highly concentrated within states. The Bureau of Immigration Research (1990) notes that between 80 and 95 per cent of the Vietnamese within each state reside in the capital city. As a result, 96 per cent of all Vietnamese live in the eight capital cities, and 72 per cent live in Sydney and Melbourne alone. Only 4 per cent do not live in cities with populations of more than 100,000, and the Vietnamese are relatively absent from recreational, retirement or industrial centres.

Even within cities, the Vietnamese are spatially localised. Hugo (1990a), for instance, notes that the Vietnamese record Indices of Dissimilarity (ID) of 66 within the metropolitan parts of New South Wales and 63 within the comparable zones of Victoria and South Australia. He also demonstrates how, within Adelaide in 1986, 61 per cent of all Vietnamese were found in only three of the metropolitan Local Government Areas, and Vietnamese resided in less than 40 per cent of the area's Census Districts. Five years previously they had recorded an ID of 78 at this finer CD-scale. Burnley (1989) commented upon similar levels of concentration within Sydney, with a 1981 ID of 65 and major 1986 concentrations in the LGAs of Fairfield, Canterbury, Marrickville and Bankstown.

Whilst concentration within Australian cities has thus been shown, it remains important to consider its causes and the location of the resulting ethnic enclaves since these are likely to be greater determinants of life-chances. Again Australian researchers have given a good deal of thought to these issues. Hugo (1990b) described five processes shaping segregation in Australian cities, and these can be amplified by reference to the work of others. The timing of the peak of the wave of immigration is important since it determines which employment and housing opportunities are on offer at the time: whilst the main location of cheap rental accommodation in Australian cities in the immediate post-war years was in the inner-city, by the 1970s this had changed, with modern speculative 'unit' developments in the outer suburbs being the most affordable and available. Refugee groups arriving in Australia at these two different times would therefore be channelled to different parts of the city by the housing system alone. The same might also be said of employment opportunities, with the concentration of semi-skilled and unskilled manufacturing work in the industrial suburbs of Melbourne, Sydney and Adelaide. Secondly, the scale of immigration is a determinant of whether ethnic areas develop and persist or whether spatial clustering is a temporary phenomenon. Coughlan (1989a) shows how the fifteen-fold increase in Indochinese in Australia from 1976 to 1981 was associated with the formation of ethnic neighbourhoods, such as Cabramatta in Sydney with its own ethnic services and facilities: by 1981 the LGA containing Cabramatta housed nearly 9 per cent of all Australia's Vietnamese, and the Keys Young Report (1980) showed that concentration there was likely to increase since it was the preferred destination for those refugees newly arrived in the country and for those migrating within Australia. This latter point introduces a third process: the attraction of an ethnic community once it has become established. Keys Young also demonstrated why those newly-arrived refugees leaving Migrant Centres were choosing to settle in Fairfield LGA. Forty-five per cent were opting for Fairfield because they were going to friends/relations or to accommodation arranged by them; 36 per cent wished to be near to community services; 28 per cent wanted to be close to the area in which their friends or relations lived; whilst 24 per cent felt proximity to the ethnic community was important. In other words, the early ports-of-entry develop a settlement momentum which is a powerful magnet for later arrivals.

The location of the earliest centres of settlement is critical to the later settlement pattern of any group. Burnley (1982) is firmly of the opinion that the siting of Migrant Centres in the outer industrial suburbs of the state capitals was critical to the subsequent settlement of post-war refugees in nearby neighbourhoods. He argues that refugees were largely without their own transport and therefore came to know only adjacent neighbourhoods; as a result it was to these areas that they looked for their first accommodation. This appears to have been borne out by the Vietnamese experience. Wilson (1990) describes how most of his sample of Sydney Vietnamese leaving a Migrant Centre settled within 11 km of it, whilst 60 per cent of respondents moved less than 5 km, even though adjacent neighbourhoods also contained cheap accommodation and manual employment opportunities. Hugo (1990a) demonstrates how the inherited location of the Pennington Migrant Centre in Adelaide was critical to the subsequent development of Vietnamese settlement in the adjacent Woodville, Enfield and Salisbury LGAs in the north west of the city. It is not surprising, therefore, that one of the main conclusions of the Keys Young report (1980) was that 'it would appear ... little thought has been given to the implications for thousands of migrants and refugees – as well as the rest of the community – of a seemingly simple decision of where to physically locate a Migrant Centre'. The final process shaping settlement patterns in Australian cities is the issue of language. Hugo (1990b) argues that those not able to speak English seek greater initial spatial concentration in order to ensure that their action space is dominated by people who speak the same language.

The social corollaries of Vietnamese spatial concentration in the outer suburbs near to the Migrant Centres can be seen in the types of housing occupied and the employment opportunities available in these areas. Using ecological correlation, Hugo (1990a) concludes that 'there is a strong positive association between the distribution of the Vietnamese and the distribution of a number of indexes of low socio-economic status – low incomes, high levels of unemployment, [and] state government housing'. Others, such as Coughlan (1989b), the BIR (1990) and Burnley (1989) have derived similar conclusions from analysis of individual or household data.

Table 9.3 Regional distribution of the Vietnamese in the UK at resettlement and in 1985–88 (%)

	Resettlement	1985–8
South East	45	53
East Anglia	3	2
South West	8	3
West Midlands	9	18
East Midlands	4	4
Yorkshire	6	2
North West	9	14
North	4	1
Wales	6	0
Scotland	5	3

Source: Robinson and Hale, 1989

British research into the spatial dimensions of Vietnamese resettlement is still in its infancy, no doubt handicapped by the absence of a 1986 census. Nevertheless, authors have been able to assemble alternative data-sets which provide a clear and detailed picture both of settlement and longitudinal changes in settlement (Robinson and Hale, 1989). Britain's Vietnamese are also concentrated within particular (economic) regions of the country (Table 9.3), with around half of all households being found in the South East. Table 9.3 also indicates a trend not seen in the Australian data, namely the very sharp increase in concentration at the regional level over time. It is clear that the geographical margins of the country have lost the majority of their Vietnamese populations to the major industrial regions of the South East, West Midlands and North West. Wales, for example, saw its share of the Vietnamese population fall from 6 per cent at resettlement to less than 0.5 per cent by the period 1985–88 and the North experienced losses of 75 per cent. These trends are contrary to those recorded by the indigenous white population and demonstrate how, even at this coarse spatial level of analysis, the Vietnamese are becoming increasingly polarised within the UK. This is confirmed by the finding that Vietnamese were present in 81 per cent of the country's Local Labour Market Areas at resettlement but only 56 per cent four years later.

The Vietnamese in the UK are almost exclusively urban dwellers, with only 2 per cent of all households being resettled in truly rural areas. Indeed, despite the government's dispersal policy, 56 per cent of all Vietnamese were resettled in only ten metropolitan areas (Table 9.4). Spatial concentration of the Vietnamese has grown further since that time, 82 per cent of households being located within the same ten cities by 1985, with three-quarters of all Vietnamese being found in London, Birmingham or Manchester. It is instructive to note that these are the very urban areas which are losing indigenous population through counterurbanisation, and are also experiencing the most savage job losses through recession and restructuring.

Table 9.4 Urban concentration of the Vietnamese in the UK at resettlement and in 1985 (%)

	Resettlement	1985
London	29.0	47.9
Birmingham	6.4	17.5
Liverpool	4.2	1.8
Manchester	3.7	9.2
Bristol	3.2	1.4
Newcastle	2.3	0.9
Leeds	2.1	1.4
Glasgow	1.9	0.9
Cardiff	1.7	0.0
Edinburgh	1.4	1.4

Source: calculated from around 11,000 entries extracted from Charity records

Concentration is equally marked within these urban areas, although there has been little research at this level as yet. Robinson and Hale (1989) and Robinson (1990) have both demonstrated how the Vietnamese population in London is very unevenly distributed with particular concentrations in Southwark, Lambeth, Greenwich, Tower Hamlets and Bexley, all of which are inner-zones losing white population. Charity records indicate an equally high degree of concentration within Birmingham in 1988, with 47 per cent of all Vietnamese found in Handsworth and a further 15 per cent located in Aston, both inner-city wards characterised by social deprivation, poor fabric and pre-existing ethnic minority settlement. These concentrations have maintained their relative importance since resettlement and have been consistently attracting new Vietnamese households from outside the city: over 70 per cent of households moving into Birmingham have settled in these two wards, most having moved directly over long distances from the north of

England or from Scotland. This highlights the considerable redistribution of Vietnamese which has occurred since, and because of, dispersed resettlement. Research by Robinson and Hale (1989) and Robinson (1992) has, for instance, shown that 51 per cent of all Vietnamese households have opted to leave the security of accommodation found for them during resettlement, and that approximately one-third of movers had relocated within two years of settlement. Some households had moved six times in as many years, often over a long distance to a major city and then frequently over short distances within that city in the search for suitable accommodation.

Some of the social corollaries of the pattern of Vietnamese settlement within the UK can be gathered from comparing the urban distribution of Vietnamese with recent national quality of life studies. Rogerson *et al.* (1988) attempted to develop a rank order of the quality of life within the thirty-eight largest cities in Britain. They found that the three main centres of Vietnamese settlement recorded uniformly low ranks (denoting poor quality of life): London was 34th, Birmingham 38th, and Manchester 30th. Much the same conclusions can be derived from analyses at the intra-urban level. When a national typology of the socio-economic characteristics of all the UK's census Enumeration Districts (ED) was applied to Birmingham, it revealed that nearly 48 per cent of the city's Vietnamese lived – at resettlement – in only one neighbourhood type, characterised by large young families, containing semi-skilled and unskilled workers living in cramped owner-occupied or rented housing. A further 12 per cent lived in EDs described as containing unskilled families, high unemployment, ethnic groups and council flats. In contrast less than one per cent of the Vietnamese lived in the two most prestigious neighbourhood types. By 1988 the situation had changed little, with the respective percentages of Vietnamese in the different neighbourhood types being 51, 12 and 0.8. Clearly, Vietnamese are not only concentrated, but they are concentrated into some of the least prosperous or desirable parts of the country. It is perhaps not surprising that a national survey of Vietnamese households in 1990 found only 25 per cent in employment, 7 per cent illegally squatting in order to gain housing and a further 7 per cent without any permanent shelter.

Conclusion

At a practical level, this study has raised a number of issues which need to be considered by any government or agency planning refugee reception and resettlement in an advanced capitalist society. Four main issues stand out as being particularly important.

First, governments have to decide whether they are seeking refugee assimilation or integration, and therefore whether they are willing to accept the development of ethnic concentrations within particular regions, cities and parts of cities. The British government appears unwilling to do so (Robinson, 1992), and has consequently forfeited the potential advantages offered to refugees by the evolution of their own communities. These advantages are now well documented in both the British and Australian literature, and appear to have been accepted by an Australian government genuinely committed to multiculturalism.

Secondly, administrations then need to decide whether they wish to impose patterns of resettlement on refugees or allow them to develop their own. In Britain, resettlement was directly managed by the Home Office and the JCRV, who imposed a particular settlement pattern. This barely lasted two years, was destroyed by the Vietnamese whom it was ostensibly designed to assist, and produced few, if any, tangible benefits. In Australia the outcome of the CRS scheme depended upon small groups making the decision to host refugee families and this therefore also produced an externally driven pattern of settlement in which the Vietnamese had no say. Again, secondary migration has undermined its long-term benefit. In contrast, the conventional Migrant Centre resettlement route pursued by many migrants and most refugees in Australia involves individual resettlement to an adjacent neighbourhood of the refugee's choice: the settlement patterns produced by this process have been enduring and have been shown to be valuable in the process of adaptation. This suggests that imposed settlement patterns rarely produce satisfactory outcomes for the refugees, who then also have to bear their subsequent economic, social and psychological costs. However it is also true that where refugees have been allowed to determine their own settlement patterns, concentrations have often occurred in cities and parts of cities which do not offer optimal economic or housing opportunities. The ideal might be to allow refugees to make their own resettlement choices after leaving a Migrant Reception Centre but to ensure that the location of these centres is monitored and adjusted to structural changes in local space-economies, so that appropriate opportunities are available in the adjacent neighbourhoods.

Thirdly, receiving societies need to establish clear and sensible goals against which their refugee resettlement policies can be evaluated. In Australia, refugees are allowed to establish their own priorities. The Vietnamese have demonstrated that their self-defined goals are the recreation of an ethnic community and economic and social mobility. In Britain, the measure of resettlement success for the Vietnamese programme was again imposed: it was the proportion that found housing, regardless of the location of that accommodation or its quality. Surely, the achievement of economic independence through language acquisition and employment in the labour market would have been more appropriate goals, especially at a time of deep recession?

Fourthly, mechanisms of achieving goals are also at issue. How, for instance, should governments respond to public concerns about immigration and refugees? Should they try to change public opinion through education and through opening the resettlement programme to volunteer host groups as they have in Australia with the CRS scheme? Or should they bow to public opinion, as the British government did in 1979, and seek to make the Vietnamese invisible by dispersing them throughout the land? Should governments adopt front-end loading and leave refugees to negotiate their own long-term resettlement with the attendant risks of isolation, misunderstanding and lack of understanding? Or should they, as the Australians have, create a set of institutions and facilities that are there in the long term, such as the Migrant Centres, the Migrant Resource Centres and the Telephone Interpreter Service? Should administrations rely upon general welfare services and hope these can be adequately accessed by newly-arrived refugee groups, as the UK has done, or is it better to have targeted programmes of resourcing such as those suggested by Galbally and made possible by the reeducation of the general public to see refugees as genuinely deserving?

Lastly, if resettlement policy is going to be refugee-driven, it is vital to ensure that those who are being asked to make choices are well informed. If refugees decide to live in one city or one neighbourhood because they know no other, they are really no better off than those who are directed to an area by an interventionist administration.

At a different level, the comparison of the Vietnamese programmes in Australia and Britain highlights that analysis of refugee issues should not and cannot be marginalised from broader processes at work in a given society. This case study demonstrates how the reception and resettlement of refugees in any advanced society must be seen against the background of that society's experience of and general policy towards immigration, its belief in and commitment to multiculturalism, its preferred role for the individual versus the state in welfare provision, and the political and racial ideologies which underpin these factors. The multiculturalism issue provides us with an excellent example of how it is only possible to understand refugee resettlement policies when these are seen in relation to broader societal philosophies. In Australia, refugee resettlement is part and parcel of a coherent policy towards ethnic diversity, rooted in a society which is opening its horizons and celebrating its diversity. The same cannot be said of Britain with its piecemeal policy towards (black) 'immigrants', its grudging acceptance of heterogeneity, and its increasingly Eurocentric myopia.

Comparison between Australia and the UK demonstrates that it is necessary to understand why the two administrations decided to admit the Vietnamese before it is possible to understand their ensuing resettlement policies. In Britain's case, the agreement to resettle Vietnamese marked the grudging fulfilment of imperial obligations, as Britain self-consciously played its high-profile part in the solution of one of Hong Kong's most pressing problems, one which could potentially have disrupted the smooth transition of power in 1997. Admission of the Vietnamese marked the closing of an imperial door prior to a retreat into a more restrictive, selective and myopic EC refugee regime. In contrast, Australia's admission of Vietnamese (amongst other Indochinese) signifies a new departure. It reflects Australia's realisation that it is an Asian–Pacific country which has to co-exist with its neighbours and become an active member of that regional grouping. The admission of Vietnamese in unprecedented numbers is a tangible affirmation of that realisation. That is perhaps why the arrival of the Vietnamese was marked by such debate and dissension, not because of the characteristics of the Vietnamese themselves or their numbers, but because it symbolised a new destiny and the casting off of old links and sentimental attachments. Not only did the decision to admit mark a symbolic end to the White Australia Policy but it also signified that Australia was mature enough to face up to the realities of multiculturalism and to celebrate its ethnic diversity. If only Britain could do the same.

Note

1.   The 'Blainey Affair' was a heated national debate touched off in 1984 by the historian Geoffrey Blainey, who argued that mass Asian immigration would impact upon levels of unemployment and community tolerance.

References

BIR (Bureau of Immigration Research), 1990, *Community profiles: Vietnam born*, Australian Government Publishing Service, Canberra.

Burnley, I., 1982, *Population, society and environment in Australia*, Shillington House, Melbourne.

Burnley, I., 1989, 'Settlement dimensions of the Vietnam-born population in metropolitan Sydney', *Australian Geographical Studies*, **27** (2): 129–54.

Coughlan, J.E., 1989a, *The spatial distribution and concentration of Australia's three Indochinese-born Communities*, Griffith University CSAAR, Nathan, New South Wales.

Coughlan, J.E., 1989b, *A comparative study of the labour force performance of Indochinese born immigrants in Australia*, Griffith University CSAAR, Nathan, New South Wales.

DIEA (Department of Immigration and Ethnic Affairs), 1982, *Please listen to what I'm not saying*, Australian Government Publishing Service, Canberra.

DILGEA (Department of Immigration, Local Government and Ethnic Affairs), 1989a, *Australia's refugee resettlement programs*, Australian Government Publishing Service, Canberra.

DILGEA, 1989b, *The Community Refugee Settlement Scheme*, Australian Government Publishing Service, Canberra.

DILGEA, 1991, *Our good friends: Australians helping refugees to a new life*, Australian Government Publishing Service, Canberra.

Dowty, A., 1987, *Closed borders: the contemporary assault on the freedom of movement*, Yale University Press, London.

Galbally, F., 1978, *Migrant services and programs*, Australian Government Publishing Service, Canberra.

Godley, M., 1980, 'A Summer cruise to nowhere: China and the Vietnamese Chinese in perspective', *Australian Journal of Chinese Affairs*, **4**: 35–59.

Hale, S., 1992, 'The reception and resettlement of Vietnamese refugees in Britain' in V. Robinson, ed., *The international refugee crisis: British and Canadian responses*, Macmillan, Basingstoke.

Hugo, G., 1986, *Australia's changing population*, Oxford University Press, Oxford.

Hugo, G., 1990a, 'Adaptation of Vietnamese in Australia', *South East Asian Journal of Social Science*, **18** (1): 182–210.

Hugo, G., 1990b, 'Demographic and spatial aspects of immigration', in M. Wooden *et al.*, eds, *Australian immigration: a survey of the issues*, Australian Government Publishing Service, Canberra.

Jayasuriya, L. and Sang, D., 1990, 'Asian immigration: past and current trends', *Current Affairs Bulletin*, **66** (11): 4–14.

Kelly, P., 1988, 'Vietnamese settlement', in J. Jupp, ed., *The Australian people*, Angus & Robertson, North Ryde, New South Wales.

Keys Young, 1980, *The settlement process of the Vietnamese, Lao, Kampuchean and Timorese in Sydney*, Department of Immigration and Ethnic Affairs, Sydney.

Liffman, M., 1988, 'Multicultural policy', in J. Jupp, ed., *The Australian people*, Angus & Robertson, North Ryde, New South Wales.

Panayi, P., 1992, 'Refugees in twentieth-century Britain', in V. Robinson, ed., *The international refugee crisis: British and Canadian responses*, Macmillan, Basingstoke, UK.

Peach, C., Robinson, V., Maxted, J. and Chance, J., 1988, 'Immigration and ethnicity', in A.H. Halsey, ed., *British social trends since 1900*, Macmillan, Basingstoke, UK.

Price, C., 1981, 'Immigration policies and refugees in Australia', *International Migration Review*, **15** (1–2): 99–108.

Rivett, K., 1988, 'Refugees', in J. Jupp, ed., *The Australian people*, Angus & Robertson, North Ryde, New South Wales.

Robinson, V., 1985, 'The Vietnamese reception and resettlement programme in the UK', *Ethnic Groups*, **6** (4): 305–30.

Robinson, V., 1987, 'Regional variations in attitudes to race', in P. Jackson, ed., *Race and racism*, Allen & Unwin, London.

Robinson, V., 1990, 'Up the creek without a paddle? Britain's boat people ten years on', *Geography*, **74** (4): 332–8.

Robinson, V., 1992, 'British policy towards the settlement patterns of ethnic groups', in V. Robinson, ed., *The international refugee crisis: British and Canadian responses*, Macmillan, Basingstoke, UK.

Robinson, V. and Hale, S., 1989, *The geography of Vietnamese secondary migration in the UK*, Warwick University Centre for Research in Ethnic Relations, Coventry, UK.

Rogerson, R.J., Findlay, A. and Morris, A.S., 1988, 'The best cities to live in', *Town and Country Planning*, **57** (10): 270–73.

Rose, E.J.B., 1969, *Colour and citizenship*, Oxford University Press, London.

SSCFAD (Senate Standing Committee on Foreign Affairs and Defence), 1976, *Australia and the refugee problem*, Australian Government Publishing Service, Canberra.

Touche Ross, 1987, *Report on the effectiveness of the Community Refugee Resettlement Scheme*, Department of Immigration and Ethnic Affairs, Canberra.

Viviani, N., 1980, *The Vietnamese in Australia: new problems in old forms*, Griffith University CSAAR, Nathan, New South Wales.

Viviani, N., 1984, *The long journey: Vietnamese migration and settlement in Australia*, Melbourne University Press, Melbourne.

Wilson, W., 1990, 'Residential relocation and settlement adjustment of Vietnamese refugees in Sydney', *Australian Geographical Studies*, **28** (2): 155–77.

Further reading

Burnley, I., 1989, 'Settlement dimensions of the Vietnam-born population in metropolitan Sydney', *Australian Geographical Studies*, **27** (2): 129–54.

Clark, C., Peach, C. and Vertovec, S., eds, *South Asians overseas: migration and ethnicity*, Cambridge University Press, Cambridge, UK.

Cox, D.R., 1986, 'Australia: a record of generosity', *Refugees*, **33**: 17–20.

Robinson, V., 1990, 'Up the creek without a paddle? Britain's boat people ten years on', *Geography*, **74** (4): 332–8.

Rogge, J.R., 1987, 'The Indochinese diaspora: where have all the refugees gone?', *Canadian Geographer*, **29** (1): 62–72.

PART IV

New directions, new developments

10 Refugees and the environment

JoAnn McGregor

Introduction

This chapter considers the link between environmental change and forced migration. The first part focuses on the recent trend of using the term 'environmental refugee' in describing environmental disruptions as causes of migration. It is argued that, although commonly used, the category 'environmental refugee' confuses rather than clarifies the position of such forced migrants, since it lacks both a conceptual and a legal basis. The second part of the chapter then considers the natural resource needs and ecological impact of refugees. The misleading nature of the usual stereotypes and general statements of environmental damage caused by refugees is clear in the few specific, local studies available.

The dynamic of local ecological change in areas affected by refugees requires an understanding of the local ecology, the relationships between refugees and their hosts, and broader patterns of economic change. Failing this, the situation can be wrongly presented as a battle between increased population and available land, rather than as a negotiated, and often conflictual, partitioning of resources between different groups.

Are there environmental refugees?

'Environmental refugee' is a term used to describe people displaced through natural and man-made disasters, and environmental degradation (El-Hinnawi, 1985; Jacobson, 1988; Tickell, 1989a; 1989b). El-Hinnawi (1985) offers a definition of environmental refugees as 'people who have been forced to leave their traditional habitat, temporarily or permanently, because of a marked environmental disruption (natural and/or triggered by people) that jeopardised their existence and/or seriously affected the quality of their life'. He continues by drawing a contrast with people 'displaced for political reasons or by civil strife, and migrants seeking better jobs purely on economic grounds', whom he does not consider to be environmental refugees. Although this analysis excludes war-displaced people from the category 'environmental refugee', El-Hinnawi does make exceptions, such as those displaced during the Indochinese war due to the effects of chemical herbicides, or in other contexts due to the 'remnants of war' such as unexploded mines, bombs, and shells. Ecological change and displacement may result from the disruption (either during war or peacetime) of the economy, of resource-use patterns, and of trade networks, but this is not considered in his analysis.

Different types of 'environmental refugee' are generally distinguished in the literature. One type comprises those temporarily displaced as the result of sudden environmental change which is reversible. This group lumps together those who flee natural disasters and industrial accidents. A second type includes people permanently displaced through long-term or irreversible environmental change, such as those forced to move by dam construction or sea level rise (some authors also include desertification). A third type is defined as those who leave in search of a better quality of life as environmental degradation has eroded their resource base, for example through salination of the soil or deforestation.

The addition of the prefix 'environmental' to the category 'refugee' is unhelpful for a number of reasons. First, there is the misleading implication that environmental change as a cause of flight can be meaningfully separated from political and economic changes. Secondly, there is in any case no legal basis for the definition of 'environmental refugee': indeed the prefix 'environmental' can undermine current trends towards using broad human rights criteria in determining refugee status. Thirdly, issues arise from these conceptual and legal problems which concern international and governmental responsibility for humanitarian assistance. These points are elaborated below.

Ambiguity of the term 'environmental'

The use of the term 'environmental' can imply a false separation between overlapping and interrelated categories. For example, the implication of using the term 'environmental refugee' is that political, economic, and environmental causes of migration can be separated. In practice, this is seldom the case, as argued repeatedly in recent literature on disasters which highlights the role of human agency, either in the disaster itself, or in causing populations to be more vulnerable to disasters (Wijkman and Timberlake, 1984; see also Hewitt, 1983).

There is a large literature on the political roots of environmental problems, which is particularly well developed in relation to drought and famine. Sen's understanding of famine is rooted not in a departure from a climatic norm, but in socio-economic processes which result in a failure of 'exchange entitlements' (Sen, 1981; Drèze and Sen, 1989). People may become victims because their coping strategies have been undermined directly or indirectly by the state, or their recovery prevented by failure to provide insurance and relief, as in the Dust Bowl disasters in the United States in the nineteenth and early twentieth century (Warrick, 1983).

Apart from economic processes, war itself also commonly interferes with people's strategies for coping with environmental variability. In the case of drought, for example, famine most commonly occurs in those countries affected by war (Duffield, 1991). On the causes of the Ethiopian famine of 1984–85, Clay and Holcombe (1985) note:

> Interviews conducted with famine victims from Tigray in eastern Sudan indicate that insects, drought and Ethiopian military policies were the three leading causes of declines in agricultural production. Most of those interviewed stated that armyworms were the main reason for crop failure in 1984–85. Armyworms can destroy a crop overnight, but the long-term stripping of the region's productive assets by the Ethiopian military was no

less debilitating. 95 per cent of the famine victims who fled to the Sudan before the end of 1984 reported that in their villages the Ethiopian army had destroyed crops in the fields and grain they had harvested. ... The army routinely attacks during planting and harvesting; attacks that delay planting increase the destruction by insect and weed pests.

On the causes of the 1987–88 Ethiopian famine, Clay *et al.* (1988, p. 3) note the correlation between famine areas and specific government policies: in Tigray and Eritrea, famine prevailed in areas outside government control and under military attack; in Tigray and Wollo, famine occurred in areas of forced resettlement; in northern Bale, Hararghe and Shoa, famine occurred as a result of the government villagisation programme; and in Wolega, Illubabor and other administrative regions the forcibly resettled were themselves unsettled and local production was disrupted.

Studies of migrants' actual decisions to flee show that they are commonly much more complicated than the simple environmental push that the term 'environmental refugee' can misleadingly imply. Migration can be one of a variety of survival strategies pursued by families either simultaneously or consecutively with others, such as eating bush foods, selling assets, wage-labour, or short-distance migration to less affected areas. Pankhurst's (1992) description of livelihood changes in the 1987–88 drought in Ethiopia and their relation to migration shows how coping strategies were undermined by state restrictions on travel, declining opportunities for both rural and urban wage-labour and increasingly unfavourable terms of trade as grain prices rocketed. He reveals how aid itself placed pressure on peasants to resettle.

In the context of political/economic and environmental problems, the existence of family or social networks outside the region can facilitate the decision to flee (see Colson, 1979, for a general text). Outside family networks have been shown to be important in Vietnamese refugees' decisions to leave the country (Hitchcox, 1991). Although they are not generally included in the category 'environmental refugees', for those leaving the Agricultural District of Yen Hung, salination of the soil leading to low rice yields was one factor among many (such as the unavailability of other employment, misinformation and rumours spread by confidence tricksters and boat organisers, and a fundamental lack of confidence in the future of the Vietnamese economy). In describing the on-going exodus from this agricultural district, Hitchcox (1991) notes that:

The main anchor to the community is the family group which can be very large, consisting of several households. When this group begins to divide, some relatives left behind in the original settlement, some abroad and in Hong Kong, the decision to move becomes a less weighty and difficult decision, especially if living conditions are poor.

The complexity of the relationship between environmental degradation, forced migration and war can be illustrated by recent literature on the destruction of the teak forests on the Thai/Burmese border and associated refugee flows (Caouette, 1991; Walpole, 1990; Westerbeek, 1991). Over half of Burma's territory has been controlled by local ethnic, communist, and other insurgent minorities for over forty years. Counter-insurgency campaigns by the Burmese State Law and Order Council (SLORC) and its predecessor, the Ne Win government, have, until recently, been unable to penetrate these minority-held areas. Bulldozed roads created by Thai logging companies for timber extraction following a new bilateral agreement in 1989 have, however, changed the dynamic of the conflict. Burmese forces, now allowed to amass on Thai soil, can launch their offensives against the minorities from the rear using the roads created for timber extraction. In 1989, this advantage was used effectively to attack numerous minority villages. The number of ethnic minority refugees on Thai soil doubled to a current figure of over 60,000 refugees living in camps on the Thai side of the border (Caouette, 1991). Many of the 10,000 students and dissidents who had fled the country following the clampdown on pro-democracy demonstrators in Burma had gone to the ethnic minority-held areas. Their camps were attacked in the same offensive. Timber extraction is not only affecting the war and creating refugees, but is undermining the natural resource base of the minorities' areas, and its environmental stability (Ashley, 1992).

Other case studies similarly illustrate the role played by environmental changes and the way in which they are entwined in broader political/economic persecution. Rapacious exploitation of forest resources, either directly by the state or by private companies, in areas occupied by indigenous peoples, is often linked to a policy of ethnocide or to counter-insurgency campaigns. It can be accompanied by transmigration and resettlement of majority groups into territories formerly occupied by indigenous peoples and the perpetuation of a myth that the area is underpopulated or even unoccupied. Examples of this kind include refugee flows from the Chittagong Hill Tracts in Bangladesh, refugees from West Papua and East Timor (both affected by Indonesian transmigration policies), and the situation of Guatemala's Indians (Gray, 1991).

A recent text on civil war and internal strife as causes of displacement (Cohen, 1991) cites a number of military conflicts leading to war-displacement, which are the same as those cited in another recent text (El Hinnawi, 1985) as causes of environmental disturbance leading to flows of 'environmental refugees'. The conflicts and environmental problems cited include, amongst others, those in Sudan, Ethiopia, and Mozambique. Such broad categorisations inevitably fail to reflect the specific complexities of interrelationships between conflict and environmental change.

'Environmental refugees' as a legal category

Environmental problems ranging from natural hazards (such as earthquakes, volcanic eruptions and tropical cyclones) to pollution by chemical toxins or radioactive waste can cause human displacement. Many such forced migrants, however, fall outside the categories protected by instruments of international refugee law, both in terms of the text and intent of the drafters, and in terms of current practice, particularly by Western states.

Originally intended to deal with refugees from communism following the Second World War, the current refugee definition (see Chapter 1) is, it can be argued, used to limit refugee status to those outside their country of origin owing to a well-founded fear of persecution, the latter being defined in narrow political terms. Such a definition is inappropriate for the root causes of flight in many developing nations, as a narrow political definition of 'persecution' can exclude those suffering economic and social persecution and the effects of war, as well as victims of natural disasters in countries where the state offers no protection. Hathaway (1991, p. 114) has expressed the nature of the current status quo as follows:

> Refugee law as codified in the 1951 Convention and 1967 Protocol relating to the Status of Refugees not only continues the original rejection of the notion of comprehensive assistance for all involuntarily displaced persons, but it allies international law with a series of strategic limitations determined by Western political objectives.

Some legal theorists, however, are arguing for the definition of a refugee to be rooted in human rights. This argument can be grounded in different ways. First, persecution can be defined in terms of human rights violations (as suggested by Coles, 1988; Hathaway, 1991) which, under the Covenant on Economic, Social and Cultural Rights, include the right to an adequate standard of living and the right to food (Lawyers Committee, 1991). If this is to be more widely adopted, those forcibly displaced across international boundaries as a result of 'environmental disturbance' could be eligible for international assistance and protection according to whether suffering amounted to a first order violation of human rights. Alternatively, as disasters themselves or an individual's vulnerability to them are commonly the result of human actions, rather than 'Acts of God', the state has a duty to protect its citizens from them. If the state is negligent or indifferent to meeting its obligation to protect its citizens' basic needs, this breach of the contract with the state could be grounds for international assistance to refugees (Shacknove, 1985).

In practice UNHCR has long assisted a broader group than those included by the narrow Convention definition in its mandate. Since the late 1950s, UN General Assembly (GA) resolutions have repeatedly been passed to authorise the High Commissioner for Refugees to lend his 'good offices' to assist persons outside UNHCR's competence (Kibreab, 1991). In the 1960s, this broader group were termed refugees 'of concern' to UNHCR. With respect to Sudan in 1972, the Economic and Social Council (ECOSOC) and the GA passed resolutions to enable inclusion of internally displaced (Goodwin-Gill, 1988). Later in 1976, ECOSOC and GA resolutions recognised UNHCR's activities in the 'context of man-made disasters' (UNHCR had played a key role in assistance in India/Bangladesh and Cyprus in the 1970s). Intervention is now made to assist those displaced by a combination of war, drought and changing entitlements to food and other resources. Goodwin-Gill (1988) however notes how the class of beneficiaries has expanded without any corresponding broadening of states' legal obligations.

Regional agreements also broaden the category of those defined as refugees. For example, within Africa, the Accord of the Organization of African Unity (OAU, 1969) recognises as grounds for asylum claims: 'external aggression, occupation, foreign domination or events seriously disturbing public order'. It differs from the Geneva definition in that it refers to objective conditions in the country of origin, and allows refugee status to be recognised for groups rather than individuals (Rwelamira, 1983). The Accord was drawn up in the context of liberation struggles against colonial powers and 'disturbances' were assumed by the drafters to be of a political nature (Greenfield, 1986). Drought and other natural disasters as causes of flight were not specifically intended in the drafting. Although the scope of this expanded definition is habitually applied to those for whom economic protection by the state is not forthcoming, a restrictive interpretation excluding victims of ecological and man-made disaster is by no means precluded (Rwelamira, 1983, p. 177).

Nonetheless, whether or not the category 'refugee' includes those fleeing environmental disturbances, the use of the prefix 'environmental' is redundant as it has no founding in law.

Responsibility for protection and assistance

Under the current system, refugees receive protection which goes beyond the assistance given to disaster victims. Legal obligations on the part of refugee-hosting states are well defined. Barriers against refugees being sent back to the persecuting state are at the core of refugee protection. However, states' responsibilities with respect to those in humanitarian need other than refugees are less well defined. MacAlistair-Smith (1985) has noted the inadequacies of international humanitarian law relating to relief operations in so-called natural disasters, and the need to transform 'functional humanitarian responsibilities into legal obligations', noting that 'there is still no international convention setting out obligations of states concerning the donation or acceptance of humanitarian assistance or regulating the coordination of relief in peacetime'.

In so far as the term 'environmental refugee' conflates the idea of disaster victim and refugee, its use brings with it the danger that the key features of refugee protection could be undermined and the lowest common denominator adopted. Because 'environmental' can imply a sphere outside politics, use of the term 'environmental refugees' may encourage receiving states to treat the term in the same way as 'economic migrants' to reduce their responsibility to protect and assist.

International provision for refugees' protection and assistance is made through UNHCR. In contrast, disaster planning and relief is generally coordinated by UNDRO as the 'focal point in the United Nations system for disaster relief matters', often through local UNDP offices (Siegel and Witham, 1991). Areas of functional responsibility were distinguished in a Memorandum of Understanding between UNDRO and UNHCR in 1978 such that:

> responsibility for the co-ordination of relief assistance to persons compelled to leave their homes as a result of, or as a precautionary measure against the effects of natural and other disasters such as earthquakes, volcanic eruptions, droughts, floods, storms and epidemics and also aviation, maritime, industrial or nuclear radiation accidents shall rest with UNDRO.

These terms limit UNDRO's mandate in regard to 'other disaster situations' to innocent or accidental disasters (MacAlistair-Smith, 1985), although these are commonly not exclusive.

UNHCR's protection services go beyond the relief, assistance and disaster preparedness planning undertaken by the host of UN institutions (UNEP, FAO, WHO, UNDP) and other regional organisations (such as IGADD, the Intergovernmental Authority for Drought and Desertification), or NGOs, and coordinated by UNDRO. The term 'environmental refugee' thus also confuses different types of service and institutional responsibility.

By reducing the complexity of real situations, the term 'environmental refugee' can also reinforce images of a Malthusian squeeze. Based on overgeneral and generally inaccurate conceptions of the relation between population change and environmental resource use, Malthusianism commonly underlies current literature on population and the environment in the Third World (as argued by Williams, 1992, with reference to World Bank reports). The idea of a population explosion, coupled with environmental catastrophe fuelling massive refugee outflows to Europe, contributes to the paranoia of 'Fortress Europe' and hence trends toward restrictive asylum practices.

Refugees' environmental impact

An implicit element of Malthusianism also underpins another aspect of the relationship between refugees and the environment, namely the impact of refugee migration on environmental processes. A key concept in justifying international intervention to assist refugees is the notion that refugees are a burden on the host community, and that this burden should be shared by other states (Harrell-Bond, 1986). In the 1960s, environmental impact was not specifically included in the notion of host-burdens, which were usually defined in terms of a strain on economic development and infrastructure.

However, since the energy crisis of 1973, and the concern expressed thereafter about the 'other energy crisis' (fuelwood shortages in the developing world), the environment has received much more attention in development policy and in refugee assistance. The environmental impact of refugees, particularly resulting from their demands for land and other resources, has increasingly become an explicit part of the literature on refugees' impact on their hosts (see for example, Kibreab, 1991, for a review of the literature, and Kuhlman, 1990, for an empirical study).

The minimal contribution of the international community to sharing the burden of refugees in Africa has been the subject of two international conferences (ICARA I and II). ICARA II aimed to accomplish what ICARA I failed to, namely the provision of assistance to host countries to enable them to cope with refugees and to increase their capacity for absorption (Kibreab, 1991, p. 53). The focus was on income-generation rather than natural resources, although such projects were seen to be particularly important in countries where land resources and employment opportunities are inadequate. However, only 24 per cent of the finance requested by host countries was spent on agriculture, forestry and fisheries; the main part went into infrastructure (Kibreab, 1991, p. 54).

Other aspects of refugee policy are increasingly environment-aware. For example, the EC can provide funds to alleviate the impact of refugees in areas in which they are settled through development funding arrangements with African, Caribbean and Pacific countries (Lomé III, Article 204, and Lomé IV, Article 255). Under Lomé IV, which came into effect in 1991, the emphasis on the environment has undergone a 'meteoric promotion' in comparison to Lomé III, such that it now has a section devoted to it (Commission of the European Communities, 1990, p. 5). The aim is that environmental impact should be considered before rather than after the approval of development projects. UNHCR is also increasingly vocal about the environmental impact of refugees.

Concern about the environmental costs of a refugee influx often conforms to a stereotype along the following lines (Lind and Peniston, 1991, p. 10):

> UNHCR and other agencies are becoming increasingly concerned about the negative environmental impacts of large influxes of refugees and displaced persons. UNHCR estimates that refugees ... have deforested about 36,000 ha to meet basic shelter needs. In addition, refugees consume an estimated 13 million metric tons of fuelwood annually for settlements worldwide ... Asylum and host countries, particularly those in degraded or fragile areas, cannot continue to bear these ecological costs. Some countries already refuse to accept refugees and displaced people, fearing negative environmental and social impacts.

As was the case in the earlier discussion of 'environmental refugees', generalisations such as this can result in misunderstanding of the way in which refugees interact with the environment: refugees are sometimes blamed for 'damage' that they did not cause, or is not really 'damage' at all, and projects can fail to address the actual causes of environmental problems. This is also the case in development policy more generally, and programmes to improve natural resource use have often themselves caused environmental damage (see for example Horowitz, 1988, for criticism of World Bank livestock and water resource programmes, and McGregor, 1991, for adverse ecological impacts of national land use programmes).

In some refugee situations, environmental problems attributed to the daily subsistence demands of refugees have been addressed by international agencies where none are perceived by either local people or the refugees themselves. For example, the subsistence strategies of self-settled Liberian refugees in Sierra Leone were said by agencies to have exacerbated local practices of indiscriminate forest clearance to create agricultural land, for fuel and timber. According to Leach (1991), the degradation cited by the agency was exaggerated and highly misleading for the following reasons:

> It fails to take account of the substantial amount of dead wood which is gathered, the collection of which has no negative impact on forest stocks and productivity. Dead wood is preferred as it is easier to harvest, lighter to carry and can be used immediately ... It totally ignores the ability of many species to regenerate. Indeed, studies of regeneration show that the regrowth of trees which have been coppiced can be more rapid than that of uncut trees. Disturbed forest is more highly productive of important locally-used species, and can be re-harvested ... It does not convey the fact that much of the harvested timber and firewood is a by-product of agricultural activity and would have been cut in any case.

UNHCR recommended Eucalyptus plantations to ameliorate the deforestation they perceived. However, the project failed to address the real environmental problems in the area, caused by the rapid increase in large-scale illegal logging and game shooting. Leach (1991) concludes that 'rather than through classic forestry initiatives, conservation and local interests may be better served by finding ways for local people to 'police' the activities of logging companies and hunting gangs, and strengthening local resource management institutions that already exist'. Misunderstandings of the ways in which local communities and refugees used their environment were also made in reference to other resource demands, such as those on building material, game, etc. (Leach, 1991).

In Burma, international agencies have similarly wrongly attributed environmental degradation, and thus misdirected projects. UNDP in Rangoon is planning plantations of exotic species as a remedy for destructive teak logging on the Thai/

Burma border, attributed to local shifting cultivators, displaced people and refugees. The organisation has failed to acknowledge or criticise the large-scale destructive logging operations of Thai companies: as noted earlier in this chapter, these mechanised logging operations play a key role in the government's counter-insurgency strategy, which is itself causing displacement of the indigenous populations and thus creating refugee flows. Moreover, traditional methods involve ring-barking large-girth trees and leaving them to dry. When finally felled, the tree causes less damage to the remaining standing trees in falling, as the branches are already dry. Use of elephants in extracting the timber causes less disruption to soils, understorey and hydrology than do bulldozer extraction and the new network of roads (Walpole, 1990). Former sustainable forestry practices, used in areas under supervision of the forestry commission, known as the Burmese Selective System under which only mature trees were felled, have been abandoned since military generals were put in charge of forestry (Ashley, 1992).

'Environmental' arguments are commonly used to justify policies which are convenient or politically expedient for governments or agencies. These may bear little if any relation to the actual processes of ecological change occurring in a given context. For example, in Swaziland, resource pressure and environmental degradation were given as some of a range of reasons for moving refugees out of the villages in which they had negotiated their settlement, and into camps. Allegations of resource pressure were detailed particularly in reference to land demands, to increased soil erosion and to cultivation of marginal land. Research suggests that in much of the border area, no such processes were operative (McGregor *et al.*, 1991).

It is sometimes assumed that refugees have a more pronounced effect on the environment than 'normal' communities (UNHCR, 1991, p. 1). Although a negative impact is assumed, this is rarely, if ever, translated into compensation for local populations (as recommended for resettlement in other contexts; see for example, Cernea, 1991). In practice, however, it can be difficult to distinguish the impact of refugees from other changes going on in an area; for example in Somalia, an area for refugee resettlement chosen by UNHCR was in a region where large-scale commercialised semi-mechanised farming was expanding dramatically (funded by the World Bank through the government Settlement Development Agency). These developments were proceeding with no consideration of maintaining or integrating them with local ecology, livestock and resource-use systems and other livelihoods, nor of a strategy for coping with drought for either the irrigation or dry land livelihoods (Low *et al.*, 1985).

Similarly, the impact of self-settling refugees may also be difficult to isolate. Mozambican refugees self-settling in Swaziland's border areas moved into a marginalised part of the country which had also received Swazis forcibly displaced by the development of large-scale irrigated sugar plantations over the previous ten years. Chieftainship disputes had been an additional source of internal population displacement prior to the refugee influx. Hence, many hosts had arrived not long before the refugees; indeed some had moved more than twice in the previous five years (McGregor *et al.*, 1991). Some families were uprooted with refugee guests already living with them. In such circumstances, it is difficult to separate the impact of refugees on the environment from environmental change occurring for other reasons.

The negative environmental impact of refugees is sometimes attributed to population pressure. The effects of demographic increase on resources and the way they are used, however, operate in a complex way which is locally specific, and should be analysed with reference to changes in resource tenure, patterns of trade and changing livelihoods. The scale of the influx to Malawi, for example, where one in ten persons is now a refugee (USCR, 1992), put additional strains on a country that was already suffering resource shortages. This strain was magnified because the war in Mozambique disrupted cross-border trade in natural resources (including firewood, timber, meat, honey and fish) which had been sustaining certain resource-poor and densely populated areas of Malawi (Wilson *et al.*, 1989).

The increased demand for resources which accompanies a refugee influx can be capitalised upon by local people, by charging for them when otherwise they would have been open access, or managed under common property regulations. This has been the case in many African refugee settings and is documented for Malawi (Wilson *et al.*, 1989) and Swaziland (McGregor *et al.*, 1991). The commodification and increasing privatisation of an array of resources (including gathered arable weeds, fuelwood, edible insects and fruit) has been a major modification in many refugee-hosting societies. In some cases poorer as well as wealthier hosts can benefit. In other contexts, however, privatisation can be used in an exclusionary way, which can increase pressures on the remaining open-access resources and cause ecological problems and economic hardship for segments of the local society as well as for refugees (as described by Low *et al.*, 1985, in Somalia; Kuhlman, 1990, and Bascom, 1989, in Eastern Sudan).

The environmental impact of a refugee influx can also be affected by settlement patterns. There is an on-going debate in the refugee literature over the relative benefits for refugees and hosts of putting refugees in camps and settlements, rather than allowing free settlement. There are many sides to this debate, touching issues of state security, agency accountability to donors, and economic integration, in addition to the impact on hosts. Natural resource use is sometimes included in this discussion. Kibreab (1991), in his review of the debate, notes that environmental damage may be a problem caused by refugees both in and outside camps.

This debate cannot be resolved in the absence of specific contexts. In Swaziland, the impact of refugees concentrated in camps was greater than that caused by the dispersed self-settled population. The effect of differential population concentrations was in this case reinforced by the differential topography of the areas: the self-settled border area being rocky with a relatively high proportion of the land unsuitable for agriculture, in contrast to the environs of the camps, which are either densely settled with little residual land, or are privately-owned large commercial estates. Indeed, there was no absolute shortage of trees in the vicinity of the refugee camps: rather, access to large areas of private wooded land was banned to refugees. Experiencing problems of bush encroachment, these farms were actually exporting timber from the area in the form of charcoal to South Africa. Negotiations between agency staff managing the refugee camp and neighbouring farm owners had failed to grant refugee access to this fuel and timber supply (McGregor *et al.*, 1991).

In contrast, self-settlement of Mozambican refugees in Malawi has had significant environmental costs (Wilson *et al.*, 1989). Refugees' homes and gardens have encroached on seasonal swamps where these were not privately owned. Such areas were previously used for grazing, gathering wild foods (particularly greens and rodents) and materials such as soil, clay and thatching grass. In other places refugees settled in former communally held woodland resulting in the loss of resources for fuel, construction and wild vegetables. Some camps were also built on villagers' communal resources (unlike in Swaziland where private land was given by the King).

The importance of a good relationship with local hosts for refugee access to resources is often not appreciated. Interventions and structures which fail to facilitate this relationship can jeopardise refugees' livelihoods. The lack of political integration of refugee and host communities can constrain resource access (refugees are generally administered through structures completely separate from host nation local government). Camp location is often determined on the basis of a national-level decision and can fail to solicit the goodwill of local populations. For example, refugees forcibly resettled in the remote East Awin area of West Papua were faced with acute antagonism from the local population. The opposition to refugees' presence reached such levels that road blockades were staged by local people in protest, denying refugees access to food and labour markets, as well as resources which they crucially needed (RPN, 1991). In Sierra Leone, agencies failed to understand the local multilayered resource tenure systems and interventions intended to secure land for refugees threatened to jeopardize refugees' livelihood by disrupting crucial relationships between them and their hosts.

Conclusion

As the above examples show, an understanding of refugees' impact on the environment has to be rooted in specific case studies which combine an analysis of changing ecology, resource tenure systems, and local politics. The challenge for policy makers is less to standardise interventions, as recommended by some agencies (GTZ, 1991), but rather to create systems which are sensitive to local conditions. Only through such studies can greater understanding be developed of environmental change and its relation to migration.

A feature common to both the current debate over environmental degradation as a cause of migration, and the debate over refugees' environmental impact, is that processes of environmental change are taken out of their political, social and economic context. The role of migration in environmental change, the role of environmental change in migration, and the relationship of both of these to broader processes of change can hence be misinterpreted.

A further danger is that 'environmental' arguments are used to defend every variety of political position: rooted less in empirical ecological, sociological or geographical processes than in the debate between interested parties. As a legitimation for a particular course of action, concern over environmental degradation can be used politically in many different ways: to reinforce Western paranoia of a mass influx from the South; to justify forced population removals; or to reduce governmental and international responsibility to assist and protect the forcibly displaced.

References

Ashley, C., 1992, 'War, logging and displacement in Burma (Myanmar)', *Refugee Participation Network*, **12**: 24–27.

Bascom, J., 1989, 'Refugee resettlement in the context of agrarian change: a case study from eastern Sudan', Ph.D. thesis, Department of Geography, University of Iowa.

Caouette, T., 1991, 'Burmese refugees in Thailand', paper presented at the joint FAO/Asian Studies Centre conference, 'Burma (Myanmar): challenges and opportunities for the future', Oxford, December 1991.

Cernea, M., 1991, *Bilateral donors: guidelines for resettlement in projects*, World Bank, Washington DC.

Clay, J. and Holcomb, B.K., 1985, 'Politics and the Ethiopian famine 1984–1985', *Cultural Survival Special Reports*, no. 20, Cambridge, Massachusetts.

Clay, J., Steingraber, S. and Niggli, P., 1988, *The spoils of famine: Ethiopian famine policy and peasant agriculture*, Cultural Survival Inc., Cambridge, Massachusetts.

Cohen, R., 1991, *Human rights protection for internally displaced persons*, Refugee Policy Group, Washington, DC.

Coles, G., 1988, 'The human rights approach to the solution of the refugee problem: a theoretical and practical inquiry', in A. Nash, ed., *Human rights and the protection of refugees under international law*, Institute for Research on Public Policy, Halifax, Nova Scotia.

Colson, E., 1979, 'In good years and in bad', *Journal of Anthropological Research*, **35** (1): 18–29.

Commission of the European Communities, 1990, *Lomé IV: 1990–2000. Background, innovations, improvements*, Europe Information, Commission of the European Communities, Brussels.

Drèze, J. and Sen, A., 1989, *Hunger and public action*, Clarendon Press, Oxford.

Duffield, M., 1991, 'The internationalisation of public welfare: conflict and the reform of the donor/NGO safety net', paper presented to the 'Workshop on the prospects for peace, recovery and development in the Horn of Africa', Institute of Social Studies, The Hague, February 1991.

El-Hinnawi, E., 1985, *Environmental refugees*, United Nations Environmental Programme, Kenya.

Goodwin-Gill, G., 1988, 'Refugees: the expanding mandate of the Office of the United Nations High Commissioner for Refugees', unpublished paper.

Gray, A., 1991, 'Indigenous peoples as refugees: what conditions for return?', *Refugee Participation Network*, **11**: p. 9.

Greenfield, R., 1986, 'The OAU and Africa's refugees', in Y. El-Ayouty and W. Zartman, eds, *The OAU after twenty years*, Praeger, New York.

GTZ (Deutsche Gesellschaft für Technische Zusammenarbeit), 1991, untitled article in *Rapport*, **10**, United Nations Environmental Programme, Kenya.

Harrell-Bond, B.E., 1986, *Imposing aid: emergency assistance to refugees*, Oxford University Press, Oxford.

Hathaway, J., 1991, 'Reconceiving refugee law as human rights protection', *Journal of Refugee Studies*, **4** (2): 113–131.

Hewitt, K., 1983, *Interpretations of calamity*, Allen & Unwin, London.

Hitchcox, L., 1991, 'Returnees within their communities: a pilot study of local attitudes and economy related to development policy', unpublished report.

Horowitz, M., 1988, 'Donors and deserts: the political ecology of destructive development in the Sahel', paper presented at the Symposium on Desertification and Development, IUAES Congress, Yugoslavia, July 1988.

Jacobson, J., 1988, *Environmental refugees: a yardstick of habitability*, Worldwatch Institute, Washington, DC.

Kibreab, G., 1991, *The state of the art review of refugee studies in Africa*, Uppsala Papers in Economic History, Research Report no. 26.

Kuhlman, T., 1990, *Burden or boon? a study of Eritrean refugees in the Sudan*, Zed Books, London.

Lawyers Committee, 1991, *The human rights of refugees and displaced persons: protections afforded refugees, asylum seekers and displaced persons under international human rights, humanitarian and refugee law*, Lawyers' Committee briefing paper, May 1991, Washington DC.

Leach, M., 1991, 'Refugee–host relations in local perspective: food security and environmental implications of the Liberian influx into rural communities of Sierra Leone, 1990–1991', report prepared for UNICEF, Geneva.

Lind, L. and Peniston, B.J., 1991, *Forestry projects for refugees and displaced persons: guidelines for project managers*, Office of International Forestry, Forestry Support Programme, USDA Forest Service, Washington DC.

Low, J., Hume, M., Sulikova, I., Xaji, M., Isaaq, X. and Maxamood, M., 1985, *Results of a baseline survey in Sablaale District, Lower Shabeelle Region, Somalia*, Euro Action Accord, London.

MacAlistair-Smith, P., 1985, *International humanitarian assistance. Disaster relief actions in international law and organisation*, Martinus Nijhoff Publishers, Amsterdam.

McGregor, J., Harrell-Bond, B. and Mazur, R., 1991, 'Mozambicans in Swaziland: livelihood and integration', report prepared for the World Food Programme by the Refugee Studies Programme, Oxford.

McGregor, J., 1991, 'Woodland resources: ecology, policy and ideology. A case study of woodland use in Zimbabwe's communal lands', Ph.D. thesis, University of Loughborough, UK

OAU (Organization of African Unity), 1969, Convention governing the specific aspects of refugee problems in Africa, 10.9.69, 1001, UNTS, 14691, entered into force 20 June 1974.

Pankhurst, A., 1992, *Resettlement and famine in Ethiopia: the villagers' experience*, Manchester University Press, Manchester, UK.

RPN (Refugee Participation Network), 1991, 'Voluntary repatriation? refugees from West Papua', *Refugee Participation Network*, **11**: 12–13.

Rwelamira, M.R.K., 1983, 'Some reflections on the OAU convention on refugees: some pending issues', *Comparative International Law Journal of South Africa*, **16** (2): 155–78.

Sen, A., 1981, *Poverty and famines*, Clarendon Press, Oxford.

Shacknove, A.E., 1985, 'Who is a refugee?', *Ethics*, **95** (2): 274–284.

Siegel, R. and Witham P., 1991, 'UNDP coordination of disaster and development planning', in *Managing natural disasters and the environment*, IBRD/World Bank, Washington DC.

Tickell, C., 1989a, 'Climate change could cause world refugee crisis', *British Overseas Development*, **7**: 16.

Tickell, C., 1989b, 'Environmental refugees: the human impact of global climate change', paper delivered as Natural Environment Research Council Annual Lecture, Royal Society, London.

UNHCR (United Nations High Commissioner for Refugees), 1991, *Rapport*, **19**, Autumn 1991, Special edition on the environment.

USCR (United States Committee for Refugees), 1992, *World refugee survey, 1991*, USCR, Washington, DC.

Walpole, P., 1990, *A report on the forestry activities of Burma (Myanmar) and the stability of the Moulmein watershed and Tenasserim uplands*, Environmental Research Division, Manila Observatory, Philippines.

Warrick, R.A., 1983, 'Drought in the US Great Plains: shifting social consequences', in K. Hewitt, ed., *Interpretations of calamity*, Allen & Unwin, London.

Westerbeek, E., 1991, 'The depletion of natural resources in Burma (Myanmar)', paper presented at the joint FAO/Asian Studies Centre conference, 'Burma (Myanmar): challenges and opportunities for the future', held in Oxford, December 1991.

Westing, A.H., 1984, *Herbicides in war*, Taylor & Francis, London.

Wijkman, A. and Timberlake, L., 1984, *Natural disasters: acts of God or acts of man?*, Earthscan, London.

Williams, G., 1992, 'Modernising Malthus: the World Bank, population control and the African environment', paper presented at conference on 'Population movement, food crises and community response', Delhi, January 1992.

Wilson, K., Cammack, D. and Shumba, F., 1989, 'Food provisioning amongst Mozambican refugees in Malawi: a study of aid, livelihood and development', report prepared for the World Food Programme by the Refugee Studies Programme, Oxford.

Further reading

Ashley, C. and RPN, 1992, 'War, logging and refugees in Burma (Myanmar)', *Refugee Participation Network*, **12**: 24–27.

El-Hinnawi, E., 1985, *Environmental refugees*, United Nations Environmental Programme, Kenya.

Leach, M., 1991, 'Environmental impact of refugees in Sierra Leone', *Refugee Participation Network*, **11**: 16–19.

Trolldalen, J.M., Birkeland, N.M., Bryen, J. and Scott, P.T., 1992, *Environmental refugees: a discussion paper*, World Foundation for Environment and Development/Norwegian Refugee Council, Oslo.

Timberlake, L., 1984, *Environment and conflict*, Earthscan Briefing Document no. 40, Earthscan, London.

11 Repatriation and information: a theoretical model

Khalid Koser

Introduction: official vs. self-repatriation

There is a growing body of literature and empirical research on official repatriation. However, a significant proportion of repatriation is non-official and refugee-induced. This process of self-repatriation is not clearly understood. The aim of this chapter is to place self-repatriation in the refugee cycle, and to try to understand how and when it occurs. It is suggested that self-repatriation may be understood as the outcome of a subjective comparison by refugees of conditions in exile *vis-à-vis* conditions at home. This approach highlights the importance of information about home conditions in the process. The notion of a refugee information system is introduced and modelled; and key elements such as the type of information available to refugees about their home areas, the sources of information and the accuracy of information are discussed.

Official repatriation

Repatriation is the end of the refugee cycle. It represents one option which may be taken after flight and temporary exile in a country of asylum. Other options are permanent settlement in the country of first asylum, and third country resettlement. Together these three are the tripartite of so-called 'durable solutions' promoted by UNHCR (Stein, 1986, p. 268). Perhaps the principal refugee problem today is that the sequence of 'flight – temporary asylum – permanent solution' is not reaching completion for enough refugees.

UNHCR was established to protect refugees and provide humanitarian aid. In the case of the European refugees with whom UNHCR first dealt, there was usually a finite end. Post-Second World War and Cold War refugees were expected to settle permanently in exile in Europe or America. Most did so. In contrast, contemporary refugees are predominantly from 'independent' countries of the less-developed world, who seek asylum in other less-developed countries. For most of them it has also become necessary for the international community to pursue a solution (Harrell-Bond *et al.*, 1989; Nanda, 1989). However, continued financial support has usually been necessary even after one of the three 'solutions' is chosen. Thus repatriation may be the end of the refugee cycle, but it is also the beginning of a new cycle of social, political and economic re-integration, and regional development.

The usual vehicles for official repatriation programmes are Tripartite Commissions consisting of UNHCR and the governments of asylum and origin. The political nature of official repatriation programmes has been emphasised by Harrell-Bond (1989). Given the contemporary countries of asylum and countries of origin of most refugees, repatriation has become the preferred solution of UNHCR. This is because UNHCR is a body with no mandate for action independent of the concerned countries. Indeed, it promotes repatriation as a result of pressures from all countries concerned with refugee flows: for the donor countries repatriation is perceived as the cheapest option; for the host government, there is the opportunity to remove a perceived burden; whilst for the government of the country of origin repatriation provides an opportunity to reduce international criticism of its human rights record.

The repatriation of refugees to Namibia following the Declaration of Independence on 21 March 1990 is the only recent example of a successful large-scale programme organised by UNHCR (see Chapter 4 in this volume). The framework for the repatriation exercise was laid down in UN Resolution 435. Only ten days after Independence, 43,387 returnees had been processed. They repatriated from Angola, Zambia and forty other countries under the auspices of UNHCR, and assisted by SWAPO and the governments of Angola and Zambia (Gasarasi, 1990, p. 343). However, repatriation is not necessarily a process which occurs in response to official programmes. It is also possible to view it in terms of a rational decision made by individual refugees. Rationality is subjectively defined and will depend upon the information which the refugee has.

Alternatives to official repatriation programmes

The limited research on repatriation suggests that refugees do not necessarily wish to participate in official repatriation schemes. They may ignore them and remain in exile, or may self- (spontaneously) repatriate. The failure of official schemes has often been a function of the mis-timing of their introduction.

An example of an unsuccessful official scheme occurred in the context of Ugandan refugees in Sudan. The initial flow of refugees into southern Sudan began in 1979, with the downfall of Idi Amin. By 1982 there were some 350,000 refugees in the area. They included both Amin supporters and uninvolved victims of the reprisals of the Ugandan National Liberation Army (UNLA). In 1983 the UNHCR office in Yei River District began to distribute repatriation forms. The programme was launched at a time when 'battles continued within earshot of many (refugee) settlements' (Harrell-Bond, 1986, p. 186), and was largely rejected by the refugees. Harrell-Bond (1986) asserts that the untimely introduction of a repatriation programme was a result of 'the belief that material assistance is the propelling force which moves people'.

A similar resistance to repatriation amongst Ethiopian refugees was found in Djibouti, even though they faced considerable harassment from the police (Crisp, 1984, p .5). The Tripartite Commission of UNHCR and the governments of Ethiopia and Djibouti met at the end of January 1983 and agreed to promote voluntary repatriation. However, the refugees rejected this proposal as new arrivals recounted details of continuing oppression by the Ethiopian government. The majority of refugees returned at the end of 1983 and beginning of 1984 only after they received assurances regarding their safety and the recovery of their property upon return.

Nonetheless, although they are by nature difficult to document and enumerate, it is estimated that 'each year tens or hundreds of thousands of refugees' repatriate without official assistance (Cuny and Stein, 1989, p. 296). Commonly this is described as 'spontaneous' repatriation, but the term is often inappropriate as many refugees plan in advance for these return movements. Consequently terms such as 'self-repatriation' are gaining credence. For the most part these refugees are willing to go home without material assistance and before a decisive political event at home (Harrell-Bond, 1989). These movements are based on the decision of individual refugees that they can return home (Cuny and Stein, 1989, p. 296).

Between 1985 and 1987 some 164,000 refugees repatriated from eastern Sudan to areas of northern Ethiopia controlled by the Tigray People's Liberation Front (TPLF). While their flight in 1984–85 was triggered by drought and famine, it occurred in the context of an internal war between the Ethiopian government and the TPLF. Due to the sensitivity of refugee returns to territories controlled by entities not officially recognised or represented at the United Nations, UNHCR neither formally recognised nor actively supported the moves (Hendrie, 1991, p. 200). The repatriation was supported by the Sudanese Office of the Commissioner for Refugees (COR) and the indigenous Relief Society of Tigray (REST), and in general was self-organised by the refugees. It is estimated (Cuny and Stein, 1989) that on a global scale self-repatriation accounts for more returnees than organised programmes. Given the apparent importance of self-repatriation, it is a strikingly understudied and misunderstood process.

Repatriates as return migrants

If it is not necessarily in response to official programmes, when do refugees repatriate? While there has been a limited conceptualisation of refugees in flight (Kunz, 1973), and of the integration of refugees (Kunz, 1981; Scudder and Colson, 1982; Kuhlman, 1991), there is a paucity of theory considering the return of refugees. It is proposed here that repatriation can be better understood if repatriates are viewed as return migrants.

A 'classic' refugee, who is crossing a border as a result of persecution at home, is hardly comparable to a migrant (or an economic refugee). Whilst Kunz (1973) does make the distinction between an 'acute' and an 'anticipatory' refugee, both are still fleeing in conditions of severe insecurity. A migrant, on the other hand, for whatever reason he or she may leave, is not escaping an environment of personal danger. The planning and decision-making process for each are different. However, it is possible to view a repatriate as a special type of return migrant, since for the most part refugees are not living in conditions so miserable that they return home without planning – although it is important to note that this cannot be said of victims of forced repatriation, '*refoulement*', such as those involved in recent repatriation movements in the Horn of Africa. In most cases then, light may be thrown on the process of self-repatriation by study of the circumstances under which economic migrants return home.

Individual migration results when a tension arises between an individual's aspirations on the one hand, and expectations about the current situation on the other. This tension prompts a search for opportunities elsewhere. A similar framework of analysis is applicable to return migrants (King, 1978; Cerase, 1974). Return migrants may not attain full knowledge of the range of opportunities at home. They choose according to a limited subset of possible alternatives, which are determined by the information available. Thus they can be seen as 'satisficing' rather than 'maximising' agents (Molho, 1986, p. 399). This distinction highlights the importance of the search for opportunity and received information in the decision-making process.

The theory is that repatriates, like return migrants, go home as a result of a balanced decision depending on their personal aspirations, and information available on wider structural conditions. Central to that decision is knowledge of conditions at home. The limited research considering the factors involved in a decision by refugees to go home suggests that this framework is applicable to repatriation.

Akol (1987) identifies three factors which were of importance in the decision whether to self-repatriate by Southern Sudanese refugees. First was the nature of settlement in the country of asylum. Refugees in organised rural camps are more easily mobilised than 'spontaneously settled' or urban refugees. Second was the level of socio-economic development achieved by refugees *vis-à-vis* conditions prevailing in their places of origin. Thirdly, a common ethnicity with members of the host population may reduce propensity to return. Rogge and Akol (1989) introduce another important factor: the longer the refugee has been in exile, the greater his/her acculturation in the host society.

How refugees subjectively evaluate conditions at home is clearly crucial. Basok's (1990) study of the repatriation of Nicaraguan refugees from Honduras and Costa Rica showed that more refugees returned from the former country. It also revealed that a higher proportion of *'costenos'* (indigenous Nicaraguans) than of *'ladinos'* returned. The difference in rate between countries can be explained by the fact that in Costa Rica, unlike Honduras, many refugees were provided employment and became better off in exile than they would have been in their own country. The difference in rate between populations is also explained in terms of their evaluations of conditions at home. The *costenos* received economic assistance upon return, whereas the *ladinos* were often treated with suspicion and not offered aid by the Sandinista government.

Information and repatriation

Unlike the beginning of the refugee cycle, which is initiated by processes out of the control of the refugee, he/she can play a central role in ending the cycle. The decision to repatriate involves a subjective comparison by the refugee of conditions in exile *vis-à-vis* conditions at home. This comparison is then pitched into the context of personal characteristics such as gender and age; and objective characteristics such as nature of settlement in exile, length of time in exile and so on.

What is suggested is that, like other potential migrants, refugees in exile have information about conditions at home against which to compare their present positions. It follows that the quantity and quality of that information is critical in the decision whether or not to return and, *ipso facto*, in ending the refugee cycle. In this context, an appropriate framework for understanding self-repatriation should analyse the information which refugees in exile receive, how it is circulated amongst them, and how they subjectively evaluate and react to it.

Repatriation: a theoretical model

The purpose of this section is to identify those elements in the literature of the social sciences which can be applied to a conceptualisation of an information system in the context of refugees. The most clearly applicable body of geographical literature is that on the diffusion of innovations, at the heart of which is the receipt and use of information by adopters. Refugees may be seen as adopters who receive information and then decide whether to act upon it.

Elements in the information system

The modern tradition of innovation diffusion studies started with Swedish geographer Hägerstrand in the 1950s. He emphasised the demand perspective of innovation diffusion, or the adoption behaviour of individuals. The assumption was that all have an equal opportunity to adopt. Later work emphasised the supply perspective (Brown, 1975; 1981). This perspective introduced two concepts. First, innovation is not usually freely accessible: rather, it is supplied. Second, adoption is not necessarily an available option: the ability to adopt an innovation depends upon the existence of an enabling infrastructure.

The supply perspective introduces the idea of a mediator and a facilitator. Applied to the notion of a refugee receiving information about his/her home area, it translates as follows. First, information does not simply arrive with the refugee, but is collected, carried and communicated by a mediator – for example UNHCR or another refugee. Second, a refugee cannot necessarily act upon favourable information by returning home, since return must be facilitated by a host of factors such as access to the border or adequate money for the journey home. This chapter focuses on the receipt of information rather than the use of it, and so the emphasis is on the idea of a mediator. The nature of the mediator thus becomes central to the type and accuracy of information available to the refugee.

Some geographical research has concentrated on the role of the media as a mediator (Burgess and Gold, 1985). The premise has been that the logic of the mediator will affect the information which is supplied. There may be an intentional manipulation of information as in propaganda, or a less sinister misinterpretation of information. Information has a quality which may also be affected by a mediator. Hägerstrand (1967) explained the decision to adopt an innovation or not in terms of resistance which is determined by personal or group factors: in other words the stress is on the nature of the individual. According to the supply perspective the decision may also lie in the nature of the information.

Model of a refugee information system

What is needed to understand repatriation in terms of the supply and evaluation of information is a working model. Such a model might have five components (see also Figure 11.1):

a)   home conditions which generate information;
b)   agents who collect, mediate and pass on that information to a refugee;
c)   reception of information;
d)   flows of information which connect these three components, and
e)   a series of inputs which relate the model to the external environment and cause the components to change through time. This component is related to the other four components as they are discussed in turn.

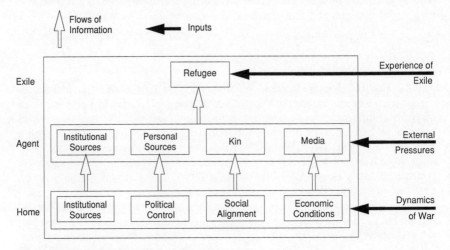

Figure 11.1 Model of a refugee information system

Models are by definition simplifications and include assumptions. In this model these are:

a)   refugees passively receive information;
b)   refugees are static in exile;
c)   refugees receive information as individuals, and
d)   refugees want to return to the place from which they came.

These assumptions are necessary for the production of the model, but in reality they may not apply. For example, refugees may actively pursue information (Christensen, 1985), in some cases by returning to their home areas. Refugees may also receive information collectively: for example, as families, in which case there may be a difference of interpretation between genders (Spring, 1982), or as communities, at which level local leaders can play an important role (Ward, 1989). Finally refugees may not wish to repatriate to the place from which they fled. Alvarez (1967) modelled the various options open to return migrants. Returnees may repatriate to their place of birth in situations where they migrated internally before internationally; or rural refugees may become urbanised and return to cities.

Home conditions The United Nations definition of a refugee (Chapter 1) is predicated on the implicit conception of a bond between a citizen and a state as the normal basis of society. In the case of the refugee, this bond has been severed (Shacknove, 1985, p. 277). Persecution is the most obvious manifestation of this severed bond, but refugees do not flee physical persecution alone. Often they flee proximate factors, which have been created or at least exacerbated by persecution.

It follows that refugees will base a decision to return upon information on a host of factors, not just security. These may include the ability to gain a livelihood in the short term (up to the next harvest) and the long term; the presence of relatives which will facilitate social reintegration; and the alignment of local authorities with whom to negotiate access to resources and facilities.

Contemporary causes of refugee flight are often low-intensity conflicts of a long duration. Spatial impact varies over time. The dynamics of war mean that the spectrum of home conditions may alter in a refugee's absence. In a highly fluid situation the frequency of information flows becomes essential.

Agents The agents in the system act as sources of information for the refugees. They can be grouped into the categories of institutional, personal, kin and the media. Of the variety of institutional sources the most active are usually UNHCR and governments of both asylum and origin. It is a self-professed aim of Tripartite Commissions to keep refugees updated on home conditions. NGOs involved in cross-border operations may also be a source of information. The Catholic Office for Emergency Relief and Refugees, for example, now regularly distributes the Ban Vinai Information Project Bulletin amongst Laotian refugees in Thailand.

During exile refugees may often interact in new social networks (Marx, 1990, p. 199) and develop a new range of personal contacts. These may be sources of information. Two sorts of relationship with personal sources can be conceived; namely uniplex relationships where the single focus of interaction is the pursuit by the refugee of information, and multiplex relationships where interaction has more than a single content and the passing of information may be incidental. Respectively these can be termed action-set and communication-set social networks (Mitchell, 1969, p. 36).

Personal sources who have information about home areas may include refugee warriors (Zolberg *et al.*, 1989, p. 276) who cross the border in order to fight and then return to recuperate and regroup in refugee camps; abortive repatriates; refugees who periodically cross the border to collect firewood or attend a funeral, for example; and refugees who work the system by repatriating for a short period of time without surrendering their ration cards and then re-apply for refugee status. In some instances trade may occur between home areas and areas of exile, in which case peripatetic traders may be information sources. Probably the most important personal source will be new arrivals, although they may be unable to provide an objective assessment of an often traumatic experience.

Some refugees may receive information from kin still at home. The Malawi Red Cross has developed a postal system in order to pass letters between refugees and relatives at home. In other cases refugees may visit home. Ugandan refugees in southern Sudan occasionally sent home scouts in order to assess conditions for return; these scouts may also pass on information from kin (Harrell-Bond, 1986, p. 191). For others the media can be an important source of information. Christensen (1985, p. 97) describes Burundian refugees in Tanzania regularly listening to broadcasts from Burundi.

Agents are mediators in the information system. Ideally, an agent will loyally relay information without altering it. The quantity and quality remain the same. But an agent may reject some information as soon as it is received, considering it irrelevant. Alternatively he/she may deliberately withhold information. Hence it cannot be assumed that information is freely available to all refugees. In any case it is impossible for an individual to communicate fully the knowledge he/she has to another (Thrift, 1985, p. 369). Thus the quantity of information decreases. An agent is also in a position to alter the quality of information. The occurrence and type of alteration will depend on the motivation of the agent.

While it is impossible to conceptualise the personal motivations of kin and individual contacts, the motivations of institutional agents and the media are largely determined by pressures external to the information system. In some cases these pressures are contradictory. UNHCR must strive to ensure that humanitarian factors are the primary determinant of its policy (Pitterman, 1987) in the context of extreme financial pressure (Coulter, 1991) which encourages them to promote certain policies over others (Harrell-Bond, 1989). For the host governments, refugees can be a cheap labour source and at the same time can exacerbate environmental, economic or social problems. The repatriation and reintegration of refugees strains home governments but also provides a potential labour force and focus for redevelopment. The limited literature on the mass media in Africa stresses its role as a mouthpiece of the government (Harrison and Palmer, 1986; Mytton, 1983).

Reception A refugee must develop some *a priori* means of assessing the reliability of an agent. This may be the perceived competence of the agent (Shibutani, 1966, p. 62) or the length of time that he/she has been known, for example. Where possible, the refugee will consider information from a number of agents: clearly, a high degree of correspondence of information from different sources will be important.

Refugees may develop a new agenda of priorities in exile (Zetter, 1988). For example, several Afghan refugee camps in Pakistan became foci for a resurgence of Islamic fundamentalism. Daley (1991) discusses the transformation of gender roles which may occur as a result of displacement in the context of Burundian refugees in Tanzania. There may be a difference of priorities between first generation refugees and later generations born in exile, particularly if refugee children are educated in the language and customs of the place of asylum. It follows that the subjective evaluation of what is relevant information and who is a reliable source may change over time.

Flows of information The flows of information in the system have quantitative and qualitative attributes. Quantitative features are morphological criteria which describe the pattern of the flows, including density and range. Qualitative features describe the nature of the information itself, especially accuracy, frequency and directedness. In the study of social networks the density of information flows compares to the concept of completeness in graph theory; in other words it describes the extent to which links which can exist actually do (Barnes, 1969). Information flows also have a range. In normal migration situations a 'bridge' of information develops between a migrant and his/her home area. It is articulated by remittances or periodic return, and is often activated by potential migrants to find accommodation or a job before they migrate. In refugee situations the development and range of 'bridges' is circumscribed by the limited access which agents have to both home areas and refugees in exile.

Accuracy is related to a series of biases (Chambers, 1980) which may occur when an agent is collecting information. These are the bias of using particular contacts in the home area; seasonal biases which mean that information has a limited temporal applicability; and biases of access which mean that information will have a limited spatial applicability. Frequency of access determines the opportunities for refugees to update their information. Directedness refers to the degree to which information targets both a specific home area and specific individuals in exile. In many cases information will be of a general nature at a regional as opposed to a specifically local scale, and be targeted at no particular individual.

Applying the model

So far, the notion of a refugee cycle has been introduced, and attention focused on how and when the cycle ends with repatriation. There are three types of repatriation: official, self, and *refoulement*; of which self-repatriation may now be predominant in accounting for refugee returns. While little is understood about the decision by refugees to return home, more is known about the decision-making of returning economic migrants. It is suggested here that the two are comparable. A subsequent analysis of self-repatriation, which draws upon literature on return migration, has highlighted the importance of information about home conditions to potential returnees. A theoretical model of a refugee information system has been presented. It is now necessary to place the model in the context of the contemporary global refugee crisis, and demonstrate the variety of circumstances and locations in which the model might be applied.

The so-called 'durable solutions' have become more difficult to apply to the contemporary refugee crisis than they were following the Second World War. The sheer volume of some flows – as many as six million from Afghanistan and two million from Mozambique, for example – and the fact that most refugees are in exile in less-developed countries, have made permanent settlement in the country of first asylum a less tenable option. Meanwhile the 'asylum issue' has re-emerged on the political agendas of the more-developed nations and consequently national policies have come to be characterised by an increase in restrictiveness (Gasarasi, 1991, p. 108) which has limited places for third country resettlement. As a result of these trends, repatriation is increasingly being seen as the preferred 'durable solution'. Indeed UNHCR described 1992 as the 'Year of Repatriation'.

For many the refugee cycle is turning full circle, and the realisation of this fact is essential if a re-conceptualisation of refugees is to escape an exilic bias and focus on the right of the individual to re-join his/her community of origin (Hathaway,

1991, p. 116). Even where official repatriation programmes are precluded due to the inflexibility of their application (Cuny and Stein, 1989), self-repatriation is occurring. As Cuny and Stein (1989) demonstrate, the majority of contemporary returnees are going home before the conclusion of the war from which they fled, and without significant political changes. However, it is important not to overemphasise the possibilities for repatriating; nor to assume that this process can be actively assisted by the international community in anything but a minority of circumstances. The model of a refugee information system provides a possible framework with which to analyse whether and how potential repatriates are receiving information about safe areas at home upon which to base their own decision to return. As such it can provide a better understanding of the process of repatriation. One example where the information system was central was the self-repatriation from eastern Sudan of Ethiopians to TPLF controlled areas; another that of Mozambican refugees from Malawi.

The case of Mozambicans in Malawi

The refugee influx into Malawi started in earnest in 1985. Most sources agree that there are at present over one million refugees, although the number is in flux as refugees both arrive and self-repatriate. They have fled the civil war launched by the rebel Mozambican National Resistance (MNR, later Renamo) against the Frelimo government which began in 1977. The conflict has generated up to two million refugees at present in exile in Malawi, Zambia, Swaziland, Zimbabwe, Tanzania and South Africa; and possibly as many internal displacees (USCR, 1992).

In the context of a severe local, particularly environmental impact of refugee concentrations, attention has turned to seeking a long-term solution to the refugee crisis. Voluntary repatriation has become the favoured option. A Tripartite Commission consisting of UNHCR and the governments of Mozambique and Malawi has met four times and commissioned an extensive Repatriation Operations Plan.

While a small number of repatriates returned under the auspices of the Tripartite Commission in 1989 and 1990, none did so in 1991. The UNHCR programme came to a standstill for a number of reasons. First, the war, an example of a 'low intensity conflict' (Cuny and Stein, 1989, p. 298) of long duration, continued in 1991 despite numerous aborted attempts to negotiate a peace settlement. Secondly, UNHCR could not negotiate with Renamo as it was not recognised by the United Nations, even though the group was powerful enough in Mozambique to be officially recognised by President Chissano, whose reforms paved the way finally for a negotiated ceasefire in 1992, and for the possibility of democratic elections between Frelimo and Renamo. Thirdly, UNHCR as an institution has faced a severe financial crisis, partly in the case of repatriation in southern Africa as a result of the considerable sums spent on the Namibian repatriation programme (see Chapter 4). This has precluded the return of many Mozambicans wishing to repatriate from both Zambia and Malawi through official programmes.

To date the lion's share of returnees have self-repatriated. The Mozambican government estimates that in 1989, for example, only 8,000 refugees repatriated officially from Malawi, compared with as many as 200,000 self-repatriates. These repatriates have sought out and returned to areas of peace, which vary in space and time as the focus of the war shifts according to the dynamics of support for each side. Such factors include 'ethnicity, religious belief, local political rivalries (and) processes of the socialization of the youth' (Young, 1990, p. 506). In this context, only a people-centred model of information available to potential returnees can begin to unravel the detailed local prospects for viable repatriation.

Policy implications and conclusion

This chapter has focused on repatriation as a solution to the refugee crisis, arguing that it is a process which is not clearly understood or conceptualised. By comparing repatriates to return migrants, it is suggested that repatriation occurs as the result of a comparison by a refugee of conditions in exile and conditions at home. The receipt of information about home conditions by the refugee is central if substantial and permanent repatriation is to occur. In this context, it is useful to draw on geographical research on innovation diffusion, in which the categories of 'adopters', and 'mediators' are crucial, as well as the notion that information has a quality as well as a quantity.

The model itself is of necessity an oversimplification. Nonetheless, it makes assumptions which are themselves worthy of research, whilst providing initial simplicity which is essential if it is to be operationalised in the field. More widely, in on-going situations such as the return of Mozambicans from Malawi, Ethiopians from Sudan or Kampucheans from Thailand, it highlights the fact that a focus upon the receipt and evaluation by potential repatriates of information about their home areas may contribute towards an understanding of the process of self-repatriation and also inform policy decisions.

The model of an information system also focuses attention upon the potential role which the international community could play as a facilitator of information flows. One option is for involved bodies to act as agents themselves. An example already mentioned is the Ban Vinai Information Project Bulletin amongst Laotian refugees in Thailand. This would certainly necessitate refugee participation, as information would be pointless unless considered relevant by the refugees themselves. Information would have to be relayed passively, without the agent suggesting what response it felt the refugee should take.

Another option is for the international community to facilitate other agents or means of information relay. Examples would be the provision of radios or newspapers in refugee settlements, or alternatively, taking representative groups of refugees back to their home areas so that they could assess conditions for themselves and report back to others. In contrast, in several cases actions by various authorities have precluded or interfered with information flows. These have included the relocation of refugee communities away from areas which border their home countries, and the systematic deregistration of and withdrawal of ration cards from refugees who attempt to cross back into their home countries and who may be seeking information or arranging their re-entry into a home society.

There have been several examples, the most recent the repatriation of Haitians from Cuba by the United States, when the genuinely voluntary nature of repatriation has been brought in to question because the international community has presumed to judge when it is safe for refugees to return home, and has apparently been incorrect. It is essential that refugees be allowed to make that decision for themselves, if one is to ensure that repatriation does not also become a 'forced migration'. In turn, such decisions by refugees must be based upon accurate, reliable and relevant information about the areas to which they plan to return.

References

Akol, J.O., 1987, 'Southern Sudanese refugees: their repatriation and resettlement after the Addis Ababa Agreement', in J.R. Rogge, ed., *Refugees: a third world dilemma*, Rowman & Littlefield, New Jersey.

Alvarez, J.H., 1967, *Return migration to Puerto Rico*, University of California Press, Berkeley.

Barnes, J.A., 1969, 'Networks and political process', in Mitchell, J.C., ed., *Social networks in urban situations*, Manchester University Press, Manchester, UK.

Basok, T., 1990, 'Repatriation of Nicaraguan refugees from Honduras and Costa Rica', *Journal of Refugee Studies*, **3** (4): 281–97.

Brown, L.A., 1975, 'The market and infrastructure context of adoption: a spatial perspective', *Economic Geography*, **51** (3):185–216.

Brown, L.A., 1981, *Innovation diffusion: a new perspective*, Methuen, London.

Burgess, J. and Gold, J.R., 1985, *Geography, the media and popular culture*, Croom Helm, London.

Cerase, F.P., 1974, 'Migration and social change: expectations and reality. A case study of return migrants from USA', *International Migration Review*, **8** (2): 245–62.

Chambers, R., 1980, 'Rapid rural appraisal: rationale and repertoire', *IDS Discussion Paper*, no. 155.

Christensen, H., 1985, *Refugees and Pioneers*, United Nations Research Institute for Social Development, Geneva.

Coulter, P., 1991, 'The cost of hospitality', *New Internationalist*, **223**: 7

Crisp, J.F., 1984, 'Voluntary repatriation programmes for African refugees: a critical examination', *Refugee Issues*, **1** (2): 1–23.

Cuny, F. and Stein, B., 1989, 'Prospects for and promotion of spontaneous repatriation', in G. Loescher and L. Monahan, eds, *Refugees and international relations*, Oxford University Press, Oxford.

Daley, P., 1991, 'Gender displacement and social reproduction: settling Burundian refugees in western Tanzania', *Journal of Refugee Studies*, **4** (3): 248–66.

Gasarasi, C.P., 1990, 'UN Resolution 435 and the repatriation of Namibian exiles', *Journal of Refugee Studies*, **3** (4): 340–64

Gasarasi, C.P., 1991, 'A report of the 2nd annual meeting of the International Research and Advisory Panel, January 1991', *Journal of Refugee Studies*, **4** (2): 105–12.

Hägerstrand, T., 1967, *Innovation diffusion as a spatial process*, University of Chicago Press, Chicago.

Harrell-Bond, B.E., 1986, *Imposing aid: emergency assistance to refugees*, Oxford University Press, Oxford

Harrell-Bond, B.E., 1989, 'Repatriation: under what conditions is it the most desirable solution for refugees?', *African Studies Review*, **32** (1): 41–69.

Harrell-Bond, B.E., Hussein, K. and Matlou, P., 1989, 'Contemporary refugees in Africa: a problem of the state', in S. Moroney, ed., *Africa, a handbook Vol.2*, Facts on File, New York.

Harrison, P. and Palmer, R., 1986, *News out of Africa*, Hilary Shipman, London.

Hathaway, J.C., 1991, 'Reconceiving refugee law as human rights protection', *Journal of Refugee Studies*, **4** (2): 113–31.

Hendrie, B., 1991, 'The politics of repatriation: the Tigrayan refugee repatriation, 1985–87', *Journal of Refugee Studies*, **4** (2): 200–18.

King, R., 1978, 'Return migration: a neglected aspect of population geography', *Area*, **10** (3):175–82.

Kuhlman, T., 1991, 'The economic integration of refugees in developing countries: a research model', *Journal of Refugee Studies*, **4** (1): 1–21.

Kunz, E.F., 1973, 'The refugee in flight: kinetic models and forms of displacement', *International Migration Review*, **7** (2): 125–46.

Kunz, E.F., 1981, 'Exile and resettlement: refugee theory', *International Migration Review*, **15** (1): 42–51.

Marx, E., 1990, 'The social world of refugees: a conceptual framework', *Journal of Refugee Studies*, **3** (3): 189–203.

Molho, I., 1986, 'Theories of migration: a review', *Scottish Journal of Political Economy*, **33** (4): 396–419.

Mitchell, J.C., 1969, 'The concept and use of social networks', in J.C. Mitchell, ed., *Social networks in urban situations*, University of Manchester Press, Manchester, UK.

Mytton, G., 1983, *Mass communication in Africa*, Edward Arnold, London.

Nanda, V.P., 1989, *Refugee law and policy. International and US responses*, Greenwood Press, Connecticut.

Pitterman, S., 1987, 'Determinants of international refugee policy: a comparative study of UNHCR material assistance to refugees in Africa, 1963–1981', in J.R. Rogge, ed., *Refugees: a third world dilemma*, Rowman & Littlefield, New Jersey.

Rogge, J.R. and Akol, J.O., 1989, 'Repatriation: its role in resolving Africa's refugee dilemma', *International Migration Review*, **23** (2): 184–200.

Scudder, T. and Colson, E., 1982, 'From welfare to development: a conceptual framework for the analysis of dislocated people', in A. Hansen and A. Oliver-Smith, eds, *Involuntary migration and resettlement. The problems and responses of dislocated people*, Westview Press, Boulder, Colorado.

Shacknove, A.E., 1985, 'Who is a refugee?', *Ethics*, **95** (2): 274–84.

Shibutani, T., 1966, *Improvised news: a sociological study of rumor*, Bobbs-Merrill, New York.

Spring, A., 1982, 'Women and men as refugees: differential assimilation of Angolan refugees in Zambia', in A. Hansen, A. Oliver-Smith, eds, *Involuntary migration and resettlement: the problems and responses of dislocated people*, Westview Press, Boulder, Colorado.

Stein, B., 1986, 'Durable solutions for developing country refugees', *International Migration Review*, **20** (2): 264–82.

Thrift, N., 1985, 'Flies and germs: a geography of knowledge', in D. Gregory and J. Urry, eds, *Social relations and spatial structures*, Macmillan, London.

USCR (United States Committee for Refugees), 1992, *World refugee survey, 1991*, USCR, Washington DC.

Ward, P., 1989, 'Local leadership and the distributional benefits wrought by illegality in third world community development', in A. Gilbert and P. Ward, eds, *Corruption, development and inequality*, Routledge, London.

Young, T., 1990, 'The MNR/Renamo: external and internal dynamics', *African Affairs*, **89** (357): 491–509.

Zetter, R., 1988, 'Refugees, repatriation and root causes', *Journal of Refugee Studies*, **1** (2): 99–106.

Zolberg, A.R., Suhrke, A. and Aguayo, S., 1989, *Escape from violence*, Oxford University Press, New York.

Further reading

Basok, T., 1990, 'Repatriation of Nicaraguan refugees from Honduras and Costa Rica', *Journal of Refugee Studies*, **3** (4): 281–97.

Crisp, J.F., 1984, 'Voluntary repatriation programmes for African refugees: a critical examination', *Refugee Issues*, **1** (2): 1–23.

Cuny, F. and Stein, B., 1989, 'Prospects for and promotion of spontaneous repatriation', in G. Loescher and L. Monahan, eds, *Refugees and international relations*, Oxford University Press, Oxford.

Harrell-Bond, B.E., 1989, 'Repatriation: under what conditions is it the most desirable solution for refugees?', *African Studies Review*, **32** (1): 41–69.

Hendrie, B., 1991, 'The politics of repatriation: the Tigrayan refugee repatriation, 1985–87', *Journal of Refugee Studies*, **4** (2): 200–18.

12 End of the Cold War: end of Afghan relief aid?

Allan Findlay

Introduction

> Increasingly abandoned and forgotten, and with the threat of further reductions in the financing of humanitarian assistance programmes, the average Afghan has understandably reached the point of despair. The figures are overwhelming and eloquent: over a million killed, over two million disabled, thousands upon thousands of orphans and widows, a standard of living below the line of abject poverty, over five million refugees and over two million displaced persons in a country which has been suffering total devastation for more than a decade. (Sevan, 1991, p.2)

Given this desperate, but accurate description of the Afghan situation in 1991, it seems remarkable that there should have been discussion at that time of scaling down and halting relief to Afghan refugees. Nevertheless, this was precisely the issue being debated by UNHCR and by other UN agencies. This chapter considers why this should have been the case. Was it simply that the Cold War was over and that international donors were uninterested in providing further aid to those who had suffered from the wars of the past? It can be argued that the decision by the USA and the former USSR to halt all further military assistance to the many factions involved in the Afghan conflict was only one of a much more complex set of factors accounting for the changing international policy which emerged towards the Afghans.

Whatever the causes, the early 1990s emerged as a critical period in international affairs which favoured a re-evaluation of the status of the world's largest refugee population. This was not an unique event and in some ways paralleled the earlier redefinition in the mid-1980s of Vietnamese refugees as economic migrants. At the time of writing in early 1992 it had become clear that in the event of an agreement on an interim government in Afghanistan to replace the socialist Najibullah regime,[1] those Afghan refugees not participating subsequently in mass repatriation to their country of origin would find themselves rapidly reclassified as economic migrants. Even prior to any such move the UNHCR had already cut its non-food assistance from over $60 million in 1985 to approximately $33 million in 1991. The High Commissioner had also stated in a letter (dated 18 June 1991) to the Prime Minister of Pakistan that the UNHCR care and maintenance programme could not be sustained indefinitely and that 'it has become imperative to pursue the developments on voluntary repatriation to Afghanistan'.

This chapter sets out to investigate the circumstances behind the changing politics of relief aid to Afghan refugees. It does this by first considering the historical context of the Afghan refugee situation, pointing out that the war in Afghanistan was not merely a conflict between two superpowers, but also involved other issues at other scales of analysis. Second, the chapter examines the role of UNHCR as an international agency and seeks to provide a basis on which to judge what lies behind its policy statements about aid to Afghan refugees. On the basis of these strands of investigation the chapter seeks to conclude whether or not the end of the Cold War did spell an end to Afghan refugee aid.

Background to the Afghan refugee situation

Afghanistan is not a nation in the same sense in which the term is used in Western Europe or North America (Anderson and Dupree, 1990). The state boundaries are artificially imposed lines which dissect pre-existing ethnic groups (Huldt and Janssen, 1988). Within the boundaries of Afghanistan lie a wide range of different language groups, each with their own cultural traits and distinctive traditions. To quote Urban (1988, p. 204), Afghanistan is a 'nation only in the xenophobic perception of outsiders'.

The so-called 'military coup' of April 1978, by Afghans sympathetic to socialist ideals, did not take over a state with a central organisation and an integrated infrastructure. In many senses resistance to the coup arose because they tried to impose the apparatus of a modern state, rather than because of their socialist ideology *per se*. There was strong resistance from pre-existing power structures. These operated at the local scale of the village in terms of tribal leaders, landowners and religious leaders, who feared that their authority would be increasingly undermined by the centralist modernising policies of Kabul. The fact that the new leaders promoted external value systems such as favouring the equality of women, which were at odds with the central precepts of Islam, reinforced the position of local leaders in the eyes of their constituencies. The initial struggle in Afghanistan in the late 1970s was therefore between many local, traditional tribal societies, and a centralist system of government seeking to overthrow these power structures and to introduce a more integrated modern state, albeit using highly unacceptable methods. Afghan refugees had begun to flee to Pakistan even before the intervention of the Soviet Union.

Failure of the original coup leaders to achieve their objectives, combined with specific political circumstances operating in the Soviet Union in the late 1970s, led the Soviet army to invade Afghanistan in December 1979. Balancing the intervention of the Soviet superpower was the infusion of billions of dollars of military aid to the local Afghan resistance (*mujahedeen*) from the USA and from conservative Arab governments. Suddenly Afghanistan was transformed from being the scene of a struggle between a centralist military regime and local traditional forces, to being the stage for a conflict between the superpowers using the latest and most destructive technologies of the twentieth century. The war which followed was merciless and costly for all involved. The death toll and refugee statistics which have been quoted at the beginning of this chapter were perhaps the inevitable tragic result for the Afghan population.

Refugee flows into Pakistan were massive in 1980 and 1981, and then began to slow down in 1982. Continuation of fighting throughout the 1980s meant that there was an influx of some refugees to Pakistan in most years. By the end of 1990 there were 3.3 million registered refugees in Pakistan and an estimated 600,000 unregistered refugees. In addition there were an estimated two million Afghan refugees in Iran, bringing the total Afghan refugee population at this date close to six million persons (Centlivres and Centlivres-Demont, 1988).

What was apparently confusing for western observers was the continuation of fighting and refugee flows into Pakistan, following the Geneva accords of April 1988 and the subsequent withdrawal of Soviet troops. In practice, what was evident was that in the period after Soviet withdrawal, the Afghan government in Kabul commanded a measure of popular support from those elements of the Afghan population who either favoured the integrating national policies of the regime or feared Najibullah less than his *mujahedeen* opponents. Continued supply of arms and economic aid to Najibullah by the former USSR throughout 1989 and 1990 meant the struggle was temporarily sustained between a central Afghan regime and the fragmented local forces of the *mujahedeen*.

During the years of the Soviet occupation the fragmented nature of *mujahedeen* fighters made it extremely hard for the Soviets to ever strike decisively against their opponents since there was no single headquarters or organising structure behind the *mujahedeen*. This seeming strength of the *mujahedeen* in a defensive situation ironically also proved to be their greatest weakness when it came to launching offensives against Najibullah. The lack of an overall coordinated strategy repeatedly led to the failure of such offensives (Huldt and Janssen, 1988). Between 1988 and 1991 they achieved no significant victories, and even when minor towns were captured by *mujahedeen* this was followed by in-fighting between different militia over the booty. Thus by early 1992, three years after the full Soviet withdrawal, the *mujahedeen* had totally failed to dislodge the central government in any significant way, despite having received continued aid from the US and conservative Arab regimes. Inversely, the brutal treatment of regional populations by some *mujahedeen* factions in areas where fighting had occurred, as for example in the Khost region, resulted in new refugee exoduses to Pakistan during 1990 and 1991, and dissuaded people from defecting to the side of the *mujahedeen*.

The net effect of the perceived stalemate in the Afghan struggle in early 1992 was an increase in status for the Najibullah regime and a growing lack of credibility for the *mujahedeen* as an alternative government. In 1991 three important aspects of the conflict did, however, begin to change. First, the ending of the Cold War ushered in what President Bush termed 'a new world order'. This so-called new world order introduced a radically different military agenda for the United States, which involved a switch from engagement in territories on the edge of the former Soviet empire to new locations of regional conflict such as the war with Iraq. The new pattern of military engagement therefore led to the emergence of new priority areas demanding international emergency relief aid in the wake of the ensuing conflicts. Another related change which took place in late 1991 and early 1992 and which affected US perceptions of the desirability of continued aid to Afghan refugees was the approaching presidential election. This in turn directed the attention of the US administration to internal over external issues, and certainly favoured US disengagement from supporting the *mujahedeen*, culminating in a total cessation of aid to certain strongly pro-Islamic groups (Hesbi-i-Islami) and a mid-summer freeze on all other US aid, officially in protest over the kidnapping of two American relief workers.

A second change came suddenly at the end of August 1991, when the centripetal dispersal of power in the former Soviet Union led to an undermining of the hard-line factions in the USSR which had supported the Najibullah regime with military and economic assistance. The Soviet Union, in seeking western relief aid supplies to solve its own internal crisis, was faced with demands for so-called 'negative symmetry' to curtail all further aid (approximately $300 million annually) to the Afghan regime.

A third significant change which took place in 1991 was that both of Afghanistan's immediate neighbours moved politically towards a position which favoured a more stable situation inside Afghanistan. Iran, faced with a new refugee influx of Kurds and with large Shiite refugee populations entering its territory after the Gulf War, was not at all unhappy at the prospect of Afghan refugees departing from its eastern provinces. Pakistan, threatened with the possibility of having itself either to provide a higher share of the relief support to the Afghan refugees in Baluchistan and in North West Frontier Province (NWFP), or to permit the permanent integration of the refugees, also became increasingly concerned about the continuation of the war. It must be said however that certain exploitative elements of the Pakistani regime still had much to gain from the continuation of the conflict.

Faced with the loss of international support both for Najibullah and the *mujahedeen*, it is perhaps less than surprising that three rounds of talks were agreed between the protagonists during 1991. The first two rounds, held in Islamabad and Tehran, showed that some flexibility did exist for compromise. For example, some prisoners were exchanged and leaders of the *mujahedeen* agreed to meet the UN Secretary General to discuss his five-point peace plan. However, the fragmentation of the *mujahedeen* position remained evident. Only four of the seven main factions were willing to take part. Moreover, assassination of the leader of one faction by another took place at the same time as the talks in Tehran.

While the logic for a settlement existed by the end of 1991 in terms of the perceptions of the international community, there remained many underlying tensions, for example between those seeking to impose a central integrating government structure on Afghanistan and local leaders seeking to maintain tribal power structures, and also between those whose primary aim was to remove all trace of the pro-Soviet socialist regime and those who sought the creation of a radical Islamic fundamentalist state. Whatever was perceived to be the future for Afghanistan by external observers, the reality of the situation from the perspective of most, though not all, Afghan refugees in late 1991 was that repatriation remained impossible.

The refugee situation in North West Frontier Province, Pakistan, 1991

Refugee statistics are notoriously unreliable (Black, 1991; Choucri, 1983). Of officially registered Afghan refugees in Pakistan, 2.24 million, or about 68 per cent, were resident in North West Frontier Province (Figure 12.1) in October

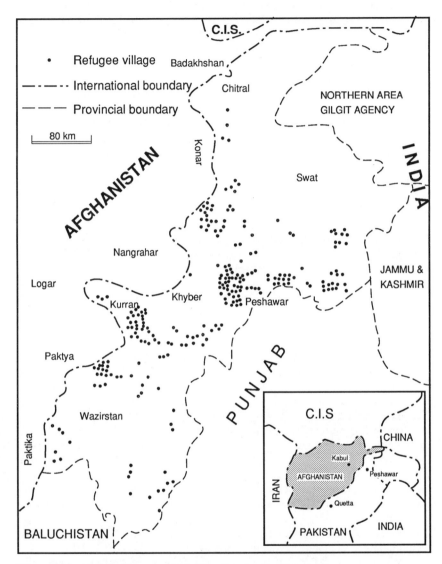

Figure 12.1 Afghan villages in North West Frontier Province, Pakistan

1989. Children comprised 48 per cent of the population, women another 28 per cent and men only 24 per cent. Despite literacy programmes in the camps, approximately 86 per cent of refugees remain illiterate (Azhar, 1990; Kushkaki, 1990; Wood, 1989).

On 1 September 1991 the total refugee population for NWFP was 2.26 million, a figure somewhat higher than that for two years previously. Despite this trend, UNHCR sources suggest that between 150,000 and 300,000 persons may actually have returned home (or between 5 and 10 per cent of the total refugee population in Pakistan.[2] The apparent contradiction of these statistics (the growing refugee total *vis à vis* the apparent pattern of a very limited scale of repatriation) can be resolved simply in terms of there being a small net inflow of refugees as a result of the continued fighting at a time when some return movement was occurring to other more tranquil regions of Afghanistan. In reality the situation was much more complex. Many 'refugees' were travelling back in the spring to fight with the *mujahedeen* or to plant their fields, before returning to Pakistan in the autumn. Relief workers visiting camps in the Chitral area in summer 1991 noted, for example, that many families had members absent in Afghanistan, but this would not have been obvious in the UNHCR statistics since they had passed on their ration books to others in the family remaining in Pakistan. This action both disguised their repatriation and kept open their option to return to Pakistan. Others had encashed their ration books under a recent UNHCR scheme (commenced in July 1990) which offered refugees 3,300 Rs and 300 kg of wheat per family for handing in their ration books and agreeing to return home. In the absence of any effective way of checking on border crossings it is impossible to tell how many of the 17,839 families from NWFP who had taken up the scheme by September 1991 had actually returned to Afghanistan as opposed to relocating elsewhere in Pakistan outside the refugee camps.

Field evidence suggests that adoption of the encashment scheme in particular, and repatriation in general, has been strongest from refugee communities in the south in Baluchistan and from those in the far north around Chitral. Return has been weakest from the Peshawar area, which was of course the location with the largest concentration of refugees. This pattern can be explained in part by the fact that Peshawar is the political control centre for the *mujahedeen*. Most of the *mujahedeen* traditionally opposed repatriation until an Islamic government is installed in Kabul, on the dual basis that prior repatriation lent legitimacy to the Najibullah regime as well as having the effect of reducing their own resource base in Pakistan. Since all Afghan refugees in Pakistan are effectively forced to register as belonging to one of the *mujahedeen* factions, and since the influence of these factions is greatest in the camps around Peshawar, it is not surprising that the pace of return was slower from this area. But it would equally be true that employment opportunities and refugee welfare services are best in the Peshawar area, and that consequently the attractions of staying in Pakistan are greatest for the refugees in these camps.

UNHCR officials interviewed by the author had hoped that 100,000 families would have accepted the encashment programme, rather than the 17,800 recorded as doing so in NWFP by mid-1991. It was believed that most refugees did genuinely want to return home as soon as possible. The 'myth of return' is however a cherished goal held by refugees and economic migrants in many different parts of the world, and research has shown that true determinants of return and repatriation may be quite independent of expressions of an intent or desire to return home. In the Afghan context, it therefore needs to be recognised that many refugees will never go home, despite claiming to hold this objective. A UNRISD survey (Christensen and Scott, 1988) has shown that two-thirds of male refugees had achieved gainful employment in Pakistan; 25 per cent had occupational skills (such as drivers, tailors, mechanics and teachers); about a sixth were self-employed, and 14 per cent earned over 1,000 Rs per month. It seems inevitable, therefore, that for some refugees the economic attractions of staying in Pakistan will far outweigh the prospects of returning to a devastated Afghanistan. Most official estimates anticipate that around 25 per cent of refugees will seek to stay in Pakistan, becoming economic migrants rather than political refugees. From an examination of the limited economic data available on the refugee community (Christensen and Scott, 1988) it seems quite possible that the figure will be much higher, reaching perhaps 40 per cent. This in itself may be a new source of conflict, with Pakistan possibly being unwilling to countenance the integration of over a million economic migrants. It seems unavoidable therefore, even given the establishment of the new government in Kabul, that the refugees will continue to be pawns in the region's complex political and economic struggle. Moreover, the needs of the refugee community will continue to be great even although their international political status may soon be modified.

Amongst those for whom repatriation in 1991/92 was a probability rather than a possibility, the necessary preconditions for their return clearly had not yet been met. These preconditions included:

1. A change in the composition of the government in Kabul which would permit as a minimum that some of *mujahedeen* leadership enter a power-sharing arrangement. This would in turn permit these *mujahedeen* factions to favour mass repatriation;
2. An increase in security for returning Afghans, both in terms of continued mine clearing operations and a restoration of a semblance of law and order, in place of on-going feuding and warring between vigilante groups;
3. A considerable degree of physical and economic reconstruction of the war torn areas of Afghanistan. Without this it will be very hard for Afghans, especially the 70 per cent of refugees who were farmers before going into exile, to return to their villages and valleys and re-establish themselves.

Having reviewed the historical context and current situation of Afghan refugee movements, it is now possible to draw some conclusions. First, it has been argued that the roots of the conflict in Afghanistan predated the intervention of the superpowers. The disengagement of the US and the Soviet Union from Afghanistan therefore only affected the scale of the conflict. The end of the Cold War between the superpowers did not provide the necessary conditions for peace to be restored to Afghanistan. Second, it has been suggested that in 1992, there remained several unfulfilled preconditions which would need to be met if successful mass repatriation of Afghan refugees were to occur. In particular, many of the refugees will find the economic imbalance between the more favourable circumstances of Pakistan and the situation in Afghanistan such that voluntary return will be unlikely on purely economic grounds.

The changing role of UN-related relief operations in Pakistan

Why did UNHCR, an organisation charged with the protection of refugee rights, adopt a programme involving cuts in relief to Afghan refugees prior to there being substantive evidence of large-scale voluntary repatriation? One answer to this question is given in the following quotation taken from the introduction to the June 1991 report of 'Operation Salam', the UN coordinated programme for humanitarian and economic assistance to Afghans:

> The international community has increasingly become immune to the war in Afghanistan and the suffering of its people, a trend which is reflected in the reduction of the overall funding of Operation Salam ... This has forced us ... to cancel, abandon or scale down 57 projects with a total value of US $31 million [including] essential activities in such fields as the rehabilitation of agriculture, immunization of children, nutrition, basic education, the disabled, the clearance of mines and unexploded ordnance (Sevan, 1991, p. 1).

In order to evaluate both the question given above and the explanation offered by Sevan for the reduction in funding, it is necessary to understand something of the nature of UNHCR as an organisation, as well as considering the political and economic implications of reducing humanitarian assistance to Afghan refugees.

UNHCR

UNHCR was established in 1951, with its immediate objective being to provide aid to the millions of displaced persons in Europe, who had fled their homes during and after the Second World War. Its expenditure was, and still is, financed mainly by voluntary contributions from sympathetic governments. In terms of the volume of income, this has meant in particular the governments of the advanced industrial nations: the US has always been a major donor.

Under international law, a refugee is defined according to the 1951 Convention on refugees (Chapter 1). UNHCR has to operate relative to this definition, and as a consequence has no remit to intervene on behalf of persons displaced within the boundaries of a state, nor on behalf of those international flows of persons not recognised by the powerbrokers of the international community as fleeing from places of persecution. Given its funding basis, it is hard for UNHCR to operate independently from its major donors in defining which groups of people can, or should, be classified as refugees. Furthermore, UNHCR and other UN agencies such as the United Nations Relief and Works Agency (UNRWA) have on occasion been criticised for contributing to the creation of permanent refugee populations, by providing an infrastructural basis for institutionalising the refugee situation, and as a consequence providing a disincentive to the emergence of a long-term 'solution' to certain refugee situations (Gordenker, 1987).

By 1991, UNHCR had provided an estimated $590 million in aid to Afghan refugees in Pakistan through its general programmes and a further $260 million under special programmes. It has been suggested that in part the reduction in UN aid to Afghan refugees reflects a trimming of budgets from a position of 'over-provision' by certain donors during the height of the superpower conflict in Afghanistan in the early 1980s. To the staggering aid statistics must be added a further $80–100 million per annum from the World Food Programme. This level of aid implies a total contribution averaging $600 per refugee.

In the early 1980s, most aid was directed towards ensuring the immediate survival of new arrivals, but by the mid-1980s attention was switching to programmes aimed at increasing the self-reliance of the refugees. Since 1988, the relief programme has tried to contemplate how repatriation might be achieved, and how UNHCR could work towards a voluntary return of the vast refugee population to an impoverished economy. The continuation of fighting in Afghanistan exacerbated what was for UNHCR an already critical problem. Changing levels of UN humanitarian and economic assistance may in part therefore be attributed to changes in the kind of assistance being provided (ACBAR, 1990).

For UNHCR, 1990 proved to be an extremely difficult year. Donor support to UNHCR reflected a growing concern by the governments of the wealthier countries, such as the UK, that international migration stimulated by extreme poverty and deprivation (undoubtedly a genuine threat to survival) was becoming increasingly difficult to distinguish from 'purely' political refugee movements. Rather than revise the 1951 Convention, UNHCR had therefore to be seen to be applying the terms of the Convention more strictly than in the past.

At the same time as UNHCR was struggling to handle an unprecedented funding crisis, refugee numbers were growing rapidly through the displacement of populations before, during, and after the Gulf War, and in relation to crises in other parts of the world. To quote UNHCR's own appraisal of the situation: 'with refugee numbers outpacing the available funds, UNHCR has been obliged to pare down its assistance budget and to focus increasingly on survival needs. As a result living conditions have deteriorated for many exiled communities' (UNHCR, 1990, p. 5).

Given the circumstances described above, it is scarcely surprising that UNHCR support to the Afghan refugees has been a matter of much debate in recent years. It has formed a very major budget item for UNHCR. Most of the aid to Afghans is perceived in UNHCR terms as relating to non-survival needs (e.g. education, developmental skills, vocational training, etc.). In addition, some have argued (Sevan, 1991, p. 5) that repatriation of refugees would speed a resolution of the conflict in Afghanistan. Why this might be true is seldom spelt out, but those who hold this opinion may be implying that aid to refugees is a form of continued covert support for the *mujahedeen*. It hence reduces the pressure on them to find a political solution. The reality of the situation, regardless of the rhetoric, is that UNHCR aid has systematically been reduced to Afghan refugees since the mid-1980s. For example, food rations to registered refugees have been cut drastically. Despite this, surveys amongst refugees suggest that most refugees are to a large degree self-sufficient after ten years in Pakistan, and that reduction of UNHCR support thus far has not threatened their survival.

To summarise the discussion presented above, there are at least three aspects of UNHCR's structure and activities which could have produced cuts in expenditure on assistance to Afghan refugees in the late 1980s and early 1990s. These are:

1.   In the middle of the superpower conflict in Afghanistan, donor aid to UNHCR was, for political reasons, very great. As a result, it can be argued that subsequent budget reductions represent an adjustment to providing only the most necessary forms of assistance, rather than what might be termed by some 'over-provision';
2.   There has been a change in the type of assistance required by the refugees over time, and this has resulted in a budget decrease;
3.   There has been an increase in pressure on UNHCR to assist in other refugee situations, combined with pressure by donors to keep UNHCR to its original

mandate, both of which may have favoured a switch in the allocation of UNHCR resources to other refugee situations.

Internal debate over reducing Afghan aid

A major element of the author's research in Pakistan in 1991 comprised interviews with high ranking UNHCR officials. One of the main objectives of these meetings was to obtain a clearer statement on UNHCR's policy directions with regard to the Afghans and to investigate the nature of the internal debate over the policy of reducing aid to Afghan refugees. It became clear in the course of the interviews that while external factors, such as those discussed above, had been influential in initiating a review of the UNHCR's single largest budget item (assistance to Afghan refugees), a strong argument existed on quite separate grounds for a reduction in aid. This argument was based on the view that a reduction in aid would contribute to resolving the refugee situation, through fostering serious discussion by all parties concerned of whether mass voluntary repatriation was probable or even possible, and to what extent measures were required to encourage long-term integration in Pakistan of those elements of the refugee population unwilling or unable to return home. The debate over future UNHCR policy to Afghan refugees seemed not only to be between the directors of UNHCR in Geneva and their staff in Pakistan, but also between different offices and officials within Pakistan.

The starting point for the debate was a statement by the UN High Commissioner in March 1990 that care and maintenance of the refugees could not be sustained indefinitely. The High Commissioner imposed a three-year time period for a political solution to be found. This statement caused anxiety for the Government of Pakistan, for NGOs operating alongside UNHCR to assist the refugees, and of course amongst the refugees themselves. In November 1990, a new High Commissioner was appointed. There followed an internal debate in UNHCR about future policy towards the Afghan refugees. In June 1991, the new High Commissioner reaffirmed aspects of her predecessor's position in a letter to the Prime Minister of Pakistan, but withdrew from the tight time schedule which had been proposed. The key elements of the letter were that 'the UNHCR care and maintenance programme could not be continued indefinitely'; that she sought 'the full cooperation of your (Pakistani) government to provide all necessary encouragement and assistance ... for their voluntary and unhindered return to Afghanistan'; and that she hoped the Pakistani government would 'appreciate the concern of the international community that the levels and modalities of international assistance foster self-reliance among the refugees and do not create disincentives to durable solutions'. Further to this, and with serious implications, the letter commented that 'it may also be timely to attempt to identify and formulate plans for the legal integration of those refugees who have achieved self-sufficiency in Pakistan and who may not return to Afghanistan'.

Prior to the conflict, Afghanistan was one of the least developed countries of the world. Even if internal security can be re-established, there will remain an immense challenge to reconstruct the country and to achieve a standard of living equivalent to that which predated the conflict. In the meantime many Afghan refugees in Pakistan have come to appreciate that it is in their economic interests to remain in Pakistan, if at all possible. A dilemma therefore faces UNHCR and other agencies concerned with refugee welfare. No one disputes the credentials of the refugee population in terms of the conditions which produced their flight from Afghanistan. It is, however, recognised by UNHCR and most others involved with the refugee community that removal of the political causes of the refugee flow may not be sufficient to make complete repatriation occur. Both within UNHCR and in some other relief agencies it is therefore argued that the provision of external humanitarian assistance to the Afghan refugees exacerbates the very economic inequalities which militate against future repatriation.

UNHCR, in making public policy statements about its declining role in refugee assistance, is both applying pressure on the government of Pakistan to support a political solution to the conflict, and warning other refugee agencies of the need to consider the imminent changes which are likely to take place in the international status of the Afghan refugee community. Once key actors in the international community perceive the situation in Afghanistan to have changed, and to be conducive to repatriation, pressure to reclassify Afghan refugees as economic migrants will become insurmountable. In declaring a 'scale-down', as opposed to a 'shut-down' situation, UNHCR is not so much trying to prevent the Afghan impasse from becoming a permanent refugee problem, as occurred with the Palestinians after 1947, but is seeking to avoid the crisis of the Vietnamese situation by which political refugees were suddenly declared to be economic migrants. Because of its mandate and circumstances, UNHCR has to avoid being accused of abandoning the Afghan refugees, while at the same time preventing any future accusation by its donors that it supports economic migrants. It has therefore moved to prepare its own echelons, the refugees, the government of Pakistan and other relief agencies for the future redefinition of 'a refugee community'. The ending of the Cold War, and the signing of a treaty in September 1991 by the US and the former Soviet Union to cease providing arms to the two sides in Afghanistan, brought this redefinition much closer. In Afghanistan, like Vietnam, it may not ultimately be internal acceptance of economic and political conditions, but international perceptions which will determine when the Afghan refugees must either return home or become redefined as economic migrants.

Conclusion

The case of Afghan refugees serves well to illustrate the ways in which refugee events have altered in a very radical fashion since the initial establishment of UNHCR in 1951. Three differences in particular stand out. First, the Afghan refugees, like most contemporary refugee movements, have moved as a result of group rather than individual decisions. Not only tribal leaders, but also political groupings such as the factions of the *mujahedeen* have strongly determined Afghan refugee movements.

Second, whereas UNHCR began its operations in Europe, most refugee flows in the 1980s and 1990s have been between countries of the less developed world. In the case of Afghan refugees in Pakistan, UNHCR is now faced with asking a state which itself remains classified as a less developed country (76 per cent of the population are illiterate, and infant mortality rates are still more than 100 per 1,000 births), to consider absorbing a refugee population of many millions of people who have come from a neighbouring and even poorer state.

Thirdly, increased inequalities between countries have meant that many genuine refugee flows also result in the transfer of people to destinations where they have the possibility of appreciably improving their standard of living. Many movements thus involve complex decision-making procedures, with refugees leaving home primarily, but not uniquely, because of a fear of persecution. Anyone even superficially familiar with the history of Afghanistan in the 1980s would agree that large portions of the Afghan population had substantial grounds to flee their homeland. It was also the case, however, that they fled from one of the least developed countries of the world. Provision of further external humanitarian assistance to the Afghan refugees may exacerbate the economic inequalities between Afghanistan and Pakistan and reduce the chances for future repatriation, while failure to continue the UNHCR programme will produce further suffering for the most vulnerable parts of the refugee community.

This chapter has sought to explain why the end of the superpower conflict in Afghanistan did not produce the immediate repatriation of the world's largest refugee population. It has also sought to explore the paradox that the Afghan refugee population received declining assistance from the UNHCR at a time when the size of the refugee population was still growing. Although the timing of events upholds the suggestion that the end of the Cold War will spell an end to Afghan aid, interpretation of the way in which UNHCR has acted to scale down humanitarian and economic assistance to Afghans would indicate that its actions and policies represent much more than a simple response to the pressures of key donor states.

Notes

1. The Najibullah regime was removed from power in late April 1992.
2. After the fall of the Najibullah regime, the level of repatriation grew, with some sources putting the total figure at 70,000 per week by mid 1992 (see for example, Girard, 1992). Nonetheless, over two million refugees remained in Pakistan at the time this book went for printing in late 1992.

References

ACBAR (Agency Coordinating Body for Afghan Refugees), 1990, *Overview of NGO assistance to the people of Afghanistan*, ACBAR, Peshawar, Pakistan.
Anderson, E. and Dupree, N., eds, 1990, *The cultural basis of Afghan nationalism*, Pinter, London.
Azhar, S., 1990, 'Afghan refugees in Pakistan: the Pakistani view', in E. Anderson and N. Dupree, eds, *The cultural basis of Afghan nationalism*, Pinter, London
Black, R., 1991, 'Refugees and displaced persons: geographical perspectives and research directions', *Progress in Human Geography*, 15 (3), 281–98.
Centlivres, P. and Centlivres-Demont, M., 1988, 'The Afghan refugee in Pakistan', *Journal of Refugee Studies*, 1 (2), 141–52.

Choucri, N., 1983, *Population and conflict*, United Nations Fund for Population Activities, New York.

Christensen, H. and Scott, W., 1988, *Survey of the social and economic conditions of Afghan refugees*, United Nations Research Institute for Social Development, Geneva.

Girard, S., 1992, 'Afghanistan: the will, but not the means', *Refugees*, **90**: 20–23.

Gordenker, L., 1987, *Refugees in international politics*, Croom Helm, London.

Huldt, B. and Janssen, E., eds, 1988, *The tragedy of Afghanistan: the social, cultural and political impact of the Soviet invasion*, Croom Helm, London.

Kushkaki, S., 1990, 'Afghan refugees: the Afghan view', in E. Anderson and N. Dupree, eds, *The cultural basis of Afghan nationalism*, Pinter, London.

Sevan, R., 1991, 'Introduction', in *Operation Salam Programme for 1991: progress report, Jan–June 1991*, Office for the Coordination of UN Humanitarian and Economic Assistance Programs Relating to Afghan Refugees, Islamabad.

UNHCR, 1990, 'A critical moment: the challenges confronting UNHCR' (editorial), *Refugees*, **81**: 5

Urban, M., 1988, *War in Afghanistan*, Macmillan, London.

Wood, W., 1989, 'Long time coming: the repatriation of Afghan refugees', *Annals, Association of American Geographers*, **79** (3), 345–69.

Further reading

Girard, S., 1992, 'Afghanistan: the will, but not the means', *Refugees*, **90**: 20–23.

Girardet, E., 1985, *Afghanistan: the war*, Croom Helm, London.

Greenway, D., 1987, 'Prospects for resettlement of Afghan refugees in Pakistan', in J.R. Rogge, ed., *Refugees: a Third World dilemma*, Rowman & Littlefield, Totowa, New Jersey.

Huldt, B. and Janssen, E., 1988, *The tragedy of Afghanistan*, Croom Helm, London.

Fair, G.M. and Merriam, J.G., eds, 1986, *Afghan resistance: the politics of survival*, Westview Press, Boulder, Colorado.

13 Forced migration and ethnic processes in the former Soviet Union

Zhanne Zayonchkovskaya, Alexander Kocharyan
and Galina Vitkovskaya

Introduction

One of the most dramatic events of recent years has been the unexpected resurgence of ethnic conflict and mass migration within the former Soviet Union. There are two outstanding questions about these developments which have considerable significance. These are: to what extent are these developments unique; and to what extent have they developed out of pre-existing circumstances?

Within the former Soviet Union there are no accurate data concerning the ethnic composition of migrants. The censuses only allow approximate estimations of national migrations through indirect means, namely comparison of the growth of ethnic population numbers in particular localities. Even using this approach, however, problems arise from the existence of differential levels of fertility and assimilation.

Ethnic diversity within the USSR

Within the period 1959-89 the ethnic structure of the population in the Soviet Union underwent noticeable change, as can be seen from the statistics contained in Tables 13.1 to 13.3. Table 13.3 in particular reveals that in the period between the last two Soviet censuses of 1979 and 1989, five republics – including the Russian Federation, the Ukraine, Byelorussia, Latvia and Estonia – saw growth in the native population accounting for less than two-thirds of all population growth; indeed, this proportion was, if anything, in decline. As a result, in each of these five republics, the native population was forming a smaller proportion of the population in its home republic.

Such an increase in the non-native population of republics can be accounted for in a variety of ways. In the Russian Federation, this situation was mainly the result of the natural increase of the Russian population declining more rapidly than that of other ethnic groups. Migration of non-Russians into the Russian Federation was also a contributory factor, to which we refer below. In the Ukraine and Byelorussia, where almost the entire population is Slavic, the decline in the importance of this group was due to losses from it through assimilation of Slavs into the Russian ethnic group, rather than through the more rapid natural increase of the latter. In

Latvia and Estonia, a third set of factors is at work. Here intensive inflows of migrants over an extended period have been responsible for the dramatically shifting balance of ethnic groups.

Table 13.1 Increase in population of indigenous nationalities of the former Soviet Union republics, 1959–70

Republic	Population 1959 (thousands)	Growth rate 1959–70 (% per annum)	Proportion of increase contributed by indigenous nationality (%)
Russian Federation	117,534	1.0	79
Ukraine	41,869	1.1	59
Byelorussia	8,056	1.1	80
Lithuania	2,711	1.4	85
Latvia	2,093	1.2	16
Estonia	1,197	1.2	20
Georgia	4,044	1.4	82
Azerbaijan	3,698	3.5	90
Armenia	1,763	3.8	90
Uzbekistan	8,119	4.1	73
Kirghizia	2,066	3.8	52
Tadjikistan	1,981	4.2	63
Turkmenia	1,516	3.8	77
Kazakhstan	9,295	3.6	39
Moldova	2,885	2.3	58

Source: Calculated from data from USSR Central Statistical Committee (Goscomstat), Moscow

In Latvia, Latvians only accounted for some 27 per cent of total population growth, whilst in Estonia, the native group only contributed 15 per cent of growth from 1979–89. Not surprisingly the ratio of native to non-native residents has declined sharply. What is more, this trend has been apparent for some time, with ratios declining consistently between 1959 and 1978. In Lithuania, the situation is not as severe, with the native population providing some 85 per cent of total population growth between 1959 and 1970, although even here, the trend is similar. It is important to note, therefore, that there have been long-standing social tensions in these states arising from immigration. This was one reason for the tough migration laws adopted in these countries in recent years.

In ten other republics, the native populations are contributing a rising proportion of total population growth. The main reason for this is high natural increase, but migration also plays a significant role. The Azerbaijani case illustrates this well. As shown in Tables 13.2 and 13.3, growth in the Azerbaijani population actually outnumbered total population growth: this is a clear indication of the size of out-migration by other nationalities and their replacement by Azerbaijani natural increase. A similar trend is apparent at a lower level within Kazakhstan: in the period 1959–70, Kazakhs contributed one of the lowest proportions of total population growth of any ethnic group in their native republic (39 per cent). By the period 1970–79 this had increased by a half to 63 per cent, with further growth to 70 per cent being recorded in the most recent time period for which we have data. By this time, the native Kazakhs were making the eighth largest contribution to population growth of any ethnic group in their own republic.

Table 13.2 Increase in population of indigenous nationalities of the former Soviet Union republics, 1970–79

Republic	Population 1970 (thousands)	Growth rate 1970–79 (% per annum)	Proportion of increase contributed by indigenous nationality (%)
Russian Federation	130,079	0.6	79
Ukraine	47,126	0.6	48
Byelorussia	9,002	0.7	52
Lithuania	3,128	0.9	78
Latvia	2,364	0.7	16
Estonia	1,356	0.9	21
Georgia	4,686	0.7	98
Azerbaijan	5,117	2.0	102
Armenia	2,492	2.4	95
Uzbekistan	11,799	3.4	79
Kirghizia	2,934	2.2	68
Tadjikistan	2,900	3.5	67
Turkmenia	2,159	3.1	78
Kazakhstan	13,009	1.4	63
Moldova	3,569	1.2	58

Source: Calculated from data from USSR Central Statistical Committee (Goscomstat), Moscow

Migration flows and spatial redistribution

In both Kazakhstan and Azerbaijan, the movement towards a mono-ethnic republic reflects the scale of Russian outmigration. This latter trend was a reversal of traditional patterns of Russian migration between republics. These had been characterised by the outward expansion of Slavic peoples – Russians, Ukrainians and Byelorussians – over the whole territory of what had been the Soviet Union. The 1989 census, however, demonstrated that this trend had been replaced by new patterns of migration, distinguished by the ousting of Russians from the Transcaucasian republics, the Central Asian republics and from Kazakhstan. In Armenia, for example, the number of Russians decreased by 27 per cent over the decade 1979–89 (Table 13.4), whilst in Azerbaijan it fell by 18 per cent and in Georgia by 9 per cent. The same was also true of Central Asian republics, but here the decline of the Russian minority has accelerated more recently under the influence of nationalistic movements. From 1979 to 1989, Russians also continued to leave the Baltic countries, Byelorussia and to a lesser degree the Ukraine and Moldova, all flows which predate the 1979 census.

Table 13.3 Increase in population of indigenous nationalities of the former Soviet Union republics, 1979–89

Republic	Population 1979 (thousands)	Growth rate 1979–89 (% per annum)	Proportion of increase contributed by indigenous nationality (%)
Russian Federation	137,551	0.7	65
Ukraine	49,755	0.4	48
Byelorussia	9,560	0.6	53
Lithuania	3,398	0.8	75
Latvia	2,521	0.6	27
Estonia	1,466	0.7	15
Georgia	5,015	0.8	88
Azerbaijan	6,028	1.6	110
Armenia	3,031	0.9	134
Uzbekistan	15,391	2.9	80
Kirghizia	3,529	2.1	74
Tadjikistan	3,801	3.4	73
Turkmenia	2,759	2.7	84
Kazakhstan	14,684	1.2	70
Moldova	3,947	1.0	69

Source: Calculated from data from USSR Central Statistical Committee (Goscomstat), Moscow

In sharp contrast to the spatial retrenchment of the Russians, Ukrainians and Byelorussians still continued to move to almost all the republics during the period 1979–89. For instance, while the total number of Ukrainians in the former Soviet Union increased by only 4 per cent between 1979 and 1989, the number of Ukrainians in the Baltic countries increased by around 35 per cent, in Byelorussia by 26 per cent and in Uzbekistan by 35 per cent. At the same time, the number of Byelorussians in Central Asia, Georgia and Azerbaijan increased by approximately 50 per cent against a national increase of only 6 per cent, although they continued to represent less than 1 per cent of the population in all of these republics except Kazakhstan. However, in 1989 itself, Ukrainians, as well as Byelorussians, began to retreat back within their own national borders.

Between 1979 and 1988 there was an intensive exchange of peoples between the Slavic republics, with Russia and Byelorussia being net beneficiaries. In 1989, this exchange continued but net movements were now focused upon the Ukraine and to a lesser extent Byelorussia. Russia itself lost Slavic nationalities.

Other groups were engaged in a process of spatial retrenchment towards the close of the 1980s. The Kazakhs who emigrated intensively to the west of the country in 1979–88 are currently moving back to their republic. In Transcaucasus the delimitation process started a long time ago, but in 1988–89 it sharply accelerated due to the influence of the Armenian massacre in Sumgait and Baku as well as the Karabakh conflict. In 1988 about 57,000 Azerbaijanis returned from Armenia to the cities of Azerbaijan only, whilst less than half that number (22,500) moved in the opposite direction. The emigration of the Azerbaijani and Armenians to their national republics from Georgia was also apparent. In 1979–88 the peoples of the Transcaucasus intensively migrated to all the republics of the European part of the former Soviet Union. In 1989 the outflow of these peoples was observed only to Russia and that of the Armenians also to the Ukraine.

Table 13.4 Index of population change of different nationalities of the former Soviet Union republics, 1979–89 (1979=100)*

Nationality			Republic		
	Russian Federation	Ukraine	Byelorussia	Lithuania	Latvia
Indigenous	105	102	104	107	103
Russians	–	108	118	113	110
Ukrainians	109	–	126	139	138
Byelorussians	115	108	–	110	107
Lithuanians	–	–	–	–	92
	Estonia	Moldova	Georgia	Azerbaijan	Armenia
Indigenous	102	110	110	123	113
Russians	116	101	91	82	73
Ukrainians	134	107	–	–	–
Byelorussians	118	–	–	–	–
Azerbaijanis	–	–	120	–	53
Armenians	–	–	97	82	–
	Uzbekistan	Kirghizia	Tadjikistan	Turkmenia	Kazakhstan
Indigenous	134	132	142	133	123
Russians	99	100	98	96	104
Ukrainians	135	99	113	96	100
Byelorussians	–	–	–	–	101
Azerbaijanis	–	–	–	142	–
Armenians	–	–	–	120	–
Uzbeks	–	129	137	136	126
Kirghiz	123	–	132	–	–
Tajiks	157	–	–	–	–
Kazakhs	130	–	–	110	–

Source: Calculated from data from USSR Central Statistical Committee

Note: * Index only included where national group constitutes over 1 per cent of total population of Republic.

Thus 1989 marked a shift towards ethnic concentration in national homelands. The same was also true for Moldavians. Traditionally they had settled throughout the Union but by 1989 emigration only continued to two republics, namely Russia and, to a lesser extent, Ukraine. Population exchange with other republics had virtually ceased.

In the case of the Baltic nations, ethnic retrenchment was associated specifically with the early move to national independence, and the break with the Russian Federation. As a result the number of Latvians in the Federation fell by 30 per cent during the period 1979–1988, and that of Estonians by 16.5 per cent.

Other groups were engaged in spatial redistribution through migration, but in their case, the outcome was spatial diffusion, not concentration. The native peoples of Central Asia were spreading beyond the borders of their region. This process did not involve large numbers of people and was, perhaps, only transient, but it was important since it created new flows, not hitherto seen. The 1989 census was the first to record this new movement, but during the remainder of 1989 the emigration of the Uzbeks, Kirghiz, Tajiks and Turkmen to Russia and the Ukraine intensified and the numerical imbalance of the exchange increased: for instance, in 1989, 5.3 million Uzbeks emigrated back to the cities of Uzbekistan from the Russian Federation, while 10.3 million people arrived in the cities of the Russian Federation from Uzbekistan. The corresponding figures for the exchange between Uzbekistan and the Ukraine were 0.75 million and 2.3 million.

Summing up, it can be noted that 1989 marked a significant turning point in migration within the former Soviet Union, characterised by an overall return of ethnic groups to their traditional homelands. Compared with the period 1979–88, migrations became more limited in scale and spatial diversity and more oriented towards native republics; there was therefore a trend towards national isolation. The diffusion of the peoples of the Transcaucasus, Moldova and Kazakhstan effectively stopped. This is likely to aggravate the problem of rural-urban migration and the growth of unemployment in Central Asia and the Transcaucasus, with commensurate increases in tension and the likelihood of social conflicts. It also indicates that migration is particularly sensitive to social change in the former Soviet Union, with migration responding directly to new social and political tensions.

However, one feature which has remained fairly constant throughout the turmoil of 1989 is the position of Russia as a receiving area for inward migration from other Republics. In 1979–88 the population of all nations (excluding the Baltic nations) actively migrated to a wide range of other republics, amongst which Russia, the Ukraine, Byelorussia, Latvia, Estonia and Moldova were particularly important. By 1989, though, the Ukraine drew population only from a limited number of other republics, and the other receiving republics sharply reduced their intake. In contrast, Russia still remained open to migrants from all other republics. It is important that this role of 'home for everybody' is maintained in the 1990s if relations between the nations of the former Soviet Union are to be normalised.

Forced migration and refugees in the former Soviet Union

In the period since the Second World War the former Soviet Union has experienced forced migration for a number of reasons, namely: inter-ethnic relations; ecological catastrophes which have threatened life and health; and changes in the political situation and structure of some areas of the country.

Estimates of the number of refugees in the former Soviet Union currently range between 0.7 and 1 million people, or between 0.23 and 0.35 per cent of the total population. This proportion is very much in line with the international average of 0.29 per cent (excluding the former Soviet Union). The explosion in the number of refugees in the former Soviet Union has been stimulated by two main factors. First, the collapse of the totalitarian state has allowed open manifestations of social tensions, with some groups being forced to flee as a result. At the same time, the intensification of the struggle for power between different social strata during *perestroika* has also been significant.

The fact that there is no accurate estimate of the number of refugees in the former Soviet Union reflects the different views of the situation taken by different official bodies. The figure of 0.7 million people is thus derived from the number of refugees registered by the State Labour Committee, Ministry of the Interior, KGB and the War Ministry of the USSR in 1991. The figure comprises 420,000 refugees from Armenia and Azerbaijan who migrated during the winter of 1988/1989; 63,000 Turko-Meskhitines from Uzbekistan and about 9,000 people of the Northcaucasian nationalities from Kazakhstan; about 100,000 refugees from Baku in Azerbaijan, who migrated in January 1990, including 75,000 Russian-speaking people of which 48,000 were members of soldiers' families; and also about 100,000 Ossetians and Georgians forced to migrate as a result of the South Ossetia conflict.

The higher estimate of refugee numbers – 1 million people – is also only an approximation but it attempts to include unregistered refugees. The latter include Turko-Meskhitines from Uzbekistan; forced migrants (mainly Russians) from Tadjikistan, Kirghizia and Tuva; migrants who left areas of environmental disaster, such as the Chernobyl zone and the Aral region, for other republics; and some Armenian and Russian-speaking peoples from Azerbaijan and the Baltic countries.

Although none of these groups can be quantified exactly, and for some regions (the Northern Caucasus, Moldova, Turkmenia) there are no reliable data on refugee outflows at all, the estimate of a total of one million refugees is likely to be reasonably accurate. However, it is important to note that this total does not include those people who have been forced to migrate but who have not crossed into another republic. Included amongst this group are those from the earthquake zone in Armenia and the localised zones of ecological catastrophe around Chernobyl and the Aral area; native Kirghiz peoples from the city of Osh in Kirghizia, and the Georgians from Southern Ossetia.

Few parts of the former Soviet Union have been left unscathed by forced migration. Almost all the Union republics and more than half the territory of the Russian Federation have generated refugee flows or acted as destinations for refugees. According to the official data, there were, at the end of 1991, 236,000 refugees in Armenia, 191,000 in Azerbaijan, 117,000 in the Russian Federation,

17,000 in the Ukraine, 26,000 in Kazakhstan, and 2,000 in Byelorussia.

Moscow has been the most important single destination for many refugees from other republics. By the beginning of 1990 about 90,000 people had arrived in Moscow and the Moscow district from Azerbaijan alone, although around a third of these were in transit to another location. Within this total, 40,700 were civilians, the remainder being soldiers' families. The civilian population comprised 18,000 Russians, 14,900 Armenians and 7,900 drawn from elsewhere. The most recent estimates suggest that approximately one quarter of all civilian arrivals eventually settled permanently in Moscow and its district. Twenty thousand returned to Azerbaijan and 3,000 migrated on to Armenia.

The northern Caucasus has also been an important destination for refugees. More particularly Krasnodar, Stavropol and Rostov have all attracted significant refugee populations. Azerbaijan was the major source area for these flows, and it has been estimated that 38,700 people were involved, including 23,900 who moved to the Krasnodar region, 11,700 who moved to the Stavropol region and 3,100 who went to the district of Rostov. However, these numbers represent only a part of the real refugee flows to these areas since many people do not apply for official residential passport registration.

The excessive flow of refugees to certain areas, such as those described above, results in the growth of social tension and the possibility of new acts of violence against refugees. According to our estimates the refugee problem is likely to become more important as there will be a sharp increase in the number of forced migrants in the near future. This will be stimulated by both ecological and political factors. We envisage forced emigration from the entire zone of the Chernobyl catastrophe involving 1–2 million people; flows of 500,000 people from Kara-Kalpakia (the Aral zone); and relocation of 500,000 soldiers with their families from Eastern Europe and Mongolia. As a result we estimate that the overall number of forced migrants, including those currently registered, will amount to 3–4 million people. Some researchers are inclined to add a further one million to this total to include those who will lose their homes during economic stagnation in some regions of the former Soviet Union.

Policies for the reception of refugees

The experience of recent years has demonstrated that the republics are completely unprepared to deal with the problems of mass forced migration. Our survey of the refugees from Azerbaijan conducted in Moscow in March and April 1990 reveals, for instance, that only 26 per cent of the respondents were involved in organised resettlement schemes. Among other refugee groups the ratio was even lower. As a result, 34 per cent of the refugees from Azerbaijan were not even offered temporary accommodation, 32 per cent were allocated accommodation within one to three months of arrival in Moscow and only 34 per cent were accommodated immediately. Two-thirds of all respondents were not offered the right of permanent residence or a job. Twenty-nine per cent *were* made offers of employment and accommodation, but these were largely located in the rural areas of Nechernozyemye, or in remote regions of Siberia. In contrast, a considerable majority (80 per cent) of the respondents were former residents of the city of Baku.

The offers also failed to take account of the occupational and educational skills of the migrants. According to the survey 29 per cent of respondents were skilled workers, 31 per cent were office workers and 31 per cent were technical specialists and scientific workers. Thirty-eight per cent were educated to the general secondary level, 20 per cent to the secondary technical level and 42 per cent to the level of higher education.

Just over half the respondents received governmental financial assistance equal to 100 roubles per person whilst 35 per cent received one-off grants of aid from charities or public organisations: these ranged in amount from 25 to 75 roubles. Ten per cent did not receive any financial aid whatsoever.

Not surprisingly, given the economic and social conditions under which the forced migrants must live, many are considering emigration to the West. Most will have to wait until the new Emigration/Immigration Law comes into force in 1993, since prior to that there is little prospect of officially sanctioned large-scale emigration. Even so, the intensification of the internal problems of the former Soviet Union have resulted in a sharp increase in emigration. Between 1988 and 1990 international emigration increased twelve-fold across the whole of the former Soviet Union, and in some republics it rose forty-fold. Most of these new emigrants, however, came from specific national, ethnic or religious groups, such as Jews who have moved to Israel (44.7 per cent), ethnic Germans who have a constitutional right to settle in Germany (41.8 per cent), and the Pontian Greeks, who have a similar right to move to Greece (4.6 per cent). In total, a further 6 per cent of migrants have moved to the US.

Meanwhile, the legal position of forced migrants who remain within the former Soviet Union is not yet clear. It remains a priority to define a refugee-determination procedure either for groups or individuals, and to decide upon the obligations and rights of those so defined. Equally, states must decide what their obligations are to forced migrants and establish administrative structures and programmes to ensure that these are delivered. Until now work with refugees has been conducted under the aegis of *ad hoc* decrees and decisions taken by Central and Republican Governments and even local government. Human rights abuses can result.

Conclusion

This chapter has demonstrated how population redistribution within the former Soviet Union has been transformed in the period since 1989. Population is now moving in directions and volumes which could not have been predicted even five years ago. Underpinning this massive redistribution of population are ethnic sentiments, and in particular the movement towards mono-ethnic nations. Increasingly, these movements are neither voluntary nor accidental but are the result of pre-existing and long-standing ethnic tensions which are only now being allowed to surface. Migration flows are consequently becoming refugee flows, with tens of thousands of people feeling they are being pushed between republics and towards the West. Perhaps the greatest tragedy is that this is all occurring at a point in time when the West is adopting deliberately more restrictive asylum-policies and when the command economy is collapsing in the East.

Further reading

Akiner, S., ed., 1991, *Cultural change and continuity in central Asia*, Kegan Paul, London.

Anderson, B. and Silver, B., 1989, 'Demographic sources of the changing ethnic composition of the Soviet Union', *Population and Development Review*, **15**: 609–56.

Broxup, M., ed., 1992, *The north Caucasus barrier: the Russian advance towards the Muslim world*, St Martin's Press, New York.

Smith, G., ed., 1990, *The nationalities in Gorbachev's USSR*, Longman, London.

Titma, M.K. and Tuma, N.B., 1992, *Migration in the former Soviet Union*, Bundesinstitut für Ostwissenschaftliche und Internationale Studien, Köln.

PART V

Conclusion

14 Retrospect and prospect: where next for geography and refugee studies?

Vaughan Robinson

It is a measure of the rapidity of political and social change in the world today that in their original form, several of the chapters in this book were already out of step with events, even before the book was published. Findlay's chapter on the ending of the superpower conflict in Afghanistan noted the durability of the Najibullah regime, yet Najibullah has since gone and the *mujahedeen* are now in control of Afghanistan. Zayonchkovskaya, Kocharyan and Vitkovskaya wrote of the Soviet Union when that body now no longer exists. And Robinson argued that the relative absence of large-scale programme resettlement of quota refugees in the west made 1991 a particularly good juncture for quiet reflection on past programmes and policies. Yet in the months since that chapter was written, Germany has already received and is resettling 350,000 refugees from the East, and is arguing, as yet with little success, that other members of the European Community should accept a quota of Yugoslavian and other refugees. By the time this book actually appears, a quota of Yugoslavian refugees may already have been accepted for settlement in the UK and be embarking on long-term resettlement programmes of the type used for the Ugandan Asians, the Chileans and the Vietnamese. Such is the pace of change and lack of predictability of refugee issues.

Whilst the rapidity of change in refugee issues makes the field a nightmare for policy-makers and book-editors, it also demands of researchers a quicker response than is usually provided by academic commentators. For the decision-makers, yesterday's crises and policies are just that. It is interesting therefore to look back to previous attempts to review the field of refugee research and to ask whether any of the current wave of work addresses the weaknesses and lacunae identified by previous reviewers.

In 1990, the writer was asked to act as rapporteur at the first meeting of the International Research and Advisory Panel on Refugees (Robinson, 1990). The task involved synthesising and summarising the discussions of the sixty or so international delegates whose work was within the field of refugee research. I chose to undertake this task through the methodology of a SWOT analysis, in which the Strengths, Weaknesses, Opportunities and Threats to an enterprise are enumerated in order to create a programme of change. Eleven weaknesses of current research were identified, nine of which have direct relevance for the current discussion. First, refugee studies appeared to have a lack of credibility with policy-makers, academics and refugees themselves. There was a shortage of historical or longitudinal studies of refugee groups. There was little truly multidisciplinary and interdisciplinary research in the field. There had been only a very limited attempt to develop theory specific to the field, and instead, theory had been borrowed without modification from other kindred disciplines. There was a paucity of internationally comparative work and a scarcity of genuinely applied research as opposed to broadly applicable work. Those who had been forced to migrate received the majority of our academic attention, whilst the institutions involved remained under-researched, as did those people who did not flee, the attitudes and reactions of the populations of receiving societies, and the refugee determination procedures. Finally, the specialism was criticised for dehumanising the experiences of refugees and of reducing these to numbers.

Assuming that there was some measure of agreement about these weaknesses – although I am sure that not all researchers agreed with all of the criticisms made – I then proceeded to make a number of suggestions as to how refugee research might be developed in the 1990s. These included the need for more longitudinal research, more interdisciplinary work, more overt theory-building, more tailoring of research to the needs of the clients (interpreted broadly), more consideration of research ethics, and a broader definition of refugee studies than simply those people who fled: such a definition would include the study of causes of flight and the reasons why different people might respond to these in different ways, the study of institutions which are involved in refugee determination, reception and resettlement, the study of the psycho-social needs and characteristics of refugees, and the response of the indigenous populations of nations of first and subsequent settlement.

The following year, Black (1991) attempted a similar task but he focused his review on the written contributions of scholars, and in particular of geographers. He argued that geographers are capable of making three distinctive contributions to the refugee studies literature, namely a contribution to understanding the causes of refugee flows, evaluation of the consequences of refugee flows for Less Developed Countries, and the analysis of refugee resettlement patterns in the developed world and how these might reflect and shape patterns of adaptation. He went on to review work in these three fields and to point to areas in need of further geographical attention. More particularly, he argued for a larger volume of applied work, both as an aid to policy formulation and as a way of stimulating theoretical developments. More work was also needed on refugee adaptation and the structural location of refugees in the employment and housing markets of the countries in which they eventually settled. And he suggested the need for research which demonstrated the positive value of refugees to these societies, in order that the stereotype of refugees as helpless burdens could successfully be challenged.

At the close of 1991 I attempted to review the geographical work presented at the conference from which this volume grew (Robinson, 1992). Like Black, I argued that geographers had much to offer refugee studies. We can, firstly, assist in the delineation of the causes of refugee flows, through our longstanding interests in geopolitics and the balance between people and natural environment. Secondly, we have the necessary spatial skills and tradition of research to quantify, chart, and monitor patterns of refugee generation, refugee flows and refugee resettlement. Thirdly, the discipline has a century-old tradition of directly assisting decision-makers through the provision of information, the evaluation of policy alternatives and the monitoring of policy once implemented, and there is no reason why such applied skills cannot be used in the field of refugee policy. And, lastly, geographers have a passion for place, as well as space, a concern which can throw much light on topics such as why some individuals become refugees whilst others do not, why some refugees eventually return whilst others do not, and why refugees 'choose' the resettlement destinations which they do. Despite these skills and potential contributions, I argued that geographical work was still deficient in some respects. Like many academics, geographers use implicit, loose and shifting definitions of what constitutes a refugee, thereby hindering the international and historical comparisons which could be so fruitful. In addition, we have failed to agree on whether refugees should be treated as a separate entity from other migrants, and we therefore still possess an ambivalent attitude towards the field of migration studies, and its concepts, theories and methods. We have failed to address the intersection of racism and refugee definition, determination, and resettlement policy despite the fact that ethnic relations is often a central determinant of refugee flows and the treatment of refugees after flight. And we have, perhaps, spent too much of our energy upon freestanding empirical case studies, rather than upon comparative work and, even more importantly, theory-building.

Three reviews by two authors can hardly reflect the diversity of opinion within any field of academic enquiry, but they do suggest common themes and concerns, which should already be apparent to the reader. Perhaps we can now ask to what extent those academic researchers within geography who have written for this volume, and those with a geographical perspective to their work, have responded to the needs and criticism of refugee studies outlined above.

Several of the contributors have addressed the issue of refugee definitions. Bascom, for example, questions the wisdom of defining refugees only in terms of those who have fortuitously crossed an international boundary and who have therefore made themselves refugees under the UN definition. He argues forcibly that those who are internally displaced often move for similar reasons, and are therefore as deserving of assistance as international refugees. He also points out that the former are at least equal to the latter in global numbers. Van Hear addresses the same theme when he describes the complexity of the forced migrations arising from the Gulf conflict and the limited recognition of those displaced by the war as formal refugees: he goes on to describe the moves afoot to broaden internationally recognised definitions of refugees. McGregor argues that the term environmental refugee, which is increasingly becoming common parlance, confuses the position of those involved rather than clarifying it. And Findlay describes how the ending of superpower conflict in Afghanistan encouraged a redefinition of Afghan refugees in Pakistan as economic migrants rather than as refugees from war and persecution.

Other chapters use a variety of methodologies to investigate the cause of refugee flows. Daley uses an historical and structuralist perspective to trace the roots of her particular case study back to the uneven spread of capitalism under colonial rule. Van Hear looks at how geopolitics and strategic interest can stimulate the flow of some four or five million people as an immediate response to armed conflict. Monzel approaches her analysis on a very different level, but also points to the importance of war as a precipitator of refugee flows. Black looks at how the flows of refugees into Western Europe have been transformed in content and volume by the thawing of the Cold War and the collapse of state socialism in the East. Zayonchkovskaya, Kocharyan and Vitkovskaya look to ethnic tensions within the newly separated republics of the former Soviet Union and to the nuclear disaster of Chernobyl as causes for the displacement of peoples. And McGregor notes how environmental degradation can form part of a wider set of stimulants to flight.

Several of the chapters directly address the decision-makers, either through providing newly collated information or through the monitoring and evaluation of policy. Black draws our attention to the new patterns of refugee movements forming within Europe. Van Hear chronicles one of the largest mass displacements of recent times. Hammar evaluates the Swedish government's policy of geographically dispersing refugees throughout the country. Robinson evaluates the reception and resettlement policies employed by the Australian and British governments and finally makes practical recommendations about good practice. And Simon and Preston both describe and evaluate UNHCR's policy of repatriating Namibians.

Two chapters specifically choose to address a different phase of the refugee experience, namely repatriation. Koser's suggestions about the importance of information flows and Simon and Preston's study of Namibia deliberately focus our attention away from flight and its immediate aftermath, and point to the need for long-term analysis of refugee groups many years after initial flight. Although very under-researched at present, it is important to remember that repatriation is currently the preferred choice from the three 'durable solutions' recognised by UNHCR. This clearly also underpins the trends and redefinitions described by Findlay in Pakistan and Afghanistan, in his consideration of why repatriation did not occur when expected by policy-makers.

Monzel has deliberately chosen to reject the 'value-free' scientific model and has instead opted for an involved humanistic account of the experience of becoming a refugee, the experience of temporary settlement in countries of first asylum and the experience of eventual resettlement in the West. She describes these experiences, and their implications, through the lens of three Hmong women in Syracuse and provides us with a moving and powerful account of the content of 'refugeeness' in these particular circumstances. She also portrays the way in which her three subjects have regained some control over their destinies and in doing so challenges the stereotype of refugees as helpless victims and therefore burdens. A similar message is developed in Black's very different chapter, for he tries to demonstrate the positive economic value of the refugees now moving east into Western Europe, as consumers, entrepreneurs and waged labour.

Like Monzel, Koser, too, has opted for *terra incognita* in his deliberate search for explanation through models and theory-building. He also seeks to link refugee issues back into migration studies, with its far more developed literature and greater theoretical armoury. The search for linkage rather than isolation, and the need to contextualise case studies, events and policies is also the theme of Robinson's chapter, for he argues that the resettlement policies of the Australian and British governments cannot be seen in isolation from the ideology of those governments about race, immigration and racial integration. In doing so, he deliberately builds bridges between refugee studies and the study of ethnic relations, and illustrates his point through international comparison. Zayonchkovskaya *et al.* are obviously engaged in a similar enterprise but one which is perhaps implicit in their work rather than explicit. And Hammar could be argued to be studying how the Swedish government's dispersal policy was an attempt to maintain their liberal ideology towards refugee determination and acceptance.

The chapters of this book do, therefore, provide us with clear examples of the way in which geographers – and those adopting a geographical approach – are addressing some of the key contemporary issues in refugee studies. We are researching the question of definitions and labelling, and the implications which arise from individuals being given different labels. We are considering the causes of forced migration and we are undertaking this at a variety of geographical scales and from a variety of political perspectives. We are responding to the needs of policy-makers through applied research. We are shifting our gaze from the early stages of refugee flows to the longer-term issues of repatriation. We are challenging stereotypes of refugees as burdens and passive victims. We are taking tentative steps in the direction of formulating theory and thinking about our work in a more rigorous manner. We are beginning to contextualise our empirical work and seek meaningful comparisons between different societies, different historical eras and different policy instruments. And we are reaching out to other kindred disciplines in an effort to benefit from their expertise and to move towards genuine multidisciplinary and then interdisciplinary work.

Given the relative youth of refugee studies, exemplified by Black's (1991) observation that few if any of the texts on human geography mentioned the field even as late as the 1970s, the achievements outlined above are considerable. They indicate through their depth and diversity of approach that geography and geographers can respond to the needs of society when they are called upon to do so, and that this response can be rapid and effective. Moreover, that those working in the field of geography and refugees can retain both their enthusiasm and their diversity of interests and approaches says much about the value of working in a post-modernist intellectual environment. However, lest we become complacent we need only remind ourselves that there are perhaps 40 million refugees and displaced people in need of protection and/or assistance in the world today, that the number is growing daily, and that the imprint of becoming a refugee will, as Monzel graphically illustrates, stay with these people for the remainder of their, often short, lives. Our best is not yet good enough.

References

Black, R., 1991, 'Refugees and displaced persons: geographical perspectives and research directions', *Progress in Human Geography*, **15** (3): 281–98.

Robinson, V., 1990, 'Into the next millennium: an agenda for refugee studies. A report of the 1st annual meeting of the International Advisory Panel, January 1990', *Journal of Refugee Studies*, **3** (1): 3–15.

Robinson, V., 1992, 'Geographers and refugee studies: a report on the international conference "The refugee crisis: geographical perspectives on forced migration" held at King's College London, September 18–20, 1991', *Journal of Refugee Studies*, **5** (1): 68–72.

Index

acculturation 174
acute refugees 173
adaptation 50, 94, 150, 212
Afghanistan 4, 12, 43, 185–96, 211, 213, 214
Afghans 185–96, 192, 213
agriculture 28, 36
aid 17, 23, 27, 28, 185–96
Albanians 5
Angola 47, 54, 55, 57, 58
anticipatory refugees 68, 173
assimilation 39, 142, 149, 198
Asylum Bill, UK 5
Aussiedler 89, 98
Australia 12, 119, 135–51, 214
Austria 89, 90, 98

Bangladesh 67, 78, 161
Belgium 97, 98, 116
Bhutan 3
black economy 95
Bosnia 3
Burma 3, 159–60, 165–5
Burundi 17, 19, 21, 24, 25
Burundians 178

Cambodians 90
Canada 135
capitalism 17, 19, 25
Chad 51
Chernobyl disaster 204, 205, 214
Chileans 106, 111, 211
children 38–9, 50, 55, 56, 57, 123, 178, 189, 192
China 119, 128, 137
colonialism 17, 18, 19, 20, 21, 22, 25, 29, 30, 47
compensation 78, 79, 165
Congo 4
Costa Rica 174
Croatia 3
Croatians 45

crime 95, 96
Cubans 96
Cyprus 99, 161
Czechoslovakia 136

de facto refugees 64, 69, 94
deforestation 158, 164
demographics 198, 199, 200
demographic impact of refugees 76
demographics of refugees 55, 138, 139, 140
demolition of refugee settlements 39–42
deportation 74, 91, 104, 109
detention 68
detention centres 94
Denmark 94, 95, 97
Development 9, 10, 17, 19, 20, 23, 29, 30, 136, 163, 164
disabled 52, 56, 136, 138
disasters 158
discrimination 60, 74, 79, 94, 96, 144
dispersal 10, 23, 104–17, 142, 144, 150, 166, 214, 215
drought 33, 158, 159, 161, 173
durable solutions 42, 48, 171, 179, 214

earthquakes 160, 204
economic integration 60
education 50, 52, 74, 94, 98, 99, 121, 192, 193, 206
Egypt 77
Egyptians 67
El Salvador 43
employment 37, 41, 51, 74, 94, 95, 113, 141, 144, 145, 146, 163, 190, 205, 212
Environment 10, 23
Environmental refugees 10, 12, 79, 157–62, 213
environmental degradation 35, 158, 159, 214
environmental impact of refugees 163–7

Eritrea 42, 159
Ethiopia 43, 91, 104, 111, 159, 160, 172, 173
Ethiopians 38, 172, 180, 181
ethnic clustering 39, 203
ethnicity 4, 7, 22, 35, 39, 41, 174, 181, 186, 198–206, 214
Europe 12, 88–100, 186, 192, 195, 213, 214
European Community 8, 105, 136, 163, 211
European Volunteer Workers 135
expatriate workers 66
ex–combatants 51, 60, 61, 73–4, 79, 177, 205

family reunion 57, 60, 106, 107, 136
famine 33, 35, 37, 158, 159, 173
Finland 94, 106
food 28, 29, 37, 39, 40, 119, 161, 192, 193
forced labour 21
forced relocation 39–42, 43, 73, 159
forced settlement 19, 25
'Fortress Europe' 93, 163
France 89, 94, 95, 96, 98, 119
front–end loading 141, 142, 150

gender 97, 113, 118–32, 138, 174, 176
Germans 90
Germany 88, 89, 90, 91, 95, 96, 97, 98, 99, 106, 211
Greece 94, 98
Greeks 90
Grenada 4
Gulf war 3, 11, 44, 64–83, 188, 193, 213

Haitians 5
harassment 68
Health 19, 69, 74, 123, 129
Health care 56, 144
Hmong 12, 118
homelessness 56, 118, 119
Honduras 174
housing 37–8, 39, 56, 94, 96, 99, 106, 108, 141, 142, 143, 144, 146, 147, 149, 150, 205, 212
Hong Kong 90, 137, 151, 159
Human rights 3, 40, 43, 44, 74, 161
    violations of 161
Hungarians 136

illegal immigrants 68

illegal immigration 98
illegal labour 95
immigration policies 4, 22, 23, 73
India 67, 78
Indians 67
Indonesia 78
information flows 49, 51, 54, 143, 171–82, 214
integration 11, 42, 59, 78, 79, 88, 93, 94, 106, 107, 110, 149, 166, 173, 194
internal migration 200–203
internal refugees 33–45, 72, 79, 161
international law 5
International Conference on Aid to Refugees in Africa 9
Iran 64, 67, 69, 70, 72–3, 79, 89, 91, 111, 187, 188
Iranians 67, 89
Iraq 4, 12, 43, 44, 64–83, 111, 187
Ireland 89, 98, 135
Irish 135
Israel 77
Italy 5, 89, 90, 95, 96, 98

Japan 119
Jordan 64, 65, 67, 69, 74, 76, 79
Jordanians 74, 77, 80

Kampuchea 4
Kampucheans 137, 181
Kurds 5, 67, 69, 70, 72, 73, 75, 79, 80, 95, 106, 188
Kuwait 12, 64, 83

labelling 35, 95, 99, 215
labour markets 17, 60, 96–9, 106, 107, 108, 135, 138, 142, 144, 150
labour migration 20, 22, 23, 28, 29, 92, 173, 185, 195
land degradation 29, 36
language 106, 147, 186
language training 107, 108, 141, 143
Laos 12, 119
Laotians 90, 126, 128, 137, 177
Lebanon 74, 91, 111
Liberia 3
literacy 189
Luxembourg 89

mainstreaming 137, 139
Malawi 166, 180, 181
marriage 122–3
media 40, 88, 135, 175

migrant workers 73, 74, 76, 79, 80
Mozambique 43, 47, 50, 51, 160, 166
Mozambicans 180, 181
multiculturalism 12, 136, 137, 141, 143,
   149, 151
myth of return 132, 190

Namibia 4, 47–63, 214
Namibians 47–63, 172, 214
natural disasters 158, 161, 162, 204
natural hazards 160
naturalisation 88
Netherlands 89, 91, 95, 98, 106
New York Protocol, 1967 7
New Zealand 135
Nicaraguans 174
nutrition 56

OAS Cartagena Declaration, 1985 7
OAU 39
OAU Convention on Refugees, 1967 7
occupational skills of refugees 55, 138,
   139, 190, 206
oral history 118

Pakistan 67, 78, 185, 186, 187, 188, 190,
   191, 192, 194, 195, 213, 214
Palestinians 74, 77, 79, 80, 195
patriarchy 122, 186
persecution 33, 160, 172, 177, 196, 213
Phillippines 78
pluralism 136
Poles 90, 106, 135, 139
pollution 160
Portugal 89, 98
powerlessness 118–32
professional workers 73, 76, 77, 79
protection of refugees 162–3
public opinion 4, 5, 72, 135, 144, 150

qualifications 139
quota refugees 89, 90, 91, 104, 116, 136,
   137, 138, 139, 141, 142

racism 136, 137
reception 50, 139–41, 205, 214
reception centres 52, 54–55, 56, 107,
   109, 110, 139, 141, 143, 145, 146,
   147, 150
refoulement 173, 179
refugees: as 'burdens' 93
  economic impact of 93–9
refugee camps 40, 41, 67, 72, 73, 74, 79,

88, 90, 104, 107, 124, 128, 139,
   165, 166, 167, 174
refugee definition 7–8, 43, 157, 213
refugee determination procedures 7, 92,
   95, 109, 138, 206, 213, 215
religion 4, 7, 35, 41, 130, 181, 206
remittances 75–9, 179
repatriation 4, 12, 17, 42, 47–63, 67, 76,
   89, 91, 135, 171–82, 185, 190,
   191, 192, 194, 195, 196, 214, 215
  costs of 58
Resettlement 10, 11, 35, 40, 42, 47–63,
   73, 88, 118, 128–30, 135–51, 160,
   171, 179, 205, 212, 213, 214
residence 127–9
return migration 11, 12, 48, 49, 64, 72–3,
   97, 173, 176, 179
  demographic impact of 77
  difficulties on 51, 60, 61
  economic impact of 76–9
  obstacles to 52
  psycho–social consequences of 51
returnees 7, 67, 70, 73, 74, 76, 79, 174,
   181
Rwanda 17, 19, 21, 23, 24

safe havens 4, 70, 72
sanctuary movement 5
Saudi Arabia 64, 65, 68, 73–4, 76, 77,
   79
secondary migration 111, 116
segregation 10, 144–6, 147–9, 203
selectivity in refugee admissions 138
self employment 96–7
self–repatriation 48, 173, 179, 180
settlement policy 25, 30, 37, 48, 109–17,
   142–51
Shias 69, 70, 72, 75, 79
Sierra Leone 164
social mobility 144, 150
Somalia 3, 104, 111, 165, 166
South Africa 9, 47, 48, 58, 61, 135, 166,
   180
South Korea 78
Soviet Union 3, 4, 13, 90, 99, 185, 186,
   187, 188, 195, 198–206, 211, 214
Spain 89, 95, 98
spatial concentration 144–6, 147–9
spontaneous settlements 39, 40
Sri Lanka 67, 78, 90
starvation 69
stereotypes 157, 164, 212, 215
Sudan 11, 33–45, 51, 67, 160, 166, 172,

173, 178, 181
Sudanese 77, 174
Swaziland 165, 166, 167, 180
Sweden 12, 89, 91, 104–17, 214, 215
Switzerland 89, 91, 98, 106
Syria 67, 69, 74, 111

Tanganyika 19, 20, 21, 23
Tanzania 11, 17–32, 178, 180
Thailand 78, 90, 122, 126, 128, 159,
    160, 177, 181
third country resettlement 42, 48
torture 68, 74
transmigration 160
tropical cyclones 160
Turkey 5, 64, 67, 69, 72–3, 79, 95
Turks 94, 99

Ubersiedler 89
Uganda 17, 21, 23
Ugandans 172, 177
Ugandan Asians 135, 139, 211
UK 5, 8, 12, 89, 94, 95, 106, 115,
    135–51, 214
unemployment 56, 60, 77, 96, 112, 147,
    149
UN 20, 28, 43, 44, 45, 49, 72, 73, 80,
    180, 185, 188, 192, 193, 213
UN Convention on Refugees, 1951 5, 7,
    70, 88, 91, 95, 104, 107, 109, 161,
    192, 193
UNHCR 4, 7, 12, 23, 26, 27, 33, 42, 49,
    53, 54, 56, 57, 58, 59, 60, 61, 70,
    72, 73, 80, 88, 95, 104, 135, 161,

162, 165, 172, 173, 175, 177, 179,
    180, 185, 186, 189, 190, 191,
    192–4, 195, 196, 214
United States 4, 8, 12, 23, 49, 70, 119,
    122, 128–30, 135, 185, 187, 195

Vietnam 67, 78, 119, 137
Vietnamese 12, 89, 90, 95, 98, 115,
    135–51, 195, 211
villagization policy 23, 26, 27
'vintages' of refugees 137
vocational training 107
volcanoes 160

War 3, 4, 11, 33, 37, 43, 44, 48, 64–83,
    88, 118, 119, 122, 124–6, 137,
    157, 158, 159–60, 161, 171, 177,
    180, 181, 187, 191, 192, 194, 202,
    204, 213, 214,
'waves' of refugees 66–75, 137, 146
welfare benefits 4, 107, 142, 143, 144
West Papua 167
White Australia Policy 135, 136, 151

xenophobia 5, 135

Yemen 67, 76
Yemenis 68, 77
Yugoslavia 3, 45, 136
Yugoslavians 211

Zaire 17, 23
Zambia 54, 55, 172, 180
Zimbabwe 48, 51, 52, 180